FORMS OF A WORLD

Forms of a World

CONTEMPORARY POETRY

AND THE MAKING OF GLOBALIZATION

WALT HUNTER

FORDHAM UNIVERSITY PRESS
New York 2019

Fordham University Press gratefully acknowledges
financial assistance and support provided for the publication
of this book by Clemson University.

Fordham University Press has no responsibility for the
persistence or accuracy of URLs for external or third-party
Internet websites referred to in this publication and does not
guarantee that any content on such websites is, or will remain,
accurate or appropriate.

Fordham University Press also publishes its books
in a variety of electronic formats. Some content that appears
in print may not be available in electronic books.

Visit us online at www.fordhampress.com.

Library of Congress Cataloging-in-Publication Data

Names: Hunter, Walt, author.
Title: Forms of a world : contemporary poetry and the making of globalization
/ Walt Hunter.
Description: First edition. | New York : Fordham University Press, [2019] |
Includes bibliographical references and index.
Identifiers: LCCN 2018010818| ISBN 9780823282227 (cloth : alk. paper) | ISBN
9780823282210 (paper : alk. paper)
Subjects: LCSH: Literature and globalization.
Classification: LCC PN56.G55 H86 2019 | DDC 809/.933553—dc23
LC record available at https://lccn.loc.gov/2018010818

Printed in the United States of America

21 20 19   5 4 3 2 1

First edition

for Lindsay

CONTENTS

Introduction   1

1. Stolen Landscapes: The Investments of the Ode
   and the Politics of Land   19

2. Let Us Go: Lyric and the Transit of Citizenship   44

3. The Crowd to Come: Poetic Exhortations
   from Brooklyn to Kashmir   65

4. The No-Prospect Poem: Poetic Views
   of the Anthropocene   90

   Coda   119

   Acknowledgments   129
   Notes   133
   Bibliography   165
   Index   183

Forms of a World

Introduction

This book shows how the forms of contemporary English-writing poetry emerge in dynamic relation to the transformations of globalization from 1970 to the present. It poses the following question: What happens when we think of poetry as a global literary genre and when we think of the global in poetic terms? I argue that poetry imagines powerful alternatives to the present and that analyses of globalization are incomplete without it. *Forms of a World* brings together a group of poets who not only make the violence of global processes visible thematically, but also renew performatively the missing conditions for intervening within these processes. Poetic acts—in this book, the rhetoric of possessing, belonging, exhorting, and prospecting—address contemporary conditions that render social life ever more precarious. Poets creatively intervene in global processes by remaking their poetry's repertoire of forms, from experiments in the sonnet to contemporary inventions of the ode. The political and economic conditions that the poets in this book engage are systemic and global. They include dispossession, commodified citizenship, financialization, precarity, ecological catastrophe, and territorial expansion. This book claims that poets register such global processes by remaking the poetic forms they have at hand.

I argue in this book that contemporary Anglophone poetry cannot be understood fully without acknowledging the global forces from which it arises. In the chapters that follow, I turn to an eclectic group of poets writing in English—including U.S., British, Ghanaian, Iraqi, Irish, Jamaican, and Kashmiri figures—whose poetry and whose lives are, in different but related ways, inseparable from the contemporary global situation. These poets emphasize the performative functions of poetry, its calls to ethical and political change. At the same time, they examine forms of agency: their ecstatic strains of poetry place the poet in the service of powers that tend to exceed or call into question individual sovereignty. *Forms of a World* argues for the recognition of a global poetics in which the global is built into the literary form of the poem itself and is inseparable from its making.

Writing about contemporary poets brings me into close contact with the danger of casually assuming a narrow, ethnocentric definition for the word "poetry."[1] Even taking the U.S. context on its own, the period from 1970 to the present has seen a proliferation of cultures of reading poetry and institutions for writing poetry.[2] While poetic performance has been central to protests, revolutions, occupations, and forms of indigenous resistance, I have chosen in this book to examine primarily Anglophone, text-based poetry and to use close textual analysis as my method. My goal in this book is to reveal how certain primarily textual subgenres or modes of poetry—the landscape poem, the ode, the hortatory poem, the prospect poem—reemerge concomitantly with structural transformations in global capitalism. Their lineages and genealogies are appraised and embedded in a politicized, material history. Each chapter investigates a particular literary form as it emerged in history and as it appears today. I hope this book renews and excites interest in the fate of English poetic subgenres such as the ode and the prospect poem, precisely by underscoring their situatedness within historical capitalism. These literary forms rise at particular moments to the imagination of poets who themselves write within and against material conditions of exploitation. The period I explore is one in which certain poetic forms have surged forward as modes of diagnosis, engagement, and the transformation of subjectivity.

In focusing on poets writing in English, I do not intend to make an equivalence between globalization and the experience of an Anglophone or Global-North elite. I argue that the poets here make visible contemporary conditions in which riot, crisis, and surplus populations have made their way into the overdeveloped and deindustrialized Global North. Studying these poets helps to reveal how crises in the capitalist world-system inflect the literary production of the United States, United Kingdom, and Europe. My object is to show how shared concerns with globalization have compelled poets to innovate within, renew, and transform text-based poetic traditions. The global appears in their work not only thematically, but also formally, as they attempt to thread global processes and subjectivities through the ode, the lyric, the hortatory poem, and the prospect poem. Taking this route also allows me to explore how poetry's global outcries subtend certain "schools" of poetry, bringing together experimental poets (Myung Mi Kim) with canonical ones (Seamus Heaney) in unexpected adjacency. While some of the poets are firmly embedded in academic discourses and practices of poetry, this book also highlights poets who challenge distinctions between text-based and performance-based practices, such as Manal Al-Sheikh, Sean Bonney, Sarah Clancy, and Danez Smith. I include these poets because they have been closely involved with immediate, public uses of poetry to create political change while producing published work and occasionally teaching in academic settings.

Anglophone poetry has been one of the last literary genres to be assimilated into the analysis of globalization, while the discourse of critical global studies continues to move from the social sciences into the humanities.[3] The novel, its relation to social thought more immediately apparent, has been a more accessible site for investigations of historical capitalism, for the politics of neoliberalism, and for the ethics of precarity. When it comes to poetry, however, a formidable hermeticism has long held sway. While criticism of other literary genres expands its grasp, most notably into new sociological approaches to literature, knowledge of poetic devices serves as a border check for those interested in poetic criticism, slowing contemporary poetry's reception, inhibiting pedagogy, and operating like a canon of revealed truths. This study of twentieth-century and contemporary Anglophone poetry argues that the major poetic innovations of the contemporary period are conditioned by global forces. Yet rather than reflect passively the sociological conditions of its production, the poetry I consider senses these conditions before they are made fully present and offers a diversity of responses to global transformation, making the conditions apparent in which action might be possible. I draw attention to poets who intervene in the making of the global through the genres and formal languages available to them. From prose poetry to the prospect poem, from the poem of the crowd to the ode, these contemporary poets write within and remake formal conventions as the global itself develops and is remade.

In his introduction to a cluster of articles on "American Poetry, 2000–2009," Michael Davidson questions the putatively natural relationship between critical theory and narrative: "Critical and cultural theory shifted to narrative as the master code through which nation, politics, identity, and race are formed, and emerging forms of cultural studies seldom referred to poetry. . . . Rather than describe this as a crisis in poetry, as many have, I would call it a division between actually existing and institutional validation of the arts."[4] Davidson is right to attribute this shift to an institutional privileging of the novel over the poem as a site of inquiry. But I also think that a refusal to incorporate these topics has been constitutive, even essential, to the production of much poetic criticism.[5] It sometimes seems as though the poetry criticism of the late twentieth century has been designed precisely to keep "nation, politics, identity, and race" out of sight, turning instead, as Christopher Nealon shows, to an "increasingly philosophical approach" as a "countermove" to the formalism of the New Critics.[6] The poetry in this book acknowledges directly and indirectly the politics, social forms, and economic processes of global capitalism. Yet Anglophone poetry criticism has largely expelled from its purview the structural, systemic, and global engagements with capitalism that form the core of social theory, from Marx and Weber to Sassen and Mitchell. In the most general terms, this book attempts to redress the absence of global theorizing, oriented by the materialist analysis of lived conditions of interlocking forms of exploitation, from the exploration of poetic subgenres and forms.

The poets in this book give form to the contemporary development of global capitalism through their reinvention of poetic traditions and can thus be misunderstood if read in isolation from histories of the global. Anglophone poetry remains in a productive but sometimes narrow critical conversation with the contending social and political projects of L=A=N=G=U=A=G=E poetry, confessional lyric, and new conceptual poetries. This book offers a broader social context for poetry that is global in sweep and that brings the literary genre into conversation with cross-disciplinary work on globalization. Heeding the call to historicize lyric poetry made by Virginia Jackson and Yopie Prins in the *Lyric Theory Reader* (2014), this study at the same time engages foundational work on twentieth-century poetry by Charles Altieri, Jonathan Culler, Marjorie Perloff, and Helen Vendler. But rather than showing how contemporary poetry emerges from philosophical debates, often rooted in modernism, over poetry and rhetoric or undecidability and symbolism, this book relocates the development of poetry in the problematics of global capitalism.[7] In my account, historical, global processes are the evolving conditions from which familiar poetic concepts emerge and within which they are transformed. *Forms of a World* thus follows in the path of recent literary-historical treatments of global capitalism and twentieth- and twenty-first-century poetry undertaken by Jasper Bernes, Michael Dowdy, Khaled Furani, and Christopher Nealon. My work also takes advantage of a broadening of the field of poetics that has brought together race, postcoloniality, and trans-nationalism with poetry.[8] Finally, in its emphasis on the social poetics of global literary forms, *Forms of a World* adds to contemporary debates over the direction of world literature, especially in the sense that these debates frequently use narrative forms rather than poems as their preferred case studies.[9]

One of the most vital political projects of contemporary theory has been the continued critique of liberalism, frequently conducted on a global scale.[10] This project involves reflecting critically on the violent founda-tions of key discursive terms and adumbrating the conditions under which a study of the theoretical and institutional "undercommons" of the Enlightenment might proceed.[11] Nowhere is this critique needed more than in studies of globalization, which all too often reproduce the planetary destructions of liberalism and humanism in celebratory terms of intercon-nection and progress. As Lisa Lowe writes in *The Intimacies of Four Conti-nents* (2015),

> Liberal forms of political economy, culture, government, and history
> propose a narrative of freedom overcoming enslavement that at once
> denies colonial slavery, erases the seizure of lands from native peoples,
> displaces migrations and connections across continents, and internalizes
> these processes in a national struggle of history and consciousness.[12]

Although Lowe does not discuss poetry, the terms that we use to think about poems are just as much products and producers of the liberal discur-sive frameworks of subjectivity, freedom, humanity, and intimacy. The development of poetry in English tracks closely, in unique aesthetic forms, the construction of liberal philosophical and economic theories, from the Renaissance sonnet's investigations of subjectivity to the nineteenth-century inventions of lyric interiority. The contemporary poets in this book propose a global poetics that contains a strong critique of Anglophone poetry's purported immunity from questions of race, class, ability, and gen-der, as well as global phenomena of colonization, slavery, and economic dispossession. But many of the normative frameworks for poetic discourse have made the work of these poets difficult to see. Thinking about poetry in English as a global form tends therefore to take place today on the flicker-ing boundaries of what counts as poetic criticism. The intention behind this book is to test those boundaries and, in the process, to show how the making of poetry and the making of the global cannot be separated.

Critiques of post-1970s globalization have long been underserved by familiar concepts for the global such as flow, hybridity, and scape.[13] These circulatory metaphors are misleading in their neutrality. Who are the agents promoting particular flows, maintaining the priority of certain circuits over others, diverting or shutting down routes, installing checkpoints? The description of the world in such terms reproduces the hierarchies that benefit more and more from their complexity, occultism, and normative posturing as accomplished fact. The current wave of critical global theory—promulgated by such thinkers as Radhika Desai, David Harvey, Greta Krippner, Timothy Mitchell, Vijay Prashad, Kristin Ross, and Saskia Sassen—seeks to think beyond these early frameworks for the global.[14] This period of globalization is distinguished by a number of common processes, manifest in diverse local forms, including dispossessions of various kinds, the commodification of national citizenship, the precariousness of life and labor, the financialization of the global economy, and the "slow violence" of ecological catastrophe.[15] To understand the poetry of the contemporary period, then, we need fresh concepts for the relation between poetry and these global forces and conditions.

This book calls for an expansion and a radicalization of poetic criticism, a project already well underway in recent work by both poets and scholars.[16] It is an argument for the continuing politicization of the global, aligning the term with the unflagging struggles underway against dispossession, settler colonialism, and systemic racism. The generic qualities created by theories of poetic influence have often been distinctly racist and capitalist in the ways they perpetuate social and civil death. As Anthony Reed writes in *Freedom Time*, "Often subtending those genealogies is an implicit transhistorical notion of poetry or of the human (which has always been a cornerstone of racial projects) that by default is white and usually male."[17] While Reed is referring to avant-garde traditions, the point applies to various other lines of poetry no less strongly. This book is one attempt to close the widening gap between the concepts available to poetry critics and the poems that people are writing and reading. To close this gap would mean to think about tropes and schemes geopolitically. It would also mean to reject the gatekeeping and the systematic exclusions that have served as a kind of immunological defense of poetic criticism. The concepts that we need to understand contemporary poetry simply cannot be found in traditions of thinking that reproduce discursively what poets are fighting with all their breath.

Part of the difficulty of laying out the coordinates for this age has to do with the recondite set of acts that have shaped it. From the perspective of geopolitical economy, these are not, primarily, major events or colorful personages, but rather contingent decisions about monetary policy. Beginning in the 1970s, U.S. monetarist policy, designed to combat intractably high inflation, forges a financialized world economy, which Leo Panitch and Sam Gindin chart in *The Making of Global Capitalism* (2012).[18] For Greta Krippner, the removal of interest-rate ceilings—and, specifically, of Regulation Q, established by the Banking Act of 1933—is decisive in shaping the contemporary period. Krippner writes,

> Free flowing—and expensive—credit reconfigured the political terrain, disorganizing a potentially broad-based coalition of middle-class homeowners and urban advocates that demanded that the burdens of inflation be more equitably shared. In this context, financial deregulation functioned both to alleviate festering social tensions and to set the stage for the financialization of the U.S. economy in subsequent decades.[19]

While Krippner, Panitch, and Gindin focus on U.S. policy as inhibiting broad-based social movements with goals of redistribution, Vijay Prashad offers a more capacious, international survey of global transformations after the 1970s. Prashad's view takes in "the breakdown of the factory regimes across the world (post-Fordism), the emergence of the new technological infrastructure (computers, satellites), and the magnetic attraction of all the planet's wealth to the all-powerful financial centers of the North (financialization)."[20] Although these three accounts are hardly representative of the expansive corpus of geopolitical economy, they do suggest a consensus. Whether contemporary globalization is understood to be a rupture with the past or rather, as Paul Jay finds, an acceleration of largely existent global processes, the early years of the 1970s mark the beginning of a distinct period of historical capitalism.[21]

The first wave of theories of globalization analyze the global as a change in the relation between space and time. In *The Consequences of Modernity* (1990), cited by nearly every work on globalization in the 1990s, Anthony Giddens defines globalization "as the intensification of worldwide social relations which link distant localities in such a way that local happenings are shaped by events occurring many miles away and vice versa."[22] Following Giddens, globalization theory is useful for its attention to processes that both deeply affect and yet extend beyond the local: mass migration, diaspora, and displacement, as well as nascent forms of solidarity and collective political organization. Today, Giddens's formulation works best not as a description, but as a continuing provocation. In her introduction to a volume of essays, *Framing the Global* (2014), Hilary E. Kahn writes, "The global is not only anchored in the broader regulatory frameworks, standards, and rules that structure our lives, but it is also embodied in essential aspects of our being that may seem to have nothing to do with globalization."[23] It is uncontroversial to claim that the individual and the local are inflected by global forces and events. But since their deliberate occlusion tends toward the advantage of a neoliberal capitalist class, detecting, preserving, or resuscitating them remains a continuing, politically vital effort, never a settled fact.

The consequences of this global contemporaneity take unusual shape when drawn into poetic forms, which can detect globality using their own resources. D. A. Powell's "Long Night Full Moon" (2016), given here in full, dramatizes the epistemological stance we might associate with a global perspective, even as it calls this stance into question for its flattening effects:

> You only watch the news to find out
> where the fires are burning, which way
> the wind is blowing, and whether
> it will rain. Forecast ahead but first:
> A mother's boy laid out
> in the street for hours.
> These facts don't wash away.[24]

There is suffering seen, or overseen, at a distance: the body of Michael Brown in the streets of Ferguson, Missouri. It is tied into, somehow connected to, climate change, to wildfires and drought in California. Perhaps this connection is as associative or as opportunistic as the news; perhaps it hints at a deeper thought, what Timothy Morton calls "the ecological thought."[25] Formally, Powell's compression is a strategy for juxtaposing as well as connecting disparate things. Yet the poem disturbs this contiguity and leveling, which may uncritically place racialized state violence and ecological disaster on the same plane—or may, perhaps, tempt the viewer to prioritize one set of political actions over another ("but first"). Regardless, the staccato self-accusation—"you only watch the news to find out"— condemns the viewer who has the security to claim a choice between catastrophes.

Along with the relational effects of distanciation, integration, compression, and "glocalization" examined by Giddens and other social thinkers, a second marker of contemporary globalization is the financialization of the current global economic system.[26] Between 1980 and 1999, there was a 597 percent increase in long-term capital markets.[27] Sassen notes that the total value of derivatives in 2013 reached more than \$1 quadrillion.[28] Theories of finance—that sphere of activity where, in Fernand Braudel's evocative metaphor, the "great predators roam"—have proliferated in the years since the world financial crises of 2007–8.[29] Giovanni Arrighi's *The Long Twentieth Century* (1994) continues to be an early reference point. Arrighi charts and analyzes the alternation of systemic cycles of trade and finance from the Florentine city-states through the end of British imperialism and the dawning of U.S. hegemony. While Arrighi's long view situates the contemporary period as one among many turns from commodities and trade to credit and militarization, Donald MacKenzie's account of the invention of financial instruments uncovers the routes by which theories of finance transformed financial markets themselves, functioning not as a "camera" to picture the economy, but as an "engine" to change it.[30]

Today, the links between poetry and finance are found not so much in the architectures of poetic form as in the rhetorical powers poets employ, question, or discard. Examining the structure of financial derivatives through the rhetorical form of the promise, Arjun Appadurai argues that we live in an age characterized by the "failure of language."[31] Poetic forms can both acknowledge and confront this failure. Recent books of poetry try to imagine what the poetic speaker will look like after the end of capital from the perspective of the current period of financialization that Krippner calls *Capitalizing on Crisis*. Here is Christopher Nealon in section 16 of *The Victorious Ones* (2015):

So look I know I won't see the end of capital

But you, child—I wonder—

Surely it won't be pretty

Yes I know   protective gear   awkward alternative currencies

But maybe also how it might be said of you/that you were the ones who saw it through

The destruction from below of all the fucked-up supply chains by those giant worms from *Dune*

The dropping like a fly of every drone

I've seen you by the window with your beautiful wide eyes as storms rolled in

I've tried to teach you the words

I've imagined you remembered at the end of a long life, circled by
  friends beneath an empty sky

Your friends who wrote the poems of the 22nd century

  The poems of storms and drones,

And hoped that when they reached the line about you it would read,

  He who loved lightning watched them fall[32]

Nealon's poem, with its cross-generational apostrophe to a young child,
is about what poems will be about after capital. The poem itself does no
more than to prepare for this future within the bounds of life under capital.
The poem's thematic matter calls for more urgent attention than an analysis of how the poem "works": the poems of the future will be poems of
storms and drones. In *The Victorious Ones*, there is a weakening sense in
which the interiority, mood, or singular mind of a fictional speaker is manifest in the formal presentation of the poem. Enjambment carries no specific tropological force or function: the line ends because that is how far it
goes in thought. The rhyme seems to be the result of a casual accident. To
imagine a poetry after the end of capital, that poetry will not be rooted in
"prophecy," as Nealon's next poem describes, but in "lists, enumeration,
inventory." And it will "choose sides." Nealon's book imagines a poem no
longer ontologized by either the fiction of a lyric subject or the decon-
structive possibilities of textuality, but rather by its adjacency to other uses
of language.

Research on financialization falls within a well-established critique of
the free-market ideology of neoliberalism. David Harvey defines neoliberalism as "in the first instance a theory of political economic practices that
proposes that human well-being can best be advanced by liberating individual entrepreneurial freedoms and skills within an institutional framework characterized by strong private property rights, free markets, and
free trade."[33] A substantial corpus of works has uncovered the intellectual
history of the term. Economist Per Jacobsson, of the Bank of International
Settlements and the IMF, uses the term in 1948 to refer to the financial
discipline of a "non-socialist majority" in Europe.[34] Workshopped in Chile
in 1973, consolidated by the "fiscal rectitude" imposed on 1975 New York,
and enacted through the 1976 IMF bailout of the United Kingdom, neoliberalism has now come to signify a relatively clear and distinct economic
blueprint. As Jodi Melamed writes,

The term *neoliberalism* commonly refers to a set of economic policies that include financial liberalization (deregulation of interest rates), market liberalization (opening of domestic markets and the dismantling of tariffs), privatization, deregulation, and global economic management through international institutions and multilateral agreements.[35]

Recent criticisms of neoliberalism worry that its heuristic use is limited and that it represents primarily an ideology and a politics rather than an underlying shift in the logic of global capital. Indeed, as economic histories of the second half of the twentieth century by Greta Krippner and Daniel Stedman Jones explain, what we now call "neoliberalism" was perhaps only the gradual product of a series of contingent responses to intractable inflation and domestic class conflict in the 1970s.

This book adopts the premise that neoliberalism is "an ideology of governance that shapes subjectivities."[36] In doing so, however, I remain mindful of contemporary challenges to the subject and to subjectivity. The radical tradition of critical black studies thus provides a third site for theorizing poetry's globality. The end of Keynesian economic policy and the spread of neoliberalism and market securitization amplify the call for transcolonial solidarity in the face of domestic racism. Analyses of poetry, lyric, and song by Saidiya Hartman and Fred Moten refer us to racialized structures of global capitalism. Yet their examinations of common poetic terms such as "subject" and "surplus" have gone largely unrecognized within strands of poetic criticism. This is not so much a matter of coincidental likeness as it is a matter of exclusion. The existence of much poetic criticism has only been possible by tacitly expelling the global from its purview. In *Scenes of Subjection*, Saidiya Hartman writes, "The slave is the object or the ground that makes possible the existence of the bourgeois subject and, by negation or contradistinction, defines liberty, citizenship, and the enclosures of the social body."[37] There have, of course, been many critiques and bracketings and returns of the poetic subject, especially in the traditions of L=A=N=G=U=A=G=E and conceptual poetries. But to follow in the line of Hartman's thought instead, the very premise, the very idea, of a bourgeois lyric subject is made possible by the existence of a (lyric) object: the commodified human, the Atlantic slave trade, and the ongoing racialized violence necessary for the continuation of capitalism. This is one way in which the process of "lyricization," through which the lyric is made by our reading it as such, occurs in concert and in complicity with global capitalism.[38]

Anti-racist global critique and poetic criticism have also explored, independently, notions of surplus. Colloquially as well as critically, the adjective "lyrical" marks language that cannot be reduced to its communicative function, but is rather a remainder, supplement, or excess. Strangely, however, this surplus in poetry has been theorized in relative isolation from surplus in global capital. One task for a global poetics is to uncover the relation between these surpluses and in the process to embed the poetic term in a material history. In some treatments of poetic surplus, the heightening of the nonsignifying order of the poem dovetails with the fading of fictions of personhood. This disappearance is what Jonathan Culler means when he writes, in his *Theory of the Lyric* (2015), that "rhythm is an event without representation."[39] Or what Geoffrey Hartman means when he calls voice in poetry "the very process of sublimation" because "voice is intrinsically elegiac."[40] In other words, the more pronounced this performance, the more unlikely the poem's investment in representation.

The relationship between rhythm, event, and representation that Culler proposes takes on a historical, global, and racialized trajectory in Fred Moten's *In the Break* (2003). Moten is a global theorist of poetry, one who places lyric firmly in the history of capital. For Moten, rhythm is where representation, as the trace of the body, occurs. In *In the Break*, Moten reads a passage from Beauford Delaney's journals, in which the painter describes both his sister's singing and the fatal illness brought on by the lack of proper shelter or living conditions: "Listen to the sentence break or break down after the invocation of Sister's singing. That breakdown is not the negative effect of grammatical insufficiency but the positive trace of a lyrical surplus." He continues, "No need to dismiss the sound that emerges from the mouth as the mark of a separation. It was always the whole body that emitted sound: instrument and fingers, bend. Your ass is in what you sing."[41] For Moten, if song is not the sublimation of body, but rather its accompaniment, then life is in and on the line.

Danez Smith's poem "Song of the Wreckage," from *[INSERT] BOY* (2014), conjoins surplus capital with one kind of lyrical surplus: the overwhelming bodily effects of grief are manifest through the tightly controlled intricacy of the sestina form. Smith begins their poem with an epigraph by James Baldwin: "How much time do you want for your progress?" The wreckage in the poem's title marks the failure of time to bring progress for black lives. It is a song of afropessimism, the body of thought extending from Orlando Patterson through Hortense Spillers and Hartman to Jared Sexton and beyond.[42] The poem takes the form of a long sestina, separated into eight poems of twenty-four lines each. Seven of these poems are in the typical six-line sestina stanza; one is in tercets, couplets, and single lines. The first stanza reads:

> I have no time for Red to be beautiful
> with summer bloodied as it is & normal
> as it's become, with the rusted, small bones
> of boys who should be my father's age
> buried under the beaming bones of boys
> who should be my age, still tinged with meat.[43]

The overdetermination of each end word is the excess of bodily grief, mourning, and sickness. Smith writes, "I mourn all the time / right out the sky."[44] Moreover, if "time" is another word for "progress," then the poem replaces time with rhythm: "Let them cypher until their song is the new sun, / give them a joint & let them build a world from smoke. / Let them build a black boy's world. Rhythm to replace time. . . ."[45] The rhythm is the frequency: the iteration of end words in a sestina-like pattern, such that the first end word is "beautiful" and the final end word is "black." The nondiscursive aspect of the poem, a complex scheme of lexical repetition, is freighted with meaning. This lexical rhythm is not an event without representation, but rather the rhythm of the "fucked-up" notes in the head, to use a phrase from later in the poem. The heightened nondiscursivity is not where the human fades, to be replaced by a figure of voice, but where the body enters the poem.

The two poems by Nealon and Smith cited earlier capture two tendencies in contemporary poetry: a division between relatively unadorned language and hypertrophied song, one that tends to crop up in most periods of English poetry. But there is something more significant than that going on in these two books, which take the rhetorical situation of address and the surplus of music and, as their titles hint, tie them directly to capitalism and racism. To read these poems, the formal qualities that are often placed in the genealogy of poetic forms must instead be treated within the contingent geopolitical and historical conditions of their emergence.

The relation between poiesis and the global can be framed in terms that are explicitly geopolitical; just as often, poetry uncovers the global dimension of something that has not earned enough attention. The poets who follow are linked by their attempts to locate the sources of poetry in sites of the global. In dialectical fashion, some of these sites only reveal themselves as global when the impulse of poetry arises. In a recent essay, "Banana Republics of Poetry," M. NourbeSe Philip turns to the regenerative, rhizomatic form of the banana leaf as an emblem for a poetry that recognizes torn and wounded states of being while investing them with the possibilities of spreading, dividing, and proliferating.[46] If the source for the poetry that follows rests in the divisive, violent splittings provoked by the global, then the promise of the poetry lies in riotous flights, unexpected assemblages, improvident alliances, and unlikely choruses.

I have chosen the poets and poems in each chapter that follows for the salience with which global processes can be detected in their unique forms and their wide-ranging subject matter. Unexpected resemblances and unresolved tensions inevitably appear when such disparate poets are placed in relation to each other. While my method risks dissonant, diagonal leaps between poets and across traditions, nations, or cultural contexts, my hope is that the benefit to the reader, in terms of uncovering a set of common global conditions that shape how poetry in English is made today, outweighs the potential for eliding important differences and unequal positions. Comparative literature, world literature, and English literary studies have all been engaged in a critique of their disciplinary foundations in Anglo- and Eurocentric canons. In the context of Aamir Mufti's stirring injunction to "forget English!" my focus on (mostly) Anglophone poets might seem untimely. Moreover, my emphasis on close textual analysis means that work on the institutions that inhibit or allow access to and production of poetry remains outside the purview of this book; the place of Anglophone poets in an unequal "world republic of letters" has yet to be fully understood.[47] I focus here on Anglophone poets because their work is imbricated in unique ways with the making of globalization and the spread of a global English. In reaching back to the literary forms central to the development of English-language poetry, the poets here remake those forms as global. Rather than offering a final word, a comprehensive survey, or a privileged set of texts, I intend for each chapter to be an experiment in understanding the special ways that global capitalism comes into view through poetic form. In the spirit of collaborative scholarship with current and future generations of scholars working on poetry, I hope that this book provides inspiration and opens up new questions about poetry and global capitalism that might inform comparativist work yet to come.

Chapter 1 begins with the contestations over land that have played a crucial role in the creation of a global capitalist system. Contemporary Irish poetry, for which landscape has been a pivotal subject from Yeats to Kavanagh to Muldoon, grapples with this politicized history of place, from the unfinished "ghost estates" to the recent monetization of water and the converted hotels used to keep asylum seekers in perpetual limbo. This chapter offers readings of Irish poetry by Paula Meehan, Mary O'Malley, Seamus Heaney, and Sarah Clancy, arguing that the landscapes of contemporary Irish poetry are the indices of dispossession. Those who write descriptively about place, in other words, also write oppositionally after having been expelled from those places. Their poetry, which inhabits specific places, local settings, landscapes, or environments, is shaped dialectically by the new enclosure tactics of global capital. The next part of the chapter takes up poetic forms of the "block" and the "grid" to look more closely at the dispossessions produced by financialized capitalism, using as case studies British poet Keston Sutherland's *Odes to TL61P* (2013) and U.S. poet Anne Boyer's "The Animal Model of Inescapable Shock" (2015). Finally, I turn to the literal displacement of forced migration, as well as its feminization and racialization, by reading the Iraqi poet Manal Al-Sheikh's prose poems.

Chapter 2 explores global citizenship as a practice of exclusion undertaken in part through policies of liberal multiculturalism. The contemporary figure of the global or world citizen, examined critically by Atossa Araxia Abrahamian, Stuart Hall, Jodi Melamed, and Immanuel Wallerstein, is brought into poetry's lyric mode by the Jamaican American poet Claudia Rankine, born the year after Jamaica's independence. In Rankine's *Citizen: An American Lyric* (2014), present-day instances of racism comprise the prose lines of a lyric "meditative space." In the twenty-first-century *Citizen*, a poetic "I" is glimpsed in the negative shape of the racialized discourse that renders it invisible. Rankine writes an experimental "American lyric" in which the confessional lyric voice is made to contain the microaggressions and minoritarian struggles situated within the United States but created by a U.S.-manipulated global capitalist economy. The poems in *Citizen* offer both a diagnosis of the failures of citizenship as an ideal and a staging of the violent beauty that emerges from these failures.

Building on Chapter 2's discussion of citizenship, Chapter 3 asks, "What special resources do Anglophone poets use to make a precarious crowd newly visible?" For the small poem to contain the world of difference, it must find some way to extend a kind of radical hospitality—in Walt Whitman's terms, a sense of hopeful expectation for "the certainty of others, the life, love, sight, hearing of others." I argue that the rhetoric of poetic exhortation has been reinvigorated in a line of contemporary poetry. This chapter charts the course of exhortation through the contemporary work of multiple poets whose lives are bound up in global processes. Exhortation is one of the modes, stances, or registers of poetry that attempts to call forth a collective "we," the "we" of lives that, in some cases, lack a state at all or, in other cases, refuse to link their identities to an oppressive regime. Yet instead of making an explicit gesture toward including an existing group or relying only on an ecumenicism of multicultural references, these poets use a hortatory aesthetics to shape the formal totality of the poem. This chapter includes a heterogeneous group of poets: Sean Bonney, Myung Mi Kim, and Agha Shahid Ali. However different in the stances they assume, Bonney, Kim, and Ali share a common endeavor to make the precarious "we" visible. They develop an implicit notion of the hortatory mode as both a political expedient and an aesthetic device.

Chapter 4, taking its cue from the ecological disasters of the current era, turns back once more to the loco-descriptive powers of poetry. The modern prospect poem, while originating in a masterly position of spectatorship, has become an attempt to confront the apparent irrevocability of globalization's damage. In this chapter, I look at poets who conjure a global subject faced with a last judgment, a full stop, or what Hannah Arendt, in her prescient commitment to the globality of a dawning age, calls an "unredeemably stupid fatality." Looking back on the lineages of post-1970 through contemporary poetry in light of catastrophic finality, this concluding chapter considers how writing by the British poet J. H. Prynne, the Ghanaian poet Kofi Awoonor, and the U.S. poets Natasha Trethewey and Juliana Spahr examines the conditions of possibility for a global subject in the light of global cataclysm: that which may no longer be prevented or undone. Individual considerations of these poets are subtended by an analysis of the modern prospect poem, in which the poet climbs the hill to get a decent enough view of the world. The view, in the case of Awoonor, is of dead Africans in the Middle Passage and of captive and exile birds. In Natasha Trethewey's prosimetric memoir, *Beyond Katrina: A Meditation on the Mississippi Gulf Coast*, the devastation of Hurricane Katrina is seen from the vantage point of the global development of the Gulf Coast.

A coda shows how the methods I use in the book uncover the globality of a U.S. poet, John Ashbery, who does not thematically engage the discourses of globalization. Then, through a brief analysis of Solmaz Sharif's *Look* (2016), I explore one of the tensions or problems for poets writing explicitly about globalization in English—namely, that the spread of English itself has been inseparable from the violence of the global and has abetted its propagation. Sharif writes about the Iran-Iraq War, the twenty-first-century U.S. invasion and occupation of Iraq, and the detainment of prisoners in Guantanamo Bay. She employs a particular kind of "global English," one that is forged in U.S. wars and military occupations in the Middle East. I conclude by reflecting more broadly on the ways that contemporary poetry has been engaged in remaking a politics of globalization and how a study of poetry changes our sense of what ethical and political actions and subjectivities are possible within the democratic crises of global capitalist regimes.

The chapters together argue that contemporary English-writing poetry is fully imbricated with and conditioned by the forms of contemporary globalization. Under the regimes of global capitalism, the violent exclusions produced by communitarian forms of belonging and by resurgent nationalisms make various calls to collective life and struggle all the more tentative and embattled. The conditions of such precarious life on earth are the grounds for the global imagination of the poetry here—which also means that these poems are able to develop a more capacious social world than has yet been attributed to genre-defining claims about interpersonal address and nondiscursivity. These global poetries bear the impress of an actual social world that has, over the last forty years, become painfully, markedly absent: it is unrepresentable, unsayable, illegible, and practically unthinkable under induced conditions of neoliberal globalization, racialized capitalism, and the contemporary precarity of life. The poets in this book are situated in conditions of precariousness, rather than in humanistic, juridical, or legal fictions of subjectivity, personhood, or individuality. However different they are in the stances they assume or the aesthetic "camps" to which they belong, they can be understood together as developing a global poetics. All these poets are chosen for the way their poems grasp and renourish the roots of poetry—song, dance, praise, exhortation, possession—by fusing them with the roots of globalization and the enclosure of economic and political spaces. At the same time that poetry is engaged in registering a social world defined by produced scarcity, various types of expulsions, and new restrictions on what might constitute personhood, the recognition of sociality also comes about, is produced, through poetry's exploration of a global revolutionary consciousness.

Ultimately, the poetry in this book, and especially the prospect poems with which it concludes, raises questions of where poetic voices and standpoints emerge, to whom the representation of a poetic subject can be extended, and how far the traditional forms of poetry can be stretched to allow the global to enter. But these poets tend not to use strategies of direct representation or recovery. Indeed, the politics of representation itself often partakes of the exclusions that a global poetics confronts.[48] While theorists from Butler to Spivak to Wilderson have emphasized an analogous point in critical contexts of gender studies, ethics, postcoloniality, and the ontology of blackness, I argue that contemporary poetry also participates in and complicates what a critical global studies might be. Without recognizing the global and the geopolitical as crucial to the very making of the poem, critics risk positioning poetry outside of the world that it endeavors to remake. The poems that follow orient their global perspectives within forms of English-writing poetry and thus within epistemologies forged in claims to a universal history. In the process, the architectural structures of the poems are unsettled and the traditions of Anglophone poetry are radically reimagined. The ecstatic, proleptic, and sometimes desperate calls to come together performed by the poems in this book become the wishful image of a future in which the rejection of the global present is at one with the revolutionary songs that the poem sustains.

CHAPTER I

Stolen Landscapes

The Investments of the Ode
and the Politics of Land

The massive global displacements, uprootings, dislocations, and migrations of the twenty-first century have emerged in tandem with a distinct set of anti-capitalist protests and poetic forms accompanying them. The enclosure of land through speculation and investment is the primary leitmotif I follow in this chapter, first through landscape poems and then through new shapes of prose poetry that critically examine the possibilities for a revolutionary space within contemporary enclosure movements. I begin with a set of Irish poets for whom the landscape poem provides a conventional vocabulary that strains under the pressures of dispossession. From the topoi of the landscape poem, I turn next to the emergence of two formal analogues in the wake of the 2007–8 financial crises: "block" and "grid" poems, poetic prose that is cast into the rectangular shapes of containment. The block and the grid register complicated forms of enclosure that are sensed without yet being conceptualized. The arc of the chapter concludes with a prose poem in translation, written explicitly from the standpoint of a displaced Iraqi poet. The meaning of dispossession today is perhaps clearest when presented in terms of forced migration, the refugee crisis, which affects nearly 65 million people at the time of writing. At the end of this chapter, my analysis of the poetics of dispossession shifts from semi-peripheral and imperial sites of the Global North to conclude with poetic voices speaking from gendered and racialized positions of global displacement.

Themes of dispossession and forced removal often accompany philosophical accounts of poetic creation. Susan Stewart describes the strange fictions of displacement that poetic performances require: she writes, "When actors become the recipients of actions, when speakers speak from the position of listeners, when thought is unattributable and intention wayward, the situation of poetry is evoked."[1] Stewart's account draws on Plato's *Ion*, in which a state of psychic displacement is one of the conditions for poetry. But these psychic displacements have political implications. In Stewart's most famous example, the poets are excluded from Plato's *Republic* precisely for the "unthought" "charm" of their work. In the Platonic account, poetry disturbs the social order of things, putting the poet in a place she should not occupy or attributing to her a form of knowledge she does not have. Complicating Stewart's Platonic expulsion, the Maghrebi poet Habib Tengour understands rhapsodic possession as a postcolonial stratagem, in which the poet adopts the pose of the madman in order to compose poetry in the language of the colonizer. The madman is believed "to speak what has been silenced."[2] Tengour brings us directly to a global poetics of dispossession: a poiesis that has been motivated by the material privations brought about by globalization. If social and political dispossession has been paired, at least philosophically, with poetic possession, today literal forms of displacement, exclusion, and expulsion shape poetic creation.

The poets in this chapter ground their sense of place in a materialist critique of dispossession. From the perspective of global political economy, a focus on dispossession helps to bring into view the transition from global development projects led by the state, ostensibly for the greater public good, to private investments in land. As the sociologist Michael Levien writes, dispossession "has been a constitutive feature of the sociospatial transformations engendered by colonial, post-colonial, and neoliberal political economies."[3] In his research on Indian "regimes of dispossession," Levien traces the process by which dispossession, once a key feature of "state-led projects of industrial transformation," becomes instead a method for "redistributing land upwards."[4] Levien's argument that dispossession has been detached from the production of commodities and linked instead to the commodification of land provides a historical through-line that connects the Irish poets in the beginning of this chapter to the U.K. and Iraqi poets with whom it concludes.

While Levien uses India as a case study, Saskia Sassen examines the expulsion from place in more general terms as a systemic global process that subtends disparate locations. Sassen emphasizes that expulsions—from eviction via land grabs and displacement by war to incarceration and "warehousing" in ghettos and slums—are both "made" and "acute," or distinguished by their current scale.[5] Sassen compiles an archive of expulsions that brings together important research from the last decade of critical global studies. While displacing and immiserating masses of people, these expulsions have also created vicious new sites for labor, including the slum and the SEZ (Special Economic Zone). Mike Davis traces the process by which "rapid urban growth in the context of structural adjustment, currency devaluation and state retrenchment has been an inevitable recipe for the mass production of slums."[6] Vijay Prashad's *The Poorer Nations* takes up the role of the SEZ. Brought to vivid life in Stephanie Black's documentary *Life and Debt* (2001), SEZs from China to Mexico to Jamaica are immune from labor and environmental laws. They attract primarily women workers "who leave the failed countryside for the glittering SEZ, where they throw in their youth for the overproduction machine that then spills out its products into the over-filled shops of the Atlantic world, where the debt-ridden consumer tries to keep up with their manufactured desires."[7] As the work of Levien, Sassen, Davis, Prashad, and Black makes clear, dispossession is not only a destructive process, looking backward at the elimination of traditional ways of life. It is also a brutally creative one, in the sense that the people displaced are put to work without protection and forced to live in positions of acutely increased precarity.

Irish poetry constitutes a capacious poetic archive of the violence of dispossession—specifically, land expropriation and housing bubbles in the early 2000s, and asylum housing crises and taxes on water in the early 2010s. The first part of this chapter surveys some of those forms in contemporary Irish poetry, arguing first that the landscapes of poems by Paula Meehan, Mary O'Malley, Sarah Clancy, and Seamus Heaney are indices of dispossession. Much more than documents of the local or nostalgic celebrations of the picturesque, Irish poems about place testify to the seizure of land by investors from afar as well as to the involvement of the Irish state in abetting speculation in land at the expense of housing and public services. Dispossessions created in familiar, though historically specific ways by "the transformation of commonly owned and managed lands into individual property" exist alongside those that have their source in a financialized economy, one that depends on "more seemingly abstract forms of privatization."[8]

From Speranza's "The Famine Year" (1848) to W. B. Yeats's "The Stolen Child" (1889) and from Patrick Kavanagh's "The Great Hunger" (1942) to Tana French's *Broken Harbour* (2012), landscapes of Irish literature are inseparable from foreclosures, evictions, ghost estates, and speculation. The term "venture capital" itself comes from British speculation in Irish land in the early 1640s.[9] The centrality of land and place in Irish literature has always been both intensely politicized and globally oriented, even if the global thrust of its politics has often been cast in the provincializing terms of cultural nationalism. Joyce's Dublin, Beckett's staging of bare life, Heaney's pilgrim sites, holy wells, and bogs, and Muldoon's roadside shrines are linked by an investigation not only of place, but also, arguably, of the global processes that have taken place away or otherwise limited its social use to an elite few. Writing about landscape in recent Irish poetry could risk the critique of an unfashionable interest in locodescriptive verse. But to think that way is to lose sight of the long history of stolen, misused, and monetized land in contemporary Ireland, from the unfinished "ghost estates" to the recent monetization of water.[10] Poetry that inhabits specific places, local settings, landscapes, or environments today cannot fail to be shaped by these "new enclosures" of global capital.[11]

Although Irish poets are far from the only writers who shape their poetry to channel these processes, it is hard to think of a corpus of contemporary poetry as vitally and diversely engaged with expulsion, displacement, and dispossession as twenty-first-century Irish poetry. Paula Meehan's "Death of a Field," from *Painting Rain* (2009), elegizes the "end of the field," which announces "the start of the estate":

> The end of dandelion is the start of Flash
> The end of dock is the start of Pledge
> The end of teazel is the start of Ariel
> The end of primrose is the start of Brillo
> The end of thistle is the start of Bounce
> The end of sloe is the start of Oxyaction
> The end of herb robert is the start of Brasso
> The end of eyebright is the start of Fairy[12]

Each line shows the conversion of land into branded commodity. But not just any commodity: these are cleaning products, suggesting housework and reproductive labor. The field of the herb, perhaps with a hint of homeopathic cures to be gathered from it, gives way to the cleaning product of the household. The knowledge encrypted in the herbs has become the unwaged labor that requires an array of specialized goods. Just as the parts of the field are highly specific, so are the brands they become, to the point that the proper names take on an anthropomorphic quality. Or perhaps an allegorical one: "Flash" and "Bounce" have something almost possessed about them, as though they are the contemporary equivalents of the allegorized figures of Virtue and Faith. The death of the field is not only the "start," but also the animation or the life of the commodity—a point to which I will return later. The catalogue concludes with Proctor and Gamble's bright green dishwashing liquid, "Fairy," a far cry from the fairy lore collected from the fields of the Great Hunger. Those dead fields, the poem suggests, have had yet another death to die. Meehan's poem brings us full circle, as it were, back to Fairy, now a fungible commodity instead of a spirit.

Meehan's poetic field stages the impossible replanting of herbs by commodities, bizarrely suggesting a one-to-one correspondence between each, and thus highlighting the exchangeability of the product as well as the worker who uses it. Her poem dramatizes what Rob Nixon calls "displacement without moving," which refers not to the removal of communities, but rather to "the loss of the land and resources beneath them."[13] In *The Enigma of Capital and the Crises of Capitalism* (2010), David Harvey defines "accumulation by dispossession" as

> all those peasant and indigenous populations expelled from the land, deprived of access to their natural resources and ways of life by illegal and legal (that is, state-sanctioned), colonial, neo-colonial or imperialist means, and forcibly integrated into market exchange . . . by forced monetization and taxation. The conversion of common rights of usage into private property rights in land completes the process. Land itself becomes a commodity.[14]

Harvey describes the kind of field-death that Meehan brings into poetic language. In doing so, Meehan animates the commodity, reanimates the fairy lore of the Hunger, and genders the subject, as well as the labor produced by this enclosure. Today, in the real fields of Athenry, once the heart of nationalist ballad and song, a different death has occurred: the end of the ballad is the start of a new server farm for Apple. The emphatic insistence on song, poetry, and performance constitutes a form of resistance to this process and an oppositional stance for poets to take.

Ireland does not come up as often as might be expected in sociologies and histories of globalization. In the first volume of *Civilization and Capitalism* (1979, 1992), however, Fernand Braudel uses Ireland's economic transformations as a key index to the development of a capitalist world economy. Braudel underscores the fact that Ireland is part of what Ian Baucom more recently calls "a migrant Atlantic modernity."[15] After acknowledging the deforestation of Ireland by the timber market in the seventeenth century, Braudel shows how Ireland's "subjection to the English market" in the eighteenth century makes it a key supplier to "not only England but the English fleet, the sugar islands of the West Indies and the fleets of other western nations, notably France."[16] The collapse of the meat market because of competition from America and Russia leads directly to the transformation of Ireland from grain importer to grain exporter, to meet the new demand for grain from an industrialized England. But as Braudel notes, Ireland can only export grain by depriving its people of it: "It is not the surplus that leaves the country, it is what anywhere else would be the vital necessity."[17] Ireland's subjection to an international division of labor leads to the Great Hunger and the genocide and emigration of over two million people. Ireland is a paradigmatic case for the exploitation that accompanies the cycles of capital in the modern world-system, cycles that Giovanni Arrighi charts in detail in the *Long Twentieth Century* (1994).

The figure of the Irish emigrant, most familiar from mid-nineteenth-century poems of the Great Hunger, assumes contemporary and mythical forms in Mary O'Malley's "Ceres in Caherlistrane," from *Asylum Road* (2001). O'Malley reappropriates the Greek myth of Persephone as a way of writing about displacement and the international division of labor. The title conflates a place-name with a mythological figure. Caherlistrane is north of Galway city; Ceres, the mother of Persephone, condemns the earth to winter while her daughter spends half the year in hell, having eaten the seeds of a pomegranate offered her by Hades. O'Malley moves the poles of the myth from earth and hell to Galway and New York: Persephone is now a busker, "somewhere near forty-second street," who "sings for a hawk-eyed man." In the summer, she returns to County Galway, where "a seed caught/in her teeth will keep the cleft between this world/and the next open." But her song, when she sings in Ireland, is now "tuned to a buried watercourse" and retains echoes of her time in the "graffiti-sprayed subway" of New York.[18]

The poem is not only about escape, but also about dependency, just as the myth is about the links between actions undertaken in hell and their consequences on earth. The construction of New York, O'Malley implies, depends on the emigration from Ireland of cheap surplus labor pools. This realization of global brutality is not directly known or thematized ("she has no idea") but rather given form in her song. The "voice of Ireland" that her listener, Hades, seems to discern in her singing is the voice of a traditional agricultural society, drawing millions of tourists to seek out an "authentic," "timeless" Irish culture: "he tastes, in the lark's pillar of sound/honey and turf-fires." When she returns to Galway, however, the brutality of the history of emigration is heard in her song. O'Malley takes the world-systemic forces of political economy, expressed through the creative economy of busking, and narrates them in mythical terms: her Irish "history from below" can only be represented in its full international implications through the existing material of Greek myth. Ceres, who causes the devastation of the land in winter, surely is a figure for the genocide of the Great Hunger, which prompts millions of Irish to emigrate or to die trying. But O'Malley also takes the collective suffering produced by global labor markets and channels it through a single voice. In "Ceres in Caherlistrane," the authentically "Irish" subject is situated within transnational flows of labor. This definition of national identity depends on a felt solidarity with others who have emigrated for a better life or for survival, only to find themselves the disposable instruments of global capitalism.

As the logic of privatization and enclosure modulates in the financial markets of the twenty-first century, the Irish field becomes securitized as well as commodified. Securitization refers to the process by which an underlying physical asset, such as land, serves as the basis for contracts between third parties. These agreements have nothing to do with the price or value of the asset itself, but nevertheless have a resounding, if indirect effect on national monetary policy, ultimately affecting prices and exchange rates, as well as the people whose lives depend on their stability. Of course, securitization coincides with and exacerbates actual dispossession from the land, such that refugees are kept endlessly in dilapidated Salthill hotels and the homeless on Grafton Street doorsteps. Greta Krippner describes how financialization in the United States arises as a means of deferring political decisions about redistribution.[19] In Ireland, under the government's austerity program, "the capital expenditure for social housing was reduced by 80 percent" from 2008 to 2013.[20] From 2008 to 2011, the number of homeless households increased by 68 percent.[21] Rather than addressing the disastrous consequences of the Irish bubble, new economic policies "have acted to delay the onset of future crises of mortgage debt while relying on market mechanisms."[22] The sharp increase in inequality has been accompanied, and exacerbated, by the rise of new financial instruments and institutions, including the National Asset Management Association and Real Estate Investment Trusts.[23] In this context, the institution of a three-hundred-euro water tax in spring 2015 is both a symbol of the Irish government's antidemocratic politics and a grave injury to a population whose lives are being sold to finance the government's debt.

In an exhortation that runs directly against the future-driven logic of land speculation, the Galway poet Sarah Clancy has demanded "we must live in these times and no other."[24] Clancy's poem "And Yet We Must Live in These Times" has been a rallying cry for those protesting the water tax. Adrienne Rich's "What Kind of Times are These," from which Clancy gets her title, ends with a description of a possessed landscape, a "ghost-ridden crossroads, leafmold paradise."[25] The poet knows "who wants to buy it, sell it, make it disappear." Clancy's poem begins in a housing office with a succinct description of housing debt: "These are the times that I live in/paying the tail end of my mortgage/with no home to show for it." The poet resists the clichés and idle chatter of Galway streets, asserting "we are not grand thanks, we are hurt/and we're making it worse by pretending we're sorted." In the middle of the poem, the poet, increasingly alienated from the crowd around her on Shop Street, suddenly gives way to skepticism:

> and I write down past-tense love affairs
> all the while getting older and worn out
> and what use is it? Resuscitating old lovers for nothing
> recycling these slogans, these dictums,
> if I can't write about this stuff why bother?

This encounter with the suspicion that writing is useless becomes the bridge first to rage—"I fool myself that one of these days I might do it/might hurt someone/and it might bring me to some other dimension." But this anger against the world, a fantasy of sovereignty, gives way to something else, a lack of self-possession. The poem concludes, "We must live in these times and no other,/I for one, might need some help with it/is that too much to ask for?" In the developing logic of Clancy's poem, dependency is not an a priori vulnerability, but a deliberate refusal of competitive self-mastery, the fantasy of which would only further the destruction of the world.

To follow both field and water through contemporary Irish poetry leads from Galway's canals to Seamus Heaney's final poem, "Banks of a Canal" (2013), which enacts its own distinct kind of field work, to borrow the title of Heaney's 1981 collection. Heaney's poem contains no explicit mention of commodification (Meehan), emigration and labor (O'Malley), or neoliberalism and the state (Clancy). Heaney approaches place far more obliquely, in part because of a felt pressure to tie the landscapes of Northern Ireland directly to political violence. In "Place and Displacement: Recent Poetry from Northern Ireland," a lecture delivered in 1985, Heaney speaks of the predicament of the Northern Irish poet as belonging "to a place that is patently riven between notions of belonging to other places."[26] Heaney questions methods of reading that draw sociological links between Northern Irish poets and "the blemished life of their country."[27] The poet, Heaney says,

> is stretched between politics and transcendence, and is often displaced
> from a confidence in a single position by his disposition to be affected
> by all positions, negatively rather than positively capable. This, and
> the complexity of the present conditions, may go some way to explain
> the large number of poems in which the Northern Irish writer views
> the world from a great spatial or temporal distance, the number of
> poems imagined from beyond the grave, from the perspective of
> mythological or historically remote characters.[28]

Heaney's defense of poetry written during emergent occasions is striking for its refusal to pit a visionary poetics against a directly political one. What he names as a "displaced perspective" amplifies rather than mutes the poem's effects. This alternate version of Nixon's "displacement without moving" is dramatized and scrutinized closely in his own coming-to-terms with poetry and violence, *Station Island* (1984), as well as in earlier poems such as "Casualty." Heaney's intention in his reading of Mahon, Muldoon, and Longley is to open a larger space for poetry in political life by preventing its pigeon-holing in one of two alternatives: either "deliberately provocative" or "culpably detached."[29]

"Banks of a Canal," published in a collection celebrating the 150th anniversary of the National Gallery of Ireland, is an ekphrastic sonnet, a rendering in words of a painting from 1872 by Gustave Caillebotte.[30] The full title of Caillebotte's painting is "Banks of a Canal near Naples," and the form of Heaney's sonnet is Italian: two abba quatrains making up an octet are followed by two tercets making up a sestet. Heaney does not use this structure to create poetic closure, nor to summon the ghosts of Petrarchan conceits, but rather to examine the painting in unexpected ways. A small structure orients the poet's eye: "the stunted concrete" on the canal's bank "mocks the classical," a phrase that plays on the older meaning of "to mock" as "to imitate." The poem begins by repeating some of the opening words, "silence and slow time," of Keats's "Ode on a Grecian Urn," an ekphrastic poem that does indeed "mock" the classical. "Say 'canal,'" the poet entreats, and the second vowel of "canal" generates a Keatsian thought-picture, "towing silence with it," "slowing time / to a walking pace, a path."

In the second quatrain, the water itself speaks, this time of dream, sleep, and peace. Finally, in the sestet, the "I" of the poem emerges to describe what the poet sees and what might be beyond the visual. At each point, the actual Caillebotte painting is not described faithfully in the poem, but rather serves as a prompt for poetic making that both echoes certain aspects of the painting (the meandering path) and exceeds them (the mysterious consonants of "verges" and "coolth," the wandering soul).

The virtues of the landscape, which include exploration, time, sleep, dream, and peace, have a value that exceeds the estimation of the land or the delineation of resources to be extracted from it. Instead of "displacement without moving," we might call this revaluation "inhabiting without possessing." But the poem does more than extol pleasure, leisure, and contemplation. The title of the poem belies its significance; the title of the painting, which includes "Naples," only slightly less so. The inconspicuous canal in fact features prominently in the early modern transformation of Europe. Particularly in Italy, the canal was the primary means by which the land of the plains was reclaimed, through irrigation and crop cultivation, to provide food for growing urban areas.[31] Canals made trade in commodities possible, even as the irrigation of land created its own forms of enslavement and seasonal migration. As Braudel puts it, bluntly, "Economic progress was assured—but at the price of social misery."[32] Caillebotte's painting and Heaney's poem lead eye and voice to the edge of the city. That border is, quite literally, their vanishing point. Yet the poem, like the painting, lingers in the foreground through a series of displacements, silences, and slowings of time. The kinds of detachment Heaney uses are poetic ones—essentially, changes in perspective—that involve the displacement of the voice. First, there is the conjuring power of a vowel, followed by the prosopopoeia of water. These throws of the voice prolong the turn, in the sestet, to the knowing "I," to the contemplative "soul," and to the city, as yet invisible beyond them. As we know from Keats's "vale of soul-making," the discovery of the "soul," still to come after Heaney's sonnet ends, is forged through repeated encounters with the crushing violence of this world.[33] If the soul in Heaney's poem "stray[s] beyond" the path, it is not to some promised paradise, but to the city.

Confronted by the democratic crises, resurgent nationalisms, and neoliberal policies of twenty-first-century Europe, this version of contemporary Irish poetry concerns itself with landscapes and local sites, but not in order to market Irishness through a nostalgic voyeurism. The landscapes in Irish poetry are landscapes that have been stolen, enclosed, or expropriated for transatlantic and European markets. The figures that inhabit these

places do so from exilic, resistant, socially marginal, or otherwise displaced
positions. The responses to these processes have taken the particular
form of poems that layer past and present landscapes. Meehan, O'Malley,
Clancy, and Heaney are not invested in sepia-tinted older views or in
postcards of present sites, but rather in the contiguity between the field
and the commodity, the canal and the city. In this way, the poems enact
a form of repossession, in which the processes of exclusion they describe
are rendered contingent, historical, and ongoing. In a world not disen-
chanted, but rather repossessed, Irish poetry speaks of the present—
"these times"—and leads us to the city, imploring us to figure out how to
live together in it.

By writing about landscape, Irish poets make contemporary use of a set
of literary topoi in order to acknowledge the undoing of the social fabric
and the human and ecological costs of the movement of capital. In Ireland as in the United States, some of the most visible repercussions of the
current age of dispossession have occurred on the ground, in subprime
housing markets.[34] But physical dispossession is only one of the forms
contemporary displacements take. The extraordinary value of long-term
capital markets has decentered the physical asset, the commodity, and the
factory from the focus of political economy. Giovanni Arrighi describes
the mid-1960s through the early 1980s in terms of "the resurgence of private high finance in the production and regulation of world money."[35] To
continue in Meehan's terms, the death of the commodity is the life of the
financial derivative, the birth of securitized assets. As Sassen, Arjun Appadurai, James Ferguson, Levien, and others have analyzed, land is far more
valuable today (in terms of global capital) as something on which one
might speculate, rather than live or subsist. This second-order dispossession of land has something eerie to it. One imagines, once again, the empty
fields, themselves now exiled and wandering through the secular transit
routes of capital. This strange new logic of possession brings the dead
commodity back to life as the credit default swap.

While the tradition of landscape poetry offers resources at hand for
poets who wish to think about land grabs or the privatization of water, the
financial markets of the global economy are so abstract and occur at such a
remove from ordinary life that poetry might seem to be an odd instrument
for thinking about them. Moreover, the precise extent of the damage of
financial instruments to political life, and especially to possibilities for collective solidarity and to the agency of individuals, has only begun to be
analyzed. Arrighi notes that "domestic social polarizations during financial
expansions were integral aspects of ongoing processes of concentration of

capital on a world scale."[36] The roots of the current period of austerity and democratic crisis in Europe can be traced to the decisive form that globalization, as the integration of capital, product, and labor markets, takes during the 1960s–80s: the combination of "U.S. restrictive monetary policy, high real interest rates, and deregulation."[37] Recent work by Franco Berardi and Appadurai departs from Arrighi in order to imagine social life in a financialized economy.[38] In Berardi's account, "semio-capitalism" comes about when "indeterminacy takes the place of the fixed relation between labor-time and value, so that the whole regime of exchange falls into an aleatory system of floating values."[39] Appadurai argues that the rhetorical structure of the promise underlies financial volatility: he writes that "no one thought to blame the linguistic and moral burden of creating a vast interlinked chain of promises that encouraged the total severance of reciprocal relations from rapid circulation and leveraged derivative assets."[40]

While Berardi and Appadurai identify semiotic and linguistic structures at play in the flow of capital, Jasper Bernes looks at the post-1970s centrality of creative labor to changes in the workplace. Bernes describes the crisis of the Fordist and Taylorist structures of labor, arguing that capitalism restructures itself in part through "artistic critique," in which "the critique of labor posed by experimental writers and artists of the postwar period became a significant force behind the restructuring of capitalism, by providing important coordinates, ideas, and images for that restructuring."[41] These accounts point to certain complicities and imbrications between art, capital, and labor. In doing so, however, they also leave open the possibility that poetry might reshape the social relations produced under capital, or at least offer a vision for doing so. Berardi's poststructuralist theory of finance, with its roots in Deleuze, should be carefully distinguished from Bernes's Marxist analysis of informal labor, which builds more directly on Brenner and Arrighi. The poetry I explore does not fit neatly into either framework, however, resisting both the external standpoint of opposition that Berardi imagines and the complicity with managing capitalism that Bernes describes.

Abstract processes of global finance create vicious material effects, innovative protest tactics, and brutal strategies of state violence deployed to contain them: these connections are brought under scrutiny by the U.K. poet Keston Sutherland. Sutherland turns to the ode, the history of which he engages and transforms in order to rethink the relevance of the commodity form, the individual, and the collective in the global economy. Sutherland's odes draw on the politics of this labile, oratorical subgenre, which from Horace to Andrew Marvell to Bernadette Mayer has been the vehicle for a mordant critique of the present and for the transformation of poetic subjectivity. In Sutherland's odes, the traditional alternation of strophes is channeled into the shape of the block instead, which comprises "every possible type of language object that could be bagged and bound into one shape."[42] Sutherland's description could apply equally to the landmarks of the Anglophone ode, many of which have provoked critics into attempts to make them cohere. The ode might be defined by a sustained and charged progression through contradictions in attitude and sentiment, perhaps best exemplified by the line of British odes that stretches from Marvell's "An Horation Ode Upon Cromwell's Return from Ireland" to its Romantic apogee in Wordsworth's "Ode: Intimations of Immortality from Recollections of Early Childhood." But for the purposes of this chapter, one of the initial reference points for Sutherland is the abolitionist poet William Cowper, for whom the ode was the vehicle for denouncing slavery.[43] Sutherland's odes are both a reprise and a departure from the political morphing of the ode's shape to confront historical capitalism: they force the ode to respond to the police tactic of "kettling" anti-capitalist protestors by establishing within the poem an aesthetic shape commensurate with the "lived physical injustice of being contained in these shapes."

One of the most elaborately ceremonial and public genres of poetry, the ode is also one of the most untimely today, a relatively minor presence in the Anglophone poetry of the twentieth century.[44] Its proliferation in the twenty-first, then, suggests a renewed historical purpose for its flexible shapes and powerful rhetoric. Unlike some poetic forms, the modern English ode has a widely agreed-upon starting date: 1656, when Cowley publishes his *Pindarique Odes*.[45] In the eighteenth century, the ode becomes associated—as least in Dr. Johnson's mind—with "sublimity, rapture, and quickness of transition."[46] The eighteenth-century ode reflects classical lyric ambitions to praise virtues and reveal vices. By the nineteenth century, as Helen Vendler shows in her study of Keats, the ode becomes a vehicle for exploring various "attitudes toward the senses, almost as though the odes were invented as a series of controlled experiments in the suppression or permission of sense experience."[47] Despite these different emphases, over time, three qualities of the ode persist: serious tone, heightened diction, and enrichment by poetic device.[48]

The subject matter of classical Greek and Latin and modern Anglophone odes varies widely: while classical odes were written as public panegyrics to gods or consummate athletes, early modern and romantic odes range from celebrations of the prodigious talents of famous friends or ambiguous attitudes about current events to hymns to emotions or reflections on urns. Attempts to define the ode as a subgenre of poetry emphasize its seriousness and its anthropocentrism or humanism. For M. H. Abrams, the defining characteristics of the ode are "lyric magnitude and a serious subject, feelingfully meditated."[49] Perhaps because the stakes of the ode are almost always quite high, its performances occasioned by dramatic historical and personal turbulence, the ode has served as the focus of foundational twentieth-century arguments over how to read poetry.[50] Indeed, the ode generally refuses to settle at rest on the page or to lend itself to satisfactory categorization as a formal structure. Its rhetoric is pitched closer to oratory than to meditative verse, yet its artifice is anything but extemporaneous.[51] And while the ode typically aspires to transcend its occasion with a statement or attitude of lasting value, it rarely loses grasp of a particular subject, person, or event.

The English ode has a history of denaturalizing the position of the poet in the world, voicing his estrangement from it in strains of both praise and lamentation; often, the ode attempts to relocate the poet at home in a world from which he has been displaced. In Abrams's well-known description, the project of the ode is "to join together the 'subject' and 'object' that modern intellection had put asunder, and thus to revivify a dead nature, restore its concreteness, significance, and human values, and re-domiciliate man in a world which had become alien to him."[52] Like the greater Romantic lyric examined by Abrams, contemporary odes locate and transform the individual in the world. But the contemporary world through which the ode must pass is particularly inhospitable, characterized by "geopolitical perturbations, ecoontological imperatives, and the operating premise of a sentient earth," or what Emily Apter appropriately calls "planetary dysphoria."[53] Odes to a dying planet, odes to precarious life and labor, odes to obsolete household objects: these are unlikely urns, inauspicious gods, devastated landscapes for the ode to worship. Yet at the same time the world has perhaps never seemed more "alien" to the human, and the possibilities of "re-domiciliation" less propitious than now, making the odal dialectic between self and object/world a strangely urgent, if uncertain way of navigating globalized life.

The complex process toward "re-domiciliation" that the ode undertakes is just as important as the actual homecoming it may or may not achieve. A dynamic, ever-changing relation between the perceiving mind and the perceived world is crucial to the ode, as Abrams argues in "Structure and Style in the Greater Romantic Lyric." Confronting the alienation of the poet from the world, the ode takes on a halting style of progression, a method of testing and probing rather than naming and defining. It engages and disengages from its object, moves forward and back, approaches from a variety of angles, retreats and circles back, invests in and divests from the authority of its speaker, proclaims its theme and then digresses. So in Keats's "Ode on Indolence" the figures seen are like figures on an urn, the turning of which brings them back into view.[54] In Hölderlin's ode to "Autumn," iconic images of the past and the seasons cycle through the stanzas, a processional that is also signaled by Hölderlin's repetition of the verb *kehren*, to turn, three times.[55] Auden, in "In Praise of Limestone," begins, "If it form the one landscape that we, the inconstant ones,/Are consistently homesick for, this is chiefly/Because it dissolves in water." He then returns again and again to the landscape, revealing that "this land is not the sweet home that it looks."[56] As the ode does its work, takes its double and triple takes, it tends to erode the certainty of a single perspective.

This formal and thematic shapeshifting endemic to the ode makes it useful as a kind of global repositioning device. Sutherland brings together Abrams's epistemology of the ode, its examination of the poetic subject, with a critique of contemporary political economy.[57] In *The Odes to TL61P* (2013), the poems commit themselves to singing odes of praise in the context of full-blown financialization; the poetic voice is raised to an ecstatic pitch. In the face of unpropitious conditions, Sutherland's odes stand as blocks of poetry, commodity fetishism, and social vulnerability. They place him in the company of other contemporary Anglophone poets, who have tuned the ode to process global crisis and catastrophe. These contemporary odes, many of which highlight themes of political economy and revolutionary struggle, build on late twentieth-century experiments in the form. Compiling "new American odes" by Frank O'Hara, John Wieners, Fanny Howe, and Bernadette Mayer, C. D. Wright notes in 1989 that "the ode . . . is one of the few literary tendencies left on the lot that admits wonder and presumes a future."[58] But the appearance of so many odes during the first two decades of the new millennium constitutes something new and global as well, an emergent social vision that differs in several important ways from previous political projects undertaken by late twentieth-century poetry.

The Odes to TL61P explores what kind of a collective political subject might exist within the current brutality of global capitalism. In five odes, Sutherland draws upon the body's sensuous reactions to the world; excavations of childhood memories, early loves, and sexual experiences; and the forging of a revolutionary subjectivity. A section marked "10/11/10" describes a walk through the London riots. Protest and riot are maligned as the unthinking spontaneity of a crowd; this narrative, which often contains a barely hidden racism, can function as a rhetorical strategy that buttresses popular condemnation of those involved. But riots are more often the deliberate product of careful preparation and long-term struggle.[59] To capture this contingent emergence of a revolutionary subjectivity, Sutherland embeds the odal block in the company of a variety of other metrical and stanzaic forms. I move through several examples from Sutherland's work, beginning with a block that gives way to an extended meditation in a lineated form. For Sutherland, a poem is neither the inert verbal icon of W. K. Wimsatt and Monroe Beardsley nor the dynamic resonance between sound and sense that Paul Valéry and Giorgio Agamben explore. Instead, it is a potentially collectivizing force that Sutherland refers to as "*the communication of energy* to the intelligence."[60] Indeed, the lingering impression of the *Odes* is one of a vast reservoir of energy, a communication of the density of language made viscerally present.

The prospect that the lonely odist beholds requires, in Sutherland's work, the strategy of description described in part by Abrams. But instead of acknowledging a fixed setting, or lauding a specific person, Sutherland's odes develop through cycles of approach and withdrawal to the matter of personal confession, to the material of prosody, trope, and scheme, and to the events of political revolution. The ode contests the separation of these realms into discrete sites of action, thought, and perception. In *The Odes to TL61P*, this inclusiveness takes on a block form that repeats at intervals throughout the collection:

> Each time you unscrew the head the truths burn out
> and fly away above the stack of basements inundated
> in aboriginal mucus, elevating the impeccable,
> hereafter congenitally depilated Janine rescaled to a
> grainy blank up on to the oblong top of the freezer
> whose shut white lid unhinged at the back alone
> preserves a pyramid of rigid meat, budget pizzas,
> devirginated arctic rolls, only ever kidding in a
> prophylactic void torn into great crates of glittering
> eye shadow, dousing all its stickiness in dark empty
> swerves, for no-one is the radius of everything we
> are, a reinforced steel artery in the very integument
> to be burst asunder, by reason of innately shattered
> strobes as soon lived as burnt out, ramming an unplanned
> crack into the door mechanism . . .[61]

Sutherland's style features the juxtaposition of incommensurable registers, the overdetermination of simple words like "unscrew" and "head," and the forced cohabitation of what he calls "the materials we work and live with." Sutherland taps the ode for its manic energy; its radical inclusiveness and seriousness in subject matter, tone, and design; its wordy, protean shiftiness that oversteps the permissions given to the poetic line by Walt Whitman, Charles Olson, John Ashbery, and J. H. Prynne and that joins other investigations of the lyric mounted by Lisa Robertson, Catherine Wagner, Claudia Rankine, Dawn Lundy Martin, and Fred Moten.

The maximalism and excess of the ode provide a jolt to the enervated subject of an economy based on global finance, speculation, options, derivatives, and securities and supported by cognitive labor. Susan Stewart describes the relation between poetry and the contemporary subject when she writes that "the physical qualities of poetic composition convey knowledge of ourselves as living beings among other living beings; they also provide relief from the suffering of disembodiment that gives rise to such a question in the first place."[62] In Sutherland's poetry, this "relief from the suffering of disembodiment" depends in large part on the sheer variety of poetic schemes he uses. Sutherland has described *The Odes to TL61P* as "a kind of album or masque of metrical variations, everything from strictly perfected tetrameters to the most psychotic arrhythmia."[63] The ode's capaciousness, its impulsive shuttling from one sensation, object, memory, persona, or register to the next, substitutes a poetics of continuous beginnings for one directed toward closure and finish.[64]

The title of the book, however, makes a claim to the historical reality of this disembodiment by drawing attention to the vanishing of the commodity. While TL61P looks at first like a reference to an obscure bit of Internet coding, it is in fact the product code for a broken door mechanism of a common, if now obsolete, domestic object: a Hotpoint dryer. The end of the first ode explains this:

> The code TL61P belongs to a Hotpoint dryer.
> You'll find out nothing if you look
> it up through the sky in the screen, the vault
> of exchangeable passion, Vertigo at
> the horizon prostrate as an outstretched
> cheek; but in the mouth that grows
> in capacity behind that overflow,
> Nobody can take away the word for it:

love, the provisional end until death;
TL61P its unconditional perfected shadow
opposite; Now go back to the start.[65]

The Odes to TL61P are addressed not to a landscape or to a famous public figure, but to a commodity. TL61P is thus more complicated than a late
modernist substitute for the ode's resplendent urn. In the well-known section on commodity fetishism from *Capital*, volume 1, Marx writes that the
commodity "appears, at first sight, a very trivial thing, and easily understood. Its analysis shows that it is, in reality, a very queer thing, abounding
in metaphysical subtleties and theological niceties. . . . But, so soon as it
steps forth as a commodity, it is changed into something transcendent."[66]
He continues by drawing an analogy with "the mist-enveloped regions of
the religious world. In that world the productions of the human brain
appear as independent beings endowed with life, and entering into relation
both with one another and the human race. So it is in the world of commodities with the products of men's hands."[67] As the preeminent poetic
form for addressing transcendent figures and gods of all kinds, the ode is
uniquely poised to capture one of the contradictions of capitalist political
economy—namely, the commodity form. Sutherland's dryer is in good
company with Jennifer Cooke's odes to parking lots, Francesca Lisette's
ode to a fork, and Joe Luna's "Having Coke with You," an allusion to Frank
O'Hara's ode to everything from yogurt to modern sculpture.

But TL61P is not exactly a commodity itself: it is the ordering code for
an obsolete part of one. In other words, Sutherland's world is still one in
which the gods have withdrawn, but the odal forms of veneration and
address remain. The missing connection between Sutherland's ode to a
dryer and Marx's account of the commodity can be found in another revision of the ode undertaken in the nineteenth century, just before Marx, by
Keats—whose odes are sometimes considered to represent a turn away
from the political.[68] In the "Ode to Psyche," the poet recovers the cult of
Psyche, a goddess who comes "too, too late for the fond believing lyre."[69]
The ode ends with the poet assuming the role of priest for Psyche and
building her temple in his mind, where there is "all soft delight / that shad-
owy thought can win, / a bright torch, and a casement ope at night, / to let
the warm Love in!" Sutherland rewrites Keats by putting an obsolete
household commodity—the "unconditional perfected shadow opposite" of
warm Love—in the place of the goddess. As Keats's ode examines the
forgetting of Psyche, so do Sutherland's odes dramatize, in their address to
a forgotten appliance, the difficulty of perceiving the social relations gen-

erated by commodities in the global economy. The complexity and violence of these relations—given synecdochal form by the ordering code
that is already obsolete, "TL61P"—necessitates the multiple approaches
to description that the odal form provides.

As Sutherland knows, the consequences of financialization are psychological and affective forms of dispossession. A response to them must find
an adequate poetics of expression. In a world in which the personality is
privatized, made to do the work of creative and affective labor, Sutherland
uses the physical language of the commons to describe psychological space.
He takes the metaphor of "occupation of the commons" to describe the
way the block-structure of the ode acknowledges through poetic form the
surge of revolutionary, anti-capitalist energy and its inevitable containment by the logic of capital, manifest in the state violence propagated by
the police. In an interview, Sutherland describes the *Odes* as "a poetry that
trie[s] energetically to occupy the commons of sensation and desire."[70]
Defending a quasi-Whitmanian notion of lyric as a capacious, communal
voice channeled through the single person, Sutherland writes, "There is
no part, or detail, or potential of experience which cannot be radically
addressed and transformed through the sheer delirious and euphoric
momentum of powerfully expressive verse."[71] This claim captures one
aspiration of the odes: to make the expression of an individual experience
into the synecdoche for a social body.

Risking the danger that the ode might call to mind a politically retro-
grade cliché of lyric subjectivity, Sutherland refashions it as a model of a
social world. While the ode's strong emphasis on a perceiving "I" could
potentially be understood as an imperializing gesture, Sutherland makes
it possible to read this "I" differently, as the sign of a multitude that cannot be identified, indicated, or named except in partial, synecdochal
form. The expressivism of Sutherland's writing often takes the shape of
erotic currents, fantasies, and encounters that the poems recall or project. A tape of an old lover or an explicit description of a sexual act transi-
tions quickly into a tender, if noncommittal gesture that recalls Auden's
"Lullaby":

Remember this: I sort through the boxes,
my first poems are there, the
drawings I made at school are
and my toys are, lead prodigies and barbarians,
paints for them, tapes of my rock band
some vinyl of Tchaikovsky and Bach, the present

photographs of my first sexual lover,
whose face is staring with intent euphoria
and deepening tenderness at the face I
was, the eyes I shone in then, the light
in them blinds me now to nothing less
than under your caress I can do still,
and do still even right now, or very soon do
when I climb into bed with you and let
my arm shrink into your waking head,
or sleeping, however you are in there,
that room of objects and that room of you.[72]

In the syntactic scheme of the final line, the genitive construction balances between its partitive ("of objects") and metaphorical ("of you") functions. The smooth symmetry and neo-Augustan closure of this line are at
odds with the awkward ambiguity of its grammatical meaning. The syntax
manages to reference, rather than to rely on, the histories of such assured
closure through parallelism, while still underscoring the sincerity of the
memory. A pastiche of Pope and Wordsworth, the lyricality of Sutherland's odes can be found here, in both the distancing effect of their formal
artifice and the metonymic associations generated by the Romantic meditations of their "I." The *Odes* are attempts to use as many of the resources
of poetic singularity as possible—the hyperbolic, confused, partly sincere
and partly ironized sensations of an individual—to figure forth in this way
the possibilities of common life.

Sutherland's centering of the poem in individual sensation not only
redresses the attenuation and marketization of personal affect and emotion. In the process, the odal "I" also creates an unexpected riposte to
contemporary global stances of universalism and communitarianism. In
the ode, the first-person "I" is placed in dynamic relation to an other. This
relation is not based on an infinite "responsibility" to the other, as Emmanuel Levinas might have it, but rather on probing, querying, testing, feeling
things out—a mutable provisionality that holds off certainty just as much
as it avoids dramatic notions of ineffable otherness and radical alterity.[73]
The ode, in its structure of approach and withdrawal, depends on a complex and dialectical relation to otherness that cannot be explained ade-
quately by the theoretical model of radical alterity. As Fredric Jameson
observes, the ethical figures of the "Same" and the "Other," given historical meaning, can be understood as allegorical manifestations of competing

claims to resources.[74] Through the ode, Sutherland critiques a notion of the "global" predicated on scarcity. As an alternative to the Levinasian metaphor of the "height" of the other, odal poetry is concerned instead with laterality, with being together in a way that extends beyond "our immediate spheres of belonging."[75] As a response to the politics and poetics of scarcity, the ode models the ethical and aesthetic forms of the search for recognition that settles neither on identity nor on difference.

The contemporary ode sets as its task a rigorous accounting of the damage done to the world and an examination of the role of the human in perpetuating that damage. In order to make this account, it retains countervailing impulses of exuberance and even praise. If we look broadly across the history of the Great Ode, however, it is not only that odes face the difficulty of praising something far greater than the poet or the poem. It is also that odes tend to treat intractable subjects that are hard for anyone to think about at all: immortality, the birth of Christ, dejection, melancholy, the coming of spring, the power of music, derivative markets. The tormented and ecstatic human subject of the ode, Coleridge bent over his cot, provides an individual, personalized locus from which to voice the damage that demands and defies thought. This resistance to prosaic summary is one of the reasons the ode has come to hand once again: the ode communicates, through the energy of an individualized "I," the sense of facing a world without access to a totalizing vantage point from which to see and interpret it.

Despite its striving toward capaciousness, the energy and eros of the ode's blithe spirit quite clearly excludes many of the most dispossessed subjects of the global economy. Among other contemporary poets, the ecstasy under late, late capitalism is especially vitiated by the gendered nature of the odal speaker. Poems by Anne Boyer and Manal Al-Sheikh, U.S. and Iraqi contemporaries of Sutherland, uncover a certain exhaustion with ethical or recuperative models of vulnerability that seek a renewal of the social based on an allegedly common sensitivity to shock, violence, contingent labor, and death. Boyer's "The Animal Model of Inescapable Shock" (2015) and Al-Sheikh's "Destitution" (2013) call the revolutionary energies of poetry into question. They charge poetry with a critical global politics that incorporates the differential experiences of gendered and racialized immigrant subjects in a global economy.

The energy that powers the ode may, in other contexts, turn into something like an electrified grid, as in Anne Boyer's prose poem, "The Animal Model of Inescapable Shock." In Boyer's poem, an animal on an electrified grid feels "deep feelings of attachment for whatever has shocked her":

If an animal is shocked, escapably or inescapably, she will manifest
deep attachment for whoever has shocked her. If she has manifested
deep attachment for whoever has shocked her, she will manifest deeper
reactions of attachment for whoever has shocked her and then dragged
her off the electrified grid. Perhaps she will develop deep feelings of
attachment for electrified grids. Perhaps she will develop deep feelings
of attachment for what is not the electrified grid. Perhaps she will
develop deep feelings of attachment for dragging. She may also develop
deep feelings of attachment for science, laboratories, experimentation,
electricity, and informative forms of torture.[76]

On the electrified grid, vulnerability is "inescapable": it is socially and
politically produced from the process of being "dragged across an electrified field." A far cry from Sutherland's rhapsodic pilfering of the ode's
prosodic toolkit, Boyer uses a coldly clinical syntax of conditional sentences. She detaches poetic tropes and schemes from fictions of juridical
personhood, private life, a first-person individual "I," and uses them instead
as material for a critique of vulnerability. Tropological and schematic conditions associated with poetic language appear: the scheme of *gradatio*,
familiar at least from Philip Sidney's first *Astrophel* sonnet, and the extended
conceit of the shocked animal, which provides a parable of life under conditions of capitalism ("shock"). The poem is composed of a series of conditional statements that begin with "if" and that create the conditions under
which the following statements can be interpreted, the responses understood. In a grim turn on the poetic rhapsode, the rhetoric of poetry is
spoken through the subject subsumed by capital, and the odal mastery over
form becomes a series of evasive maneuvers within it.

Through the gendering of the subject of the poem, Boyer particularizes
life under global capitalism in a different manner than Sutherland's odes
allow. While the induced precariousness of global capitalism becomes a
site for revolutionary agency and a rallying cry for sociality in Sutherland's
odes, the "she" of Boyer's poem experiences a life understood as attachment, dependency, vulnerability—as a suturing of the subject to the shocks
of capitalism. Such a version of the commons would be, from the perspective of Boyer's poem, a total electrification of the field of activity for the
subject who was not white, male, and writing from the Global North.
Constructed by a differential portioning of precarity, the poetic subject
"she" has no choice but to write within the conditions set by global capital.
It is not only that poetry emerges from conditions of precarious life, but
also that this conditionality is the language that poetry must speak and yet
defy. There is a double bind here, enacted by the poem: the more the con-

ditions are spoken, the more entrenched in these conditions the subject "she" becomes. To speak without conditions would mean, in Boyer's poem, to open oneself up to the model of "inescapable shock": the consequences would be "deep attachment" to capitalism, to the "electrified grid." The rigor of the poem's model is the impossibility of an external position for the subject who both speaks and is spoken by the conditions of precarity. The poem ends with two questions: "Also, how is Capital not an infinite laboratory called 'conditions'? And where is the edge of the electrified grid?"[77] We might see in this poem a different version of the contemporary poetic speaker and a different topos of the global commons. To speak with, or in, "conditions" would be both to assume the impossible language of the liberal, universal subject, the language denied to the precarious—to "bare life," evacuees, refugees, prisoners, women, and colonial subjects—and also, at the same time, to reject the process by which precariousness might become subsumed under capital.

Boyer's poem stages the danger that can follow from ethical models of precarity that elide gendered and racialized distributions of global vulnerability. A different position shapes the work of the Iraqi poet and refugee Manal Al-Sheikh, whose writing is inextricable from the global displacements and altered patterns of labor that have affected women in disproportionate degrees. Born in Nineveh, Al-Sheikh fled Iraq with her two children for Stavanger, Norway, becoming a guest writer at the ICORN Center (International City of Refuge Network). Al-Sheikh explains her relation to both the classical Arabic ode, the *qasida*, and to the prose poem as borrowing aspects from both: "It doesn't end with the same rhyme [n]or is it based on classical meter. But . . . you can feel the hidden rhythm during the reading."[78] The prose poem, she writes, loses an "organized shape" while retaining an "inner rhythm," as in "Destitution":

I'm orphan enough for a poleless tent
And desolate enough for a flying kiss in the crowd

I'm hungry enough to declare my bodily destitution on
a signboard at my tent that says:
"Organs herein are unsuitable for human feeding"

I'm passionate enough to cause your impudent ships to sink
And have of blood enough to menstruate for all the village women more
centuries to come
And have of isolation enough to continually hurl insults for every
knocking at the neighbor's door

Of wars do I have enough to offer carefully chosen heads to those hungry
for slumber and wet dreams
And of pagan heritage do I have enough to cast the flags of my Sufi
ancestors into the abyss of a desolate history

Of death do I have enough to make him an evening with neither moon to
fade nor sun to replace
Of homelands do I have enough to call all the murdered to get to their
resting place
Neither do I have graves for them nor consent to own ones

. . .

As I have much more time to put a remorseful question to death:

Why do I have all of this but you?[79]

Al-Sheikh's poem engages a global political economy of what is shared
and how it is distributed. In its inventory of contemporary figures of the
global, "Destitution" turns a logic of scarcity into an ironic catalogue of
excess. The world within the reach of Al-Sheikh's poem is a world of abun-
dance, a copious offering of wars, blood, fugitives, death, loneliness, orphans,
hunger, and violence. By the end of the poem, the pronouns "I" and "you"
stand in for the stateless refugee, within reach of everything the world offers
her—that is, nothing other than poetry—and the fictions of community,
personhood, legal status, rights, family, social welfare, and citizenship that
are denied to her.

Taken together, the poems in this chapter allow us to understand dispossession prismatically and differentially. The kinds of removal and expulsion
faced in an Irish context call upon a long tradition of landscape poetry,
transforming those topoi by forcing through them the expropriated landscapes of the present. Written from one of the centers of financial capital,
Sutherland's odes demand that we rethink the poem in terms of action,
exertion, energy, or activity, in tension with its tendencies toward artifac-
tual or formal completeness. This dream of movement and these constant
displacements are inherent to the very structure of the odal form: they
address the peculiar dispossessions of a financialized economy, which dis-
articulates the social body and monetizes the affects. The subtle replacement of *enthusiasmos* by *energeia*, of praise by communication, of awe by
alacrity, distinguishes Sutherland's work as a case study. But as Boyer's
poem makes clear, the putative ecstasy of a revolutionary poetic stance
hides the deeply gendered shock conditions of contingent labor on a global

scale: time reduced to shorter and shorter increments, contracts that expire at the end of each day, the giving way of clock time to a clock-less engulfing of activity, the exhausted body and the anxious mind that never come to rest. And as Al-Sheikh demonstrates, the non-exchangeability and euphoric excesses of the odal economy may be the negative image of the violent, unequal distribution of global vulnerability, born on the back of the female refugee.

In Al-Sheikh's contribution to a forum on global poetics, she maintains that the condition for writing poetry is not the free flight of the imagination, but rather the unfettered movement between sites of the real—impossible for the refugee. Irish poetry of place makes description the negative image of the processes of dispossession that have taken its landscapes away. In stark contrast, Al-Sheikh's poetics of displacement is written from the position of the poet's own physical displacement. Echoing Meehan's litany of com- modities, Al-Sheikh's poem catalogues the privations it does possess. These are the holdings of a "global" citizen: not one of the well-traveled elite, but rather one of the sixty-five million displaced who, in Hannah Arendt's famous analysis, lack the "right to have rights."[80] The following chapter brings the figure of the citizen to its center, turning to the work of Claudia Rankine, who uncovers the roots of lyric poetry in the global violence of racialized citizenship.

CHAPTER 2

Let Us Go

Lyric and the Transit of Citizenship

In the twenty-first century, the politics of national citizenship have failed to address the problems of statelessness and state-sponsored discrimination, producing new and violent conjunctures of neoliberalism and racism. In this context, it is not at all clear how contemporary Anglophone and European poetry has addressed citizenship or what difference a change in the meaning of "citizen" would make for poetry. Unlike the epic, soldered to the myth of national identity, or the novel, born into the scrutiny of capitalist social relations, the poem has no agreed-upon place in the history of relations between the state and the people. In *Citizen: An American Lyric* (2014), the Jamaican American poet Claudia Rankine explores the contradictions of an American citizenship that, while ever more comprehensive in form, does not ensure basic rights for racial minorities in practice. Rankine's work reveals that U.S. lyric poetry is uniquely intertwined with the history of citizenship as the racialized constitution of the subject. She examines how the racial violence of American citizenship structures ordinary encounters, sports games, news reports, emergency management, and bus routes. These forms of the everyday, which Rankine draws through lyric, wear on their surface a political neutrality and a multicultural pluralism that sets them ostensibly beyond the history of race in the United States. Through these forms and their inclusion within lyric, Rankine shows how notions of citizenship and discourses of multiculturalism are harnessed not to redress historical inequality but to aid the expansion of capitalism. Rankine's book, while focused largely on U.S. citizenship, describes the making global of an American lyric through exploitative and exclusionary politics.

By making "An American Lyric" the subtitle not only for this book, but for her previous collection as well, Rankine aligns literary genre, nationality, and citizenship. Yet these terms can only appear at first in provocative tension with each other. Their full unfolding requires, in Rankine's poetry, the transit of the Atlantic Ocean, a site that brings together the disparate sections and multimodal forms of Rankine's book. After reviewing the mutations of citizenship from the nineteenth century to the present and exploring the recent developments in lyric studies, my reading of *Citizen* focuses on two figures, or rather two heads, that Rankine juxtaposes: first, the head of the black U.S. citizen on which the Atlantic and its continual re-creation as a theater of racial ascription and violence constantly "breaks"; and second, the head of the Franco-Algerian citizen, from which a rebuttal arises against the racism of contemporary European society. The poetic transit of *Citizen* across the Atlantic, and implicitly across the Mediterranean, creates the conditions for imagining solidarity between anti-racist movements in the United States and ongoing anticolonial struggles in France and North Africa.

In what follows, I place Rankine's book at the intersection of theories of lyric and histories of citizenship. There is no doubt that the lyric reputation for solitary confession, immediacy, or personal feeling pairs awkwardly with the liberal fantasy of a "global citizen." A genre filled with character and action has more available space for deliberation about citizenship than a sonnet or an ode. Following Roland Greene, however, the English and European lyric is a poetic genre that serves historically as the vehicle for posing questions about subjectivity.[1] For Rankine, lyric poetry emerges to interrogate subjectivity at specific moments when the possibilities of being a subject are delimited and foreclosed. Noticing a marked "persistence of the lyric" in recent poetry, Jennifer Ashton finds that contemporary lyric critically examines political life defined by a "grounding in personhood."[2] She suggests that the poetry of the first decade of the twenty-first century undertakes a "serious consideration of the ground of 'scarcity' on which the recognition of persons is constructed."[3] A lyric of black life in the United States cannot partake easily of a history of thinking about the lyric based in an ostensibly universal personhood, whether that idea is attached to white supremacy or to a liberal, post-racial society. Both the subject and the person are concepts that have functioned to exclude black Americans before the law, as Saidiya Hartman and Angela Naimou argue, respectively. In *Citizen*, lyric is made to be the genre that, to paraphrase Jared Sexton, captures black life lived in social death.[4]

In U.S. poetry, writing about citizenship usually involves some transformation of the poetic tools available to do so. Whitman's catalogues shape his invention of a capacious poetic line, one that could contain what he saw as tests and types of U.S. citizenship in the nineteenth century, including the worker, the slave, the suicide, and the student. Like Whitman, Rankine employs the catalogue; hers too exceed the norms of the poetic, making the "line" into the paragraph, the soccer game, the collage, the CNN news report, and the city bus. The rhetorical devices of lyric emerge when these theaters of citizenship become visible so that the tropes of apostrophe or prosopopoeia, for instance, are the traces of historical conditions, particularly ones in which black life is expelled, mocked, destroyed, or made invisible. For Rankine, the transformation of U.S. citizenship comes about through the lyric. But Rankine also helps us to see that the lyric is best defined by a profound multiplicity and indeterminacy, one that always threatens to burst into new forms.

The terms in which lyric is theorized have often reproduced the terms in which citizenship has been circumscribed. Focusing on citizenship, this chapter also attempts a synthesizing gesture across recent studies of the lyric, some of which are in opposition to each other. I show that Rankine's lyricized citizenship comes out of a tradition of the "citizen lyric" in post–World War II U.S. poetry. Her expansion of the lyric extends in practice the theoretical work of the New Lyric Studies, which holds, in general, that "a resistance to definition may be the best basis for definition of the lyric—and of poetry—we currently have."[5] Such a "resistance to definition" mirrors the way that contemporary poets have used the term "lyric" themselves. But my reading also finds unexpected allies in Jonathan Culler's genre criticism and in Anthony Reed's intervention within the poetics of black experimental traditions. In this sense, I follow and build on the work of Reed and of Evie Shockley, who both write about *Citizen* as a lyric poem. Reed asks, "How does our understanding of literary possibility change . . . when we consider dissident practices of citation of texts and forms as transformative of those forms rather than as rejecting or mocking them?"[6] For Shockley, "Whether we think of *Citizen* as 'post-' or 'neo-' lyric, finally, may be less important than taking stock of how thoroughly Rankine has upended the genre."[7] Poets across the twentieth and twenty-first centuries claim their poetry to be lyric not because of its generic consistency with a tradition of writing or a way of reading, but rather because of the lyric's potential capaciousness as a form. Read in light of the work of Jackson, Prins, Culler, Greene, Reed, Shockley, and others, lyric poetry provides an unexpected source for thinking about the exclusions created by contemporary citizenship.

The modern European story of the word "citizen" begins, according to Immanuel Wallerstein, with the French Revolution. But the word itself appears much earlier. In English, it is used as early as 1330 to refer to inhabitants of a city or town.[8] In the nineteenth century, modern citizenship emerges, alongside equality, as an alternative to dividing society by heritage. Wallerstein tracks this emergence of citizenship as a concept after 1789:

> The nineteenth century saw the creation of our entire contemporary
> conceptual apparatus of identities. Once rule was no longer an appara-
> tus guaranteed by heritage—a system whose legitimacy, if not whose
> reality, the French Revolution had definitively undone—identities were
> required to delineate who had and who didn't have the right to power
> and wealth. The identities of the powerful were the most urgent. They
> were, however, relational—that is, they identified not only who they
> were but who they were not. In creating their own identities, the pow-
> erful thereby created the identities of others.[9]

At the very base of the notion of "equality"—liberation from heritage as a basis for belonging to a state—is the preservation of new forms of inequality, ones that are founded instead on identity. A notion of "active" versus "passive" citizenship arises at the same time, allowing some identities the power of governance and others the tenuous right to belong or live. Citizenship becomes associated with a zero-sum game, in which the provision of rights to some means that others have to be kept excluded from those rights.[10] Wallerstein writes, "Each success of a particular group seemed to make easier by example and harder in practice the attempts of the next claimants of liberation. Citizenship always excluded as much as it included."[11]

Wallerstein writes a history of nineteenth-century liberalism as a politics of exclusion on the basis of race or gender. Calling for a transformation of contemporary citizenship, Stuart Hall identifies "the coming question of the twenty-first century" as the "capacity to live with difference."[12] In his tribute to Raymond Williams, "Culture, Community, Nation" (1993), Hall writes,

We need to be able to insist that rights of citizenship and the incommensurabilities of cultural difference are respected and that *the one is not made a condition of the other.* In this sense, unless the universalistic language of citizenship, derived from the Enlightenment and the French Revolution (but long denied both women in Europe and black slaves in Hispaniola), is transformed in the light of the proliferation of cultural difference, the idea cannot and does not deserve to survive in the transformed conditions of late-modernity in which it is required to become substantively operable.[13]

As the twentieth century draws to its close, Hall worries that states will "reach for too closed, unitary, homogeneous and essentialist a reading of 'culture' and 'community.'"[14] Recent events, from police violence against black life in the United States to Brexit and the xenophobia of "Fortress Europe," prove Hall to be a prescient theorist of citizenship's shortcomings as a "universalistic language." In Hall's analysis, the language of citizenship offers the fiction of a common belonging, but only by making the expulsion of cultural difference into the "condition" for it. Audre Lorde notes that the "institutionalized rejection of difference" is central to the logic of capitalism, "which needs outsiders as surplus people."[15]

In some ways, however, twenty-first-century capitalism has found a profitable solution to the problem of difference without rejecting it at all. As studies by Jodi Melamed, Jean and John Comaroff, Roderick Ferguson, and Aihwa Ong have shown, the "proliferation of cultural difference" has been quickly and easily commandeered by institutions, universities, governments, and corporations. In *Represent and Destroy: Rationalizing Violence in the New Racial Capitalism* (2011), Melamed examines how official anti-racism becomes wedded to a global capitalist agenda. Neoliberalism, or the shift from a welfare state to "supply-side economics and market-oriented development, alongside the growing importance of finance capitalism," is perfectly compatible with multiculturalism—unlike neoconservatism, which rejects difference or covers it up. The conflation of neoliberal policy and multicultural values functions rhetorically

> to represent a certain set of economic policies as multicultural rights,
> to portray the equality of the free market as the most fundamental
> expression of equality, and to make the diversity of goods, services,
> and capital flowing across national boundaries stand for the best manifestation of multiculturalism.[16]

The expansion of citizenship is thus defined as and limited to the expansion of property rights and the free movement of capital instead of "the rights of people to a degree of security in housing, employment, or education."[17] Citizenship itself, through the selling of passports, appears today as a commodity with a market value, bought by the wealthy individuals whom Atossa Araxia Abrahamian names "the cosmopolites."[18] Abrahamian reveals the profits of global citizenship today by looking at the example of the Comoro Islands. The Comoran government, as a means of servicing its debt, sells Comoran passports to the stateless *bidoon* of Kuwait, who then face relocation en masse.[19] To study contemporary forms of citizenship, as political philosophy from Arendt and Derrida to Foucault and Agamben insists, is both to summon and to call into question the discourses, policies, and practices of human and animal rights, anti-racism, feminism, liberal globalism, and multiculturalism.

American poetry after World War II often situates meditations on civic life in the personal experience of the poetic speaker. This strain of poetry, which I will call the "citizen lyric," looks particularly closely at class and race during the period of embedded liberalism, often by using a combination of hyperlocal and distanced international perspectives. Robert Lowell's *Life Studies* (1959) is now considered a groundbreaking book of "confessional poetry" for its baring of Lowell's psychology, including his status as conscientious objector during World War II. Yet Rankine, in an interview, turns to Lowell for a social critique, one that makes his poetry part of a postwar discourse about race. For Rankine, Lowell's experimental inclusion of prose and poetry serves as the vehicle for his struggle with "the construction of whiteness."[20] The eponymous poem from Lowell's next book, *For the Union Dead* (1964), continues and heightens this work by lamenting the failure of liberal anti-racism to produce material change. Fifteen years later, as the Keynesian welfare state gives way to post-Keynesian neoliberalism, the citizen lyric gathers force and outrage, particularly at processes of deindustrialization. Richard Hugo's searing 1973 volume *The Lady in Kicking Horse Reservoir* catalogues the forms of desperate and depleted social life in small towns in Montana, counterpointing these vignettes with companion pieces set in Scotland. A collection published in the same year, James Wright's *Two Citizens*, moves between Florence, Italy, and small-town Ohio, juxtaposing love poems with ethnographies of the deindustrializing Midwest. "When I was a boy/I loved my country," concludes the first poem in *Two Citizens*. "Hell, I ain't got nothing./Ah, you bastards, //How I hate you."

In these citizen lyrics, a white, male voice diagnoses in caustic, splenetic tones the crushing poverty and inequality of the late 1960s and 1970s. These poets, Robert von Hallberg notes, benefited from the GI Bill, inherited wealth or awards to travel Europe, garner cultural capital, and look back critically at the United States.[21] Common to all these books are love and family lyrics, scenes of intimate address from an "I" to a "you." These moments of intimacy appear, however, not as a private recourse, but as scored by the larger social disintegration captured in the poems around them. A citizen lyric such as Lowell's, Hugo's, or Wright's would now have to be written across a changed domestic scene, in conditions of post-Keynesian, multicultural, global capitalism. But this configuration has naturalized, incorporated, and monetized both the values and the invectives of the citizen lyric. The logic of capitalism has passed from Lorde's "institutionalized rejection of difference" to the institutionalized recognition of difference instead.

Citizen: An American Lyric is both a break with and a continuation of the American citizen lyric. Rankine's book asks what citizenship means in an American context in which the right of *jus soli*, or citizenship by birth, replaces the right of *jus sanguinis*, or citizenship by bloodline.[22] As Peter Spiro notes, U.S. citizenship by birth was conditioned by race, so that the Fourteenth Amendment, which gave citizenship to African Americans in 1868, excluded children of Asian immigrants until 1898 and Native Americans until 1924.[23] Rankine does not lay claim to be included in the history of either citizenship or lyric, as though broadening their meaning alone would be enough to mitigate their violence. Instead, she captures an America in which the significance of citizenship has become partially undone under global mobility, the availability of dual citizenship, and the expansion of welfare to nonnaturalized permanent residents. In this context, the lyric poem brings into view the legacy of a citizenship predicated upon expelling black life and enacting a form of belonging that addresses the "increasing disconnect between the legal definition of the citizenry and strong community on the ground."[24]

The next section of this chapter lays out the common procedure of Rankine's prose anecdotes, which is to transform the situation of lyric address into a formal space for meditation, grief, and anger by threading racialized violence through the poem. The poems in the first section of *Citizen* are not recognizably "poetic": their language is the ordinary, spoken kind; there is no elaborate figuration; there is hardly a sense of stanza, or line break, or rhyme, or meter. There is no dreamlike sensation of being in a different world, a meaning that "lyrical" prose sometimes carries. One of the poems recounts a visit to a trauma therapist, who reacts to the presence of a black figure approaching her house with "Get away from my house. What are you doing in my yard?" The poem continues:

It's as if a wounded Doberman pinscher or a German shepherd has gained the power of speech. And though you back up a few steps, you manage to tell her you have an appointment. You have an appointment? she spits back. Then she pauses. Everything pauses. Oh, she says, followed by, oh, yes, that's right. I am sorry.

I am so sorry, so, so sorry.[25]

Rankine describes these anecdotal scenes "as a way of talking about invisible racism—moments that you experience and that happen really fast. They go by at lightning speed, and you begin to distrust that they even happened, and yet you know that you feel bad somehow."[26] These are microaggressions, moments that may seem insignificant, in comparison to greater moments of violence, but that come as shocking and unexpected. This poem is in the genre of the prose anecdote: someone is listening to someone else, and she is talking about a strange, violent, and disturbing thing that happened to her. Readers are situated firmly in the everyday world, a world constructed from individual misrecognitions that channel historical prejudice. Very little here is obscured through figuration or rhetoric, hardly anything that recalls lyric poetry's proclivities for lies or playful obfuscations. Still, the anecdote is more than a report or documentation of an incident, transcribed faithfully. At the moment in which the therapist realizes her error, the poet's voice interpolates a remark, "everything pauses," widening the meaning of the verb "pauses" and complicating the poetic mediation of the account. This repetition, which turns the reporting of the incident into a poetic trope, is an index not only to the realism of the language—it is common enough to have the feeling, while remembering a violent scene, that "everything suddenly froze"—but also to its constructedness, a shaping gesture of the poet.

By calling this prose poetry "lyric," *Citizen* makes an argument for the malleability of lyric as a genre. In its juxtaposition of heterogeneous forms, the book is a companion volume to Rankine's 2004 collection of poems *Don't Let Me Be Lonely: An American Lyric*. There, Rankine explores life after 9/11 by collaging citations from other texts, images captured on television screens, anatomical drawings, clip art, and logos. This "image stream" brushes against meditations on racialized violence, cancer, and Zoloft, focalized through the first-person "I."[27] Commentary on *Don't Let Me Be Lonely* reveals some of the concerns that subtend both books. For Emma Kimberley, *Don't Let Me Be Lonely* investigates the mediated nature of life in the early twenty-first century: "Rankine chooses to foreground visual and narrative frames as a comment on the fact that all representations, whether they acknowledge it or not, are framed."[28] Kevin Bell focuses on the "damaged or dead body" in Rankine's work, arguing that she "meditates on the poverty of that body's circumstances and possibilities; and further still on the inability of language to secure within its own unfolding the substance of that poverty's densities and textures."[29] Christopher Nealon notes that Rankine "makes analogies to these other media throughout *Don't Let Me Be Lonely*, using them to establish a poetic method through which the uncertain value of life can be tested out."[30] He concludes that Rankine "establishes 'lyric' as a master category meant to be intellectually powerful enough to withstand the intrusions of the image stream, even to take energy from it, even to mock it."[31]

Rankine's book opens a space of possibility for what kinds of writing might be designated as lyric. In this way, she is oddly more faithful to the tradition of thinking about lyric than it might seem. For the lyric has never had a stable set of generic traits or characteristics; the history of identifying them is checked with moments of ambivalence and resistance to genre. Succinctly defined in 1957 by M. H. Abrams as "any fairly short, non-narrative poem presenting a single speaker who expresses a state of mind or a process of thought and feeling," the lyric was just as succinctly undefined by René Wellek a decade later in the *Festschrift für Richard Alewyn*.[32] After sifting through the various claims made for the immediacy, intensity, and interiority of the lyric, Wellek writes, "One must abandon attempts to define the general nature of the lyric or the lyrical."[33] Wellek's terse dismissal is perhaps the most well-known adaptation of Samuel Johnson's remark, in his *Lives of the Poets*, that "to circumscribe poetry by a definition will only show the narrowness of the definer."[34]

This is not to say that the lyric has been without its defenses. Jonathan Culler's *Theory of the Lyric* (2016) revisits and unsettles transhistorical traits associated with the genre. Culler questions the hegemony of the "fictional speaker" in pedagogies of poetry stemming from New Criticism: thinking of the lyric speaker as a dramatic persona in a specific situation fails to explain many of the most striking details of lyric poems, from their tropological play to their intertextuality. In Culler's account, lyric poetry is a product not so much of interiority as of the sounds that the poem makes, the patterns it constructs, and the normative, putatively communal claims that it ventriloquizes or entertains. Culler argues that the more a lyric emphasizes its "vocal effects," "the more powerful the image of voicing, oral articulation, but *the less we find ourselves dealing with the voice of a person*" [italics mine].[35] Indeed, the lyric "I," to the extent that it emerges intact from the poem at all, hardly emerges in a form we would recognize using the racialized language employed for "real-world" versions of the "I": a legal person, a neoliberal individual, a human being. Culler's point might be retained and extended as a condition for approaching Rankine's book. According to Culler, the lyric comprises "events without representation." Culler's phrase refers to the schematic and tropological play of the lyric— figures that do not depend upon the fiction of a subject. To write a lyric about American citizenship, and to collate racist events where representa- tion is effaced, is to supply the missing historical and political thickness to Culler's theory. The lyric of U.S. citizenship faces a contradiction: how can a form often associated with personhood be used to stage moments of racialized violence, when personhood has been one of the conceptual the- aters for racial genocide?[36] Culler's theory of lyric complicates the New Critical dogma of the fictional speaker and dramatic scene, drawing atten- tion to rhetorical aspects of the form that link the lyric to other modes of engagement with the world.

While Culler's defense of the lyric isolates two related generic aspects of the lyric—its worldliness and its anti-discursiveness—it treats the devel- opment of the lyric as though this occurs in isolation from historical world-making.[37] The pervasive difficulty of identifying a genre called "lyric" has led some to dismiss the idea altogether, calling instead for a history of the moments in which lyric has emerged in history. In a cluster on the "New Lyric Studies" in the January 2008 issue of *PMLA*, Rei Terada argues that the publication of Chaviva Hošek and Patricia A. Parker's *Lyric Poetry: Beyond New Criticism* in 1985 marks the end of attempts to specify the nature of lyric. At present, Terada suggests, critics have moved from a defensive rejection of lyric exceptionalism to an exploration of the lyric's continuity with other discourses. After listing a series of recent MLA talks in which the lyric appears alongside rap and hypertext, Terada expresses her relief that "the lyric zone of electrification is dissipating along with belief in the autonomy of the lyric object and in the specialness of the lyric mode."[38] For Terada, the work of Virginia Jackson in *Dickinson's Misery* (2005) marks a turn toward the historicization of the lyric. In Jackson's book, the question of "why" the lyric emerges at various points in history replaces the question of "what" the lyric is and supplements the question of "how" the lyric works. Jackson focuses on the separation of lyric from its historical accoutrements. For her, this process, which she calls "lyric read- ing" or "lyricization," erases the historical ephemera (in Dickinson's case, notes, crickets, shopping lists, postcards) that accompany the production of the poem and that set up horizons for its interpretation. Jackson describes how, in the mid-nineteenth century, poetry goes through the early stages of its "lyricization" into a contextless, discrete set of texts. Following Jackson, Terada writes, "What most needs explanation in lyric occurs before and after the poem, in the motives for the materialization of lyric or lyricism."[39] Jonathan Arac, in his conclusion to *Lyric Poetry: Beyond New Criticism*, urges against essentializing the lyric as a genre: "We could usefully go on to define 'lyric' as the possibility of a certain kind of reading . . . but even if texts from any period may occasion lyric reading, the question will then be whether that mode of reading is available at all times and places."[40]

In one sense, Prins and Jackson provide the tools for a critical unmasking of the lyric as a reading practice produced by institutions. They are not interested in reading lyric as a stable genre that sits alongside the novel, a modern name for the dithyramb, that third kind of poetry that Plato adds to epic and dramatic forms. In another sense, however, the New Lyric Studies preserves and opens up the category of "lyric" by tracking its contingent historical manifestations. As Rankine embeds the lyric in a thick social and geopolitical context, she also offers a rereading of quintessentially lyric poets. Rankine describes her conception of the lyric as influenced by W. B. Yeats, Emily Dickinson, and Walt Whitman in particular. She writes,

> I think of the lyric as creating a meditative space. There's such a desire to separate our political and social condition from our domestic and private space. To me, they're intertwined; what's happening in the government determines where you live, how you live, who your neighbors are, how much money you have in the bank. I wanted to bring the entire political and social condition into a lyric meditative space. All of the best poetry—W. B. Yeats, Emily Dickinson, Walt Whitman—take on both our social and political condition and view it through their uniquely personal lens.[41]

Her sense of the lyric underscores not so much what it is as what it creates, a "meditative space." Thinking of the lyric this way allows Rankine to use the language of contemplation to draw the "entire political and social condition" into the poem. Rather than existing as a "verbal icon," a "machine," or a "pudding," as the New Criticism would have it, the lyric represents a certain procedure through which the global conditions that affect subjects differentially are manifest in private acts of mind.

Rankine's notion of the meditative space recalls what Hegel names the "lyric 'situation,'" which is also the name Rankine gives to her video scripts. Hegel remains one of the historical starting points for thinking about lyric as a dramatic monologue with a fictional speaker. In Hegel's *Introductory Lectures on Aesthetics*, lyric withdraws its relation from the external world

and sets up shop in the foul rag and bone shop of the heart. The existence
of lyric poetry can be traced back to an "inner mood." Hegel speaks about
"lyric situations" in the following way:

> There may of course be obvious some objective state of affairs and an
> activity in relation to the external world, but, all the same, the mental-
> ity as such, in its inner mood, may withdraw into itself from all external
> connection whatever and take its starting-point from the inwardness of
> the states and feelings.[42]

There is a short jump from here to Mill's more famous 1833 claim about
solitary confession of feeling. Indebted to Hegel and Mill, the kind of
agency captured by the lyric has most often been individual rather than
social or collective. In Northrop Frye's famous description of the lyric, the
poet "turns his back on his listeners."[43] The individual speaker of the lyric
has made it particularly difficult to incorporate poetry into global theories
of world literature and world-space. The notion of lyric poetry as synony-
mous with private expression—the "imperial assertion of self," to borrow
Mark Jeffreys's phrase—has identified the form with a sovereign "I," not a
global "we."[44]

The procedure of *Citizen* is to transform the "lyric situation" into the
"meditative space," making meditation, paradoxically, into a public, social
activity. In order to do this, Rankine threads multiple, daily, overheard
instances of racism through the body of the single "I." Rankine's compositional process involves first listening to the stories of others and then enfold-
ing them into her own voice: "The entire book is a collection of stories
gathered from a community of friends and then retold or folded into my
own stories."[45] However distinct Rankine's anecdotal form appears from
lyric, this statement nevertheless recalls vividly Mill's definition of poetry:
"Poetry and eloquence are both alike the expression or utterance of feeling:
but, if we may be excused the antithesis, we should say that eloquence is
heard; poetry is overheard."[46] In one passage, Rankine describes the effect as
an ocean wave breaking on the meditating head:

> Yours is a strange dream, a strange reverie.
>
> No, it's a strange beach; each body is a strange beach, and if you let
> in the excess emotion you will recall the Atlantic Ocean breaking on
> our heads.[47]

Here the "Atlantic Ocean" stands for the Middle Passage. But it also
quite literally re-calls the final line of Robert Lowell's "Man and Wife":

"your old-fashioned tirade—/loving, rapid, merciless—/breaks like the Atlantic Ocean on my head."[48] In *Citizen*, lyric is the literary form in which an individual is revealed to be a "strange beach," an embodied subject who is vulnerable at any moment to the collective and systemic violence of history. Lowell's "my" becomes Rankine's "our," substituting the collective vulnerability of the black body for the self-reliant individual voice of the New England patriarch. A "confessional" poetry such as Lowell's becomes quickly radicalized as soon as the "I" is not taken for granted.

Rankine's summoning of Lowell draws attention to more specific conventions of lyric, to which I now turn. In the following pages, I try to think through some of the ways that Rankine's poetry historicizes and geopoliticizes the familiar resources of the lyric, from collecting racist anecdotes (overhearing) to calling out to the dead of Hurricane Katrina (apostrophe) to making their faces appear (prosopopoeia). Readers of Rankine quite justly tend to focus on the pronouns "I" and "you," which might call to mind an embrace of private, lyric subjectivity. Yet Rankine uses the pronominal relation to acknowledge the way the very notion of the subject is predicated upon the denial of citizenship to black lives in the United States. Since Rankine's poetry is conditioned by the racialized history that engulfs the dreaming head, writing the lyric pronominal "I" is already a tactic of resistance. There is no separating the lyric "I" from its determination by economic status, by racial identity, by the cost of water or the price of oil or the ability to vote without having to present a voting I.D. In Michelle Clayton's terms, the lyric subject is presented as a "contingently located social subject."[49] This location might also be threatened by submergence: in Rankine's poem, "a body in the world drowns in it."[50] Rankine uses the lyric to show that having an "I" at all, being able to speak the first-person pronoun, is hardly a guarantee of personhood. She writes,

> Sometimes "I" is supposed to hold what is not there until it is. Then *what is* comes apart the closer you are to it.
>
> This makes the first person a symbol for something.
>
> The pronoun barely holding the person together.
>
> . . .
>
> Drag that first person out of the social death of history, then we're kin.
>
> Kin calling out the past like a foreigner with a newly minted "fuck you."[51]

"An American Lyric," like an "American citizen," is not something that already exists, but that has to be continually dragged out of "the social death of history." To return to Wallerstein's history of citizen in the nine-teenth century, the expansion of citizenship for some comes at the expense of the contraction of citizenship for others.[52] If the lyric is a meditative space in which the private act of the mind merges with the social condi-tions that shape it, then the "I" is not a transparent record of feeling: the "I" must be dragged out. The poem records the struggle to say "I" and to be heard at all. This procedure is what might be called the "lyricizing of citizenship," rather than the making of a citizen lyric. Rankine's open-ended lyric looks to the future for new and unbridled forms for poetry. Questioning and broadening what counts as a lyric, her lyricizing of citi-zenship proposes a more capacious category for who counts as a citizen.

In her examination of the drowning "I" and the "foreigner with a newly minted 'fuck you,'" Rankine shuttles between both poles of lyric address, the "I" and "you." One of the most striking aspects of Rankine's book is how frequently she employs the word "you," the second-person pronoun. Reading *Citizen*, there is the unshakeable feeling that each of the anecdotes comes from a particular person. Yet each of them is also made into some-thing quite different by changing the "I" to a "you" (not to a "he" or "she" or "we"). In *Citizen*, the "you" does not produce a sense of universal "relat-ability," but rather a sense of social division, as in the following poem:

When the stranger asks, Why do you care? you just stand there star-ing at him. He has just referred to the boisterous teenagers in Star-bucks as niggers. Hey, I am standing right here, you responded, not necessarily expecting him to turn to you.

He is holding the lidded paper cup in one hand and a small paper bag in the other. They are just being kids. Come on, no need to get all KKK on them, you say.

Now there you go, he responds.[53]

As this poem underscores, much of *Citizen* confronts the limitations on a universalizing ethics as a methodology for understanding human encoun-ter. Each poem expresses the historical antagonism and violence directed toward a particular set of "Americans." Rankine's book abjures theological questions about the Other in favor of difficult political questions about cohabitation, or what the Trinidadian communist poet and theorist Clau-dia Jones names "togetherness."[54] The lyric exposes what prevents an "us" from being able to identify "ourselves" with a "you." At the same time, the use of "you" encourages what Shockley calls "white cross-racial identifica-tion," so that white readers may find themselves in the position of imagina-tively experiencing racial aggression.[55] It might also be possible to present this identification not as a way of appealing to black and white readers alike, but as a desire that the poems continually summon from the white reader, only to rebuff.

The lyric serves as the space in which that "I" is continually, impossibly restated in full recognition of its own impossibility. While these prose poems rely on the lyric as an overheard conversation between the "I" and the "you," other sections draw on rhetorical devices associated with lyric instead. A section of the book entitled "Situations" comprises scripts of films. Several of these films take up systemic racism as it is channeled through sports, disaster relief, police stops, and public transportation. "August 29, 2005 / Hurricane Katrina" is a video script containing quotes from CNN broadcasts after Hurricane Katrina. The script moves between reportage of damaged houses and dead bodies to the reactions of witnesses and interviewees. The repeated line "Have you seen their faces?" occurs at intervals, making the script into the contemporary version of an *ubi sunt* lament. In this particular situation, the lyric's definition as "overheard speech" becomes conflated with the "aestheticized distancing" of the cable news coverage. The poem does more than diagnose a failure of empathy, however. The end of the poem shows how the demand for lyric arises at moments when political and aesthetic representation founder:

Call out to them.
I don't see them.
Call out anyway.

Did you see their faces?[56]

"Call out to them" both enacts and asks for apostrophe—which is to say, for the lyric, if we follow Culler's association of the lyric with the address to an absent entity.[57] Similarly, "Did you see their faces?" associates prosopopoeia, the trope of giving human attributes to nonhuman entities, with the racialized violence of the state, which abandoned black inhabitants of New Orleans to die. Following Fanon, Angela Hume reads this passage as a moment of nonrecognition.[58] It is also a moment in *Citizen* when lyric and citizenship become inseparable. The erasure of black bodies is the motive for the lyric's creation of address, "call out to them," which uses an apostrophe to mount a demand for another one. Raising the question of prosopopoeia, meanwhile, humanizes that which has been excluded from the liberal category of the human.

Apostrophe and prosopopoeia have always been about the limits of what counts within political life, and even what counts as human, though critics have disagreed about the political and ethical valences carried by the tropes. Studies of apostrophe in poetry associate the trope closely with lyric, which, for Paul de Man, is defined as "the instance of represented voice."[59] De Man argues that apostrophe, "which posits the possibility of . . . reply and confers . . . the power of speech," sets off a chain of figuration: "Voice assumes mouth, eye, and finally face, a chain that is manifest in the etymology of the trope's name, *prosopon poien*, to confer a mask or a face (*prosopon*)."[60] Influenced by the work of de Man and Riffaterre, Jackson argues against "received phenomenologies of lyric reading" and for the ambiguities of reading Emily Dickinson's apostrophes as addressed to a general audience, when in fact they have specific historical addressees.[61] William Waters emphasizes that the circuit of lyric address has an ethical valence, that "in a poem's touch" we might feel "an intimation of why poetry is valuable, why it matters to us, and how we might come to feel answerable to it."[62] In her influential essay on the politics of apostrophe, Barbara Johnson contends that "the fact that apostrophe allows one to animate the inanimate, the dead, or the absent implies that whenever a being is apostrophized, it is thereby automatically animated, anthropomorphized, 'person-ified.'"[63] She notes that "legal and moral discourses of abortion tend to employ the same terms as those we have been using to describe the figure of apostrophe."[64] Johnson's reading of apostrophe reconstructs the juridical grounds on which apostrophe already operates and on which poetry can act as an opposing form of address.

The moments of address and of anthropomorphization in Rankine are not the transhistorical traits of a genre, but the historically contingent modes of political expression. Johnson's argument about apostrophe remains productive when we shift the terrain from her case study, abortion, to U.S. citizenship and its exclusion of black lives. In this context, the lyric is present less as a genre than as a desire, something that might undo the violence of American citizenship and its construction through processes of silencing and dehumanization. Prising the lyric from a progression of white, male poets, Rankine situates it in a politicized, racialized chronology. Rankine does something analogous with the art she interpolates throughout the book. David Hammons's installation "In the Hood," on the cover of *Citizen*, references Trayvon Martin's hoodie, but the piece, as is well known, was created in 1993. As Catherine Zuromskis notes, the images provide a "vivid visual counterpoint to Rankine's episodic, meandering, and often ambiguous prose on the social and affective terrain of race, racism, and American history."[65] The artwork in the book, which includes pieces from J. M. W. Turner's *The Slave Ship* (1840) to Wangechi

Mutu's *Sleeping Heads* (2006), is prevented from settling into cloistered, homogeneous genealogies (of abstract art, of black art, of nineteenth-century British art). Rankine's method cannot be called merely "appropriation." It is a political intervention into the discourses of art and literature, the siloed genealogies of which are typically presented as natural instead of gendered and racialized.

I have shown previously how Rankine turns to the Atlantic Ocean as a figure for the transatlantic slave trade and for the accumulation of moments of racism, any one of which has a disproportionate impact on the single individual who confronts it in the present. The Atlantic Ocean is also a real geographical presence in *Citizen*, and it serves as the theater for one of the situations. "October 10, 2006/World Cup" crosses to France and transcribes the end of the 2006 World Cup soccer match between France and Italy. The FIFA World Cup represents a specific version of neoliberalism that celebrates cultural diversity while evicting thousands of residents to build stadiums, creating deadly working conditions, and militarizing cities. The sports journalist Dave Zirin has called the World Cup "a neoliberal Trojan Horse aimed at bringing in business and rolling back the most basic civil liberties."[66] The game between France and Italy, which Rankine turns into one of her "meditative spaces," illustrates the repression of French colonial history by the profit-driven logic of neoliberal multiculturalism.

While the prose poems isolate specific instances of racism, the Situations slow down the encounter in a different way, adding layers of text and thickening the narrative that leads to the explosive moment of violence. Rankine captures the irruption of European racism within the soccer game by taking footage of several seconds from the end of the game and slowing them down into a six-minute video. At the end of his final game before retirement, the French player Zinedine Zidane, who is of Algerian heritage, headbutted Marco Materazzi's chest.[67] No one could see what Materazzi said to provoke Zidane, so lip readers were hired afterward to try to discern it. A few years later, Materazzi claimed he said, "I prefer the whore that is your sister." But many had believed he had said "big Algerian shit, dirty terrorist, nigger." Rankine takes the video of this event and slows it down radically, overlaying it with Zidane's own comments, and collaging a text out of appropriated works by Ralph Ellison, Maurice Blanchot, James Baldwin, Shakespeare, and Frantz Fanon. While there is a contemporary poetic tradition of appropriating texts, this formal strategy has most often been associated with conceptual poetry, rather than with the lyric. Moreover, conceptualism has often been justly accused of racism, ignoring or effacing the context in which appropriated material has been written. For

Rankine, as I have suggested, the severing of a piece of writing or art from its context cuts the other way. Her textual appropriations work against the homogenization of a lyric tradition pictured as the latticework of a white male "anxiety of influence" or a set of hermetically sealed "other traditions." By using them as a script and voiceover, these selections become a radical archive, a kind of conjuring spell out of which a politicized act of lyric beauty irrupts.

The sudden movement from the United States to France and Algeria, in a book focused largely on domestic racism, makes sense for several related reasons. Shifting transnationally, Rankine sets up her own version of what Paul Gilroy calls "the black Atlantic," arguing implicitly that the "American citizen" has always been imbricated with the geography of the triangular slave trade.[68] A Francophone context offers a comparative vantage point from which Rankine, like Lowell, Wright, and Hugo in the 1960s and 1970s, can weigh and defamiliarize the history of American citizenship. In France, moreover, the word "citizen" has at times been part of a counterdiscourse of belonging that marks a separation from the nation. Kristin Ross argues that the Paris Commune begins in 1868 in the Vaux-Hall ballroom at Château-d'eau with a scene of disidentification from nationality: the shouting of the word *citoyen*, instead of *mesdames, messieurs*, by a heterogeneous group of workers, refugees, and veterans of the 1848 revolutions. Ross writes,

> The words *citoyen, citoyenne* no longer indicate national belonging—
> they are addressed to people who have separated themselves from the
> national collectivity. And because the words are an interpellation, a
> direct second-person address, they create that gap or division in a
> *now*, in the contemporary moment constituted by the speech act; they
> create a new temporality in the present and, essentially, an agenda . . .
> they allow an understanding of the present, in its unfolding, as historical, as changing.[69]

In Ross's account, "citizenship" does not exist prior to its creation through an act of address to those excluded from the normative citizenship of the French nation. This lyricization of citizenship is akin to a revolutionary moment in which the possibility of change accompanies the grasp of historical contingency.

The World Cup Situation brings together the rest of *Citizen* into a single emergence of the lyric. In keeping with Rankine's stretching of the lyric, it is one that takes shape from a physical gesture—the head butt—rather than a speech act. This address, directed to those not recognized as French citizens, is also an anticolonial act of redress. Following Ross, we can understand Zidane as creating an analogous "gap or division in a *now*" that permits "an understanding of the present, in its unfolding, as historical." In this Situation, what happens in an instant—the provocation and the response—is given time, slowed down, subjected to thought. The war with Algeria, which continues to structure French notions of who is French and who belongs in France, breaks like an ocean on a single head. But in this powerful moment, the head does not go under the waves; it offers a rebuttal, a head butt. What can potentially emerge, Rankine suggests, from these moments of exclusion is a response, or even a creation—what she refers to as "beauty." She employs two quotations from theorists to make this point. Rankine first quotes Fanon, who writes, "It is the White Man who creates the Black Man. But it is the Black Man who creates." She juxtaposes this quotation with one from Baldwin: "The endless struggle to achieve and reveal and confirm a human identity, human authority, contains, for all its horror, something very beautiful." The poem offers both a diagnosis of the failures of citizenship as an ideal and a staging of the "terrible beauty" potentially created from these failures.

The trans-Mediterranean head butt is a complementary image to that of the transatlantic head that feels the impact of slavery from the endless accumulation of racist aggressions. To lyricize citizenship is both to acknowledge the exclusion of certain "I's" as the means of creating the nation and to assert that "I" within a vision of alternative belonging. Ultimately, Rankine neither negates the categories of lyric and citizen, nor does she leave them in the suspension the title enacts. Angela Hume writes that

> in yoking these two questions together, Rankine suggests that acknowledging the conjectural nature of the first [question about lyric] becomes key to recognizing the answerability of the second [question about American citizenship]; through experimental, even failed "lyric" practices, one becomes capable of exposing the interrelation and co-constitution of race and environment.[70]

Hume demonstrates how Rankine improvises within a set of compromised lyric practices. But it is also possible to see how Rankine's reinvention of the lyric—a term that comprises a constellation of prose anecdotes, painting and sculpture, video script, meditative vers libre, and physical action—gives aesthetic form to what she defines as beauty. In Rankine's work, beauty is created through the political rebuttal and transformation of a notion of citizenship that has continued the U.S. project of racial genocide by brandishing the alibi of a post-racial society.

Beauty appears prominently in the title of an earlier work by Rankine called "The Provenance of Beauty: A South Bronx Travelogue" (2009), which puts the lyric to a different, but related purpose. In this performance piece, the audience boards a bus along with three narrators, who serve both as improvisational sightseeing guides and as mouthpieces for a script of Rankine's poetry. In an interview, Rankine explains why she chooses the Bronx:

> I grew up in the Bronx, so [the director and I] went and checked out
> different neighborhoods in the Bronx, and we ended up, for many
> reasons, in the South Bronx. . . . I believe that where we are, how we
> are allowed to live, is determined by the politics of the land—the big
> politics and the little politics. And it varies depending on where
> you're located. I'm very interested in the landscape in general as the
> site of living, of a place created out of lives, and those lives having a
> kind of politics and a kind of being that is consciously and uncon-
> sciously shaped. Decisions are made that allow us to do certain
> things, that give us certain freedoms and "unfreedoms."[71]

Rankine's description of "the politics of the land" conjoins the local and the global, the individual history of the lyric "I" and the massive transfor-mation of the South Bronx caused by city spending cuts in the 1970s.[72] Panitch and Gindin describe this period in New York as an inaugural moment of neoliberalism, when the city embraces "a concept of fiscal rec-titude that rejected higher taxes and instead cut social programs, froze wages, and privatized public services and assets."[73] Here, the lyric appears in a form appropriate to the investigation of the landscape it undertakes: the moving bus, with its clear connection to labor, class, everyday life, and the city politics of mass transportation.

"The Provenance of Beauty" crystallizes a present-day form of a Whit-manian lyric, taking literally the exhortation "Let us go." An excerpt from the script sounds very much like Whitman indeed: "If I sat next to you, spoke only to you, you would feel the warmth of my breath. As our shoul-ders touched you would shift, and I would know your movement as response. This is a world and we are in it."[74] Rankine telegraphs the lyric into these lines: they contain a moment of address—"spoke only to you"—that is also one of inspiration—"the warmth of my breath"—and of deixis, or the work of pointing at something—"*this* is a world." Rankine situates this epitomized moment of lyricality in the context of a group bus ride through the Bronx. To place the lyric in the service of the recognition of others, she finds an appropriate emblem and vehicle for uncovering the imbrications of neoliberalism with local communities, individuals, and daily lives.

The contemporary lyric thus directs us outward to particular kinds of engagement with the world: as Roderick Ferguson writes, Rankine "attempts to produce the conditions by which the reader can become a witness not simply to the internal properties of the text but to the social world that locates the text, the writer, and the reader."[75] This persistence of the lyric has not rendered moot the question of poetry's orientation toward the world, but has left it still largely undertheorized. The insights of the New Lyric Studies help to uncover a set of global, material, and historical "motives for the materialization of lyric."[76] Such work does not only supply an extended genealogy of lyric texts; it also offers a direction forward, freeing lyric from the history of its generic contestation. When the conditions for living negate the rich interiority that Hegel asserts as the natural property of lyric discourse, then the lyric claims the right instead of a rebuttal, a head butt, a meditative space, and a desire to question the ethical human, the legal person, the political subject, and the individual self. Soldered to the mutations of a global capitalist system, the lyric does not withdraw from the traces of consumer goods that threaten it, as Adorno would write. It is the continually reasserted voice of that which has been made into a commodity and traded. The lyric appears where Rankine's poetry forges an oppositional counter-discourse of the citizen in the neoliberal era of institutionalized difference.

The next chapter moves from the citizen to the crowd. As "The Provenance of Beauty" makes clear, the lyric's orientation toward the world can also take on the nature of an act, a performance, a desire, a song, a demand, or a call-and-response. Chapter 3 looks at some of the ways in which the rhetoric of exhortation shapes poetic forms, bringing into view a sociality, a crowd, that has been dispersed or expelled by global forces. The prospective agencies summoned by exhortation, a particularly hospitable kind of poetic address, do not always depend on a message superimposed on the poem or explicitly stated. Instead, the hortatory procedures of the poem make possible a shared recognition of an incipient, as-yet-to-be-determined friendship, a global "we." Even if this is a "provisional location" or a place to which we may not yet arrive, the poem points us there, and points to us there, as if to say that this is a world, and we are in it.

CHAPTER 3

The Crowd to Come

Poetic Exhortations from Brooklyn to Kashmir

In his analysis of Charles Baudelaire, Walter Benjamin shows that late nineteenth-century European poetry's retreat into a radical individuality is a response to changes in capitalism—in particular, new temporalities of machine work and "shocks" by the crowd.[1] This chapter brings together a group of contemporary poems that arise from conditions in which that crowd has disappeared. The hortatory mode used by these poets takes its ethical and political force not from the shock of encountering the crowd, but from realizing that crowds themselves are in jeopardy. While some contemporary hortatory poems draw on historical norms of lyric laid out in the previous chapter, my concern here is not the Anglophone lyric per se; the ballad and the ghazal also reshape the rhetoric of calling, inviting, pleading, and cursing. While the first parts of this chapter continue to explore Western European forms as they are repurposed in a globalized context, I turn at the end to the Urdu ghazal. Working within the history of the ghazal and of a divided Kashmir, the Kashmiri American poet Agha Shahid Ali threads exhortation through the poem in an attempt to bypass forms of belonging imposed by India and Pakistan. To orient these poems in relation to global capitalism today is to underscore the extent to which global capitalism renders its crowds precarious, capable of disintegration by informalized labor conditions; dispersal by a militarized police and a securitized state; or co-option by the politics of communitarianism and expulsion. In response to the globally induced vulnerability of collective life, a strain of Anglophone poetry desperately conjures a globalized "we," a crowd to come.

None of the poets in this chapter lays claim to an explicit, thematized "we," however. Suspicious of the totalizing and potentially totalitarian politics of the "we," each of them develops instead a formal and stylistic procedure for culling and gleaning the material that they include in their poetry. I use the metaphor of commoning to describe this poetics, taking my cue from the titles of the first two poetry collections in this chapter, Sean Bonney's *The Commons* and Myung Mi Kim's *Commons*. The third poem, Ali's "Tonight," serves as a limit-case for the hortatory poetics I explore in Bonney and Kim; the ghazal itself might be understood as particularly receptive to gleaning across poetic traditions, languages, and citations. Their materials are never simply equal fragments juxtaposed across gulfs of difference, but, as the terms "gleaning" and "commoning" both imply, ones scored by economic precariousness and marked by historical positions of inequality. Nor are they the remnants of a high European tradition, preserved in modernist bricolage against their ruin. The porousness of the poem to its different materials varies in degree from Bonney to Kim to Ali, depending on the unique possibilities granted by their chosen forms. The poems range from the songs, spells, and curses of the ballad to the experimental "translations" of Kim's sentences and syllables to the tightly structured ghazal with its intricate couplets and echoing rhymes. The conditions and locations in which the poems are situated are ineluctably specific: Bonney's cuckoo sings ballads about British and U.S. networks of finance; Kim's fractured and reconstituted Korean and English syntax is embedded in the violence of war and displacement; Ali's adaptation of the Urdu ghazal form becomes the occasion to critique contrasting versions of sovereignty and varieties of belief. But all three poets reinvent the forms they use through the poetic enactment of gleaning. In this way, the commoning of diverse poetic leftovers becomes the stockpile that powers a collectivity yet to come.

The invitation to a crowd is not so much marked by the imagination of a particular set of figures in Bonney, Kim, and Ali as it is by their innovations within the hortatory modes of summoning, calling together, and inciting. The rhetoric of exhortation has been reinvigorated in contemporary Anglophone poetry written under global conditions of vulnerability, exile, radical uncertainty, and expulsion from social life. Hortatory rhetoric is closely related to the lyric trope par excellence, apostrophe, which Jonathan Culler argues "makes its point by troping not on the meaning of a word but on the circuit or situation of communication itself."[2] Epideixis, or the convention of praise that is constitutive of Greek lyric poetry, can often be combined with exhortation: *The Song of Songs*, for instance, balances devotion with invitation: "Come, my beloved,/let us go out into the fields."[3] Aristotle, in the *Rhetoric*, notes that praise has the tendency to slip quickly into exhortation: "To praise a man is . . . akin to urging a course of action."[4] As early as Sappho and as late as Rankine, exhortation is one of the most recognizable ways that Greek, European, and Anglophone poetry talks to strangers, extending its intimacy to what the poet Jorie Graham calls "regions of unlikeness."[5] Exhortation is thus one of the rhetorical strategies that specific strains of poetry take toward the world as they attempt to call forth a collective "we" through the poem, a "we" of displaced, oppressed, exiled, and vulnerable lives.[6]

Modern instances of exhortation trouble a lingering twentieth-century sense of Anglophone poetry as solipsistic, instead emphasizing its communality, accessibility, and democratic aspirations. While Rankine's "The Provenance of Beauty" invites us to gather together on a bus tour through the South Bronx, Walt Whitman exhorts the cosmos from a ferry to Brooklyn and from the battlefields of the Civil War. In Whitman's exhortations, the "we" is explicitly thematized, though perhaps more as a wishful image than an assumed quantity. Whitman's "Small the Theme of My Chant," from the 1869 *Leaves of Grass*, invites lyric poetry into the modern period, but not without difficulty:

> Small the theme of my Chant, yet the greatest—namely, One's-Self—
>   a simple, separate person. That, for the use of the New World, I sing.
> Man's physiology complete, from top to toe, I sing. Not physiognomy
>   alone, nor brain alone, is worthy for the Muse;—I say the Form
>   complete is worthier far. The Female equally with the Male, I sing.
> Nor cease at the theme of One's-Self. I speak the word of the modern, the
>   word En-Masse.
> My Days I sing, and the Lands—with interstice I knew of hapless War.
> (O friend, whoe'er you are, at last arriving hither to commence, I feel
>   through every leaf the pressure of your hand, which I return.
> And thus upon our journey, footing the road, and more than once, and
>   link'd together let us go.)[7]

Whitman's exhortations point to a problem of representation at the heart of modern and contemporary Anglophone poetry: how can the singular pronoun "I" of the poem contain both "One's-Self" and the "word of the modern, the word En-Masse?" While we might think of some lyric poetry as being directed toward a single person—"O friend"—Whitman immediately makes the poem accommodate itself to the "word En-Masse": "whoe'er you are, at last arriving hither to commence." From within his intimate address, Whitman breaks open the poem to accept the unknown friend. For the small chant to contain a world of difference, it must hold out a kind of radical hospitality, a sense of hopeful expectation for "the certainty of others, the life, love, sight, hearing of others."[8]

In disparate contemporary traditions of poetry in English, the rhetoric of exhortation is strongly marked. Yet instead of appearing in the form of Whitman's encompassing catalogues and explicit invitations, the hortatory mode moves in the late twentieth century into the formal totality of the poem itself. The result is a set of poetic structures that range from examples of avant-garde L=A=N=G=U=A=G=E poetry to the cross-cultural matrix of the ghazal. Before moving into the trio of poets to follow, I want to give a brief example of what this looks like from John Ashbery's recent books. In Ashbery, there is not much of the "let us go" that we find in Whitman. Instead, exhortation might usefully describe the process of composition itself. Ashbery is sometimes thought to epitomize in his work a certain late Romantic version of Whitman's democratic "I."[9] Yet from this standpoint, much of his writing of the past twenty or thirty years has seemed almost unreadable, or at an oblique angle to the present period of globalization.[10] Here is the opening stanza from "They Knew What They Wanted," a poem in his 2009 collection, *Planisphere*:

> They all kissed the bride.
> They all laughed.
> They came from beyond space.
> They came by night.[11]

Ashbery's lines are cobbled together from invisible voices; the poems are created from bits of utterance severed from their moments of articulation—in this case, the titles of films. The compositional procedure of the poem, then, is itself an invitation to the "we" to enter into the poem: the poem invites voices in. In Ashbery's world lyric, Whitman's "word En-Masse," explicitly stated in "Small the Theme of My Chant," enters into the making of the poem itself.

Earlier readings of poetic sociality by Walter Benjamin and Theodor Adorno help to situate a contemporary hortatory poetics. Benjamin and Adorno examine a relation between the "I" of the poem and the "we" that is shaped by the altered material conditions of capitalism. For Benjamin, the "we" is the figure of the crowd, while for Adorno the "we" is shorthand for society. Benjamin's "On Some Motifs in Baudelaire" (1939) argues that modern capitalism is based on the encounter with "shock" and its deflection by the consciousness.[12] Benjamin draws a set of analogies between machine work, crowds, and gambling: "The shock experience which the passerby has in the crowd corresponds to the isolated 'experiences' of the worker at his machine . . . the reflexive mechanism that the machine triggers in the workman can be studied closely, as in a mirror, in the idler . . . the jolt in the movement of the machine is like the so-called *coup* in the game of chance."[13] A new sense of time connects the worker, the member of a crowd, and the gambler: in Baudelaire's world, Benjamin argues, "each operation . . . is . . . screened off from the preceding operation."[14] Benjamin argues that this process of "starting all over again" is inimical to the creation of experience that stretches back in time, which we perceive as the "aura" that surrounds the objects of our memory.[15] Since the aura is no longer accessible as long experience over time, Baudelaire's lyric grants its power instead to immediate experience, to the eyes that "have lost their ability to look."[16] In such a context, to write lyric at all requires a cost, which for Baudelaire is "the disintegration of the aura in the experience of shock."[17] In Benjamin's analysis, the lyric poem continues to be written, but only by acquiescing to the loss of the particular social and material conditions that had once accompanied it.

For Adorno, poetry occupies an even more strained relationship to the language of capital. In "On Lyric Poetry and Society" (1957), Adorno argues for an "immanent" approach to the lyric that avoids reducing its social efficacy to a set of political concepts or themes.[18] The explicit social themes and concepts of a poem are only evidence of its debasement, distortion, and subsumption under capital.[19] Adorno maintains that, instead, the social is "imprinted in reverse on the poetic work"[20]: "The less the work thematizes the relationship of 'I' and society, the more spontaneously it crystallizes of its own accord in the poem."[21] As Robert Kaufman explains, "The lyric poem must work coherently in and with the medium—language—that human beings use to articulate objective concepts, even while the lyric explores the most subjective, nonconceptual, and ephemeral phenomena."[22] This argument allows Adorno to steer between two social interpretations of a poetic "I." By denying that the "I" speaks from an external vantage point on society, he separates the poetic subject from that false image of an individual who has somehow escaped from "utility" and the "weight of material existence."[23] And by insisting against the thematization of the social, he prevents the "I" from becoming the mouthpiece of already existing concepts. Thus Adorno claims that "in the lyric poem the subject, through its identification with language, negates both its opposition to society as something merely monadological and its mere functioning within a wholly socialized society."[24]

Benjamin's essay begins with a hypothesis that modern European poetry receives a poor reception because of a "change in the structure of . . . experience."[25] He turns quite deliberately not to philosophy, but rather to Baudelaire's poetry itself to try to find out what this change might be. The "decisive, unmistakable experience" confronted by Baudelaire's lyric is the shock of "having been jostled by the crowd."[26] Today, much U.S. poetry directs itself to a "change in the structure of experience" as well. Yet the changes registered by the poem are the erosion, rather than the "shock" and "jostling," of sociality. The disposition toward the social modeled by some contemporary poets does not draw into the poem an oppressive encounter fraught with responsibility, as some ethical models propose, so much as it manifests as a side-by-side, adjacent, or contiguous relation.[27]

The poetry in this chapter is responsive to the global condition that Judith Butler describes as "unchosen cohabitation" and the accompanying ethical commitment "to an equal right to inhabit the earth."[28] While contemporary capitalism fictionalizes social life in terms of corporate personhood or agonistic competition over scarce resources, one strain of recent poetry enacts on the level of poetic form the jostling, prickling, energizing sensations of proximity to heterogeneous others. The poets I consider here use poetic language to summon forth a crowd that would be impossible to represent as either a homogeneous totality or something imperiously "other." In this way, their poetry aligns itself with the precarious, a term I borrow here to emphasize both the fragility of these collectivities and their position outside waged labor, political representation, and economic security.

Research in political, economic, and social thought demarcates the current period of globalization as a "new historical phase," an "age of precarity."[29] "Precarious life" and "precarity" have appeared more and more frequently as political, philosophical, and ethical terms that refer to contemporary conditions of life under specific forms of insecurity, including "the shrinkage of the social welfare state, the privatization of what had once been publicly held utilities and institutions, the increase in state, banking and corporate pension insecurity, and the ever more 'flexible' practices of contractual reciprocity between owners and workers."[30] These changes have also been accompanied, most recently, by the increasing financialization of commodities, which exacerbates the pressures put on local markets for food and other everyday items.[31]

Discussions of precarity are shaped by Paulo Virno, who describes precarity as "the chronic instability of forms of life"[32]; by Pierre Bourdieu, who examines the "absolute reign of flexibility"[33]; by Judith Butler, who considers precarious life as a common ontological vulnerability on the basis of which we might found a tentative solidarity; by Isabell Lorey, who analyzes the normalization of precarity as an aspect of neoliberal governmentality; and by Guillaume Le Blanc, who analyzes precarity as the social vulnerability created by economic and political oppression. These philosophies of precarity are complemented by the sociologies of labor undertaken by Saskia Sassen and Andrew Ross, who analyze the increasing role of sweatshops, free zones, and exploited workers in the global economy. While some discourses of globalization emphasize the placelessness of the "information economy," Sassen directs attention to the precarious bodies of workers whose labor supports the global city, especially women of color and immigrants. The precarious subject of "material conditions, production sites, and activities bounded by place," the subject moving through "counter-geographies of globalization," confronts contingency, difficulty, risk, and expulsion from social norms.[34]

As a term that describes the period following the independence of former colonies, the implementation of Cold War underdevelopment, and the crisis of U.S. legitimacy as a world hegemon, "precarity" knits together global changes in economic relations, aesthetic perception, and the social production of collectivities. Precarity is particularly important for this study of a global poetics because it calls attention to the disintegration of sociality. As Franco Berardi argues, solidarity is hard to imagine under a regime of financial speculation and cognitive labor, because "the work process is no longer based on a community of workers living together in a factory day after day, but instead takes the form of an ever-changing recombination of time fragments connected in the global network."[35] At the same time, precarity has served as a rallying cry that draws together disparate groups into a common struggle against neoliberal globalization. As Lauren Berlant notes, movements of the precarious seek "to forge transcategorical alliances (trans-local, -national, -class, -legal, -sexual, etc.) against the fading of social democratic institutions and toward the invention of new communities of care and political belonging."[36] In this sense, precarity refers not only to a general state of ontological vulnerability, but also to specific global political movements of the present.

The theorization of precarity by Berardi, Butler, Berlant, Sassen, and others is helpful because it undermines celebratory narratives of globalization that focus on a hypermobile capitalist elite. At the same time, the overdetermined figure of the precarious challenges analyses from the left that privilege the factory floor as the site for labor activism. Arguments about precarity can be situated in the broader context of social-scientific analyses of economic globalization undertaken by proponents and critics of deregulation, privatization, and speculation. By now, the costs of careless pacing, deliberate hypocrisy by certain global players, and the unthinking adoption of neoliberalism as a political ideology are glaringly evident.[37] Older arguments that economic globalization might ameliorate poverty and inequality have been refuted by careful attention to the disagreements over what these terms mean and how they are measured.[38] Anthropologists, meanwhile, continue to look closely at the failures of theoretical models of development within local communities.[39] While methodological differences certainly continue to exist—what poverty line to use, whether to measure inequality within countries or between countries— research across the disciplines bears out the claims that neoliberal policies exacerbate inequality, poverty, and precariousness. As Robert H. Wade notes, "What is striking is how little, rather than how much, the 'developing world'—outside of East Asia—has caught up with the West after 65 years of deliberate 'development.'"[40] One widely publicized concession from global development institutions in this respect is the International Monetary Fund's June 2016 report, "Neoliberalism: Oversold?" The report blames short-term capital flow liberalization and austerity policies for both exacerbating inequality and undercutting growth.[41]

The term "precarity" draws out certain elements of the historically specific configuration of capitalism and insecurity that faces contemporary poets when they try to imagine a "we." I am less concerned here with the ontological meaning of "precarity" as the shared vulnerability of existence. Recent poetry collections by the English poet Sean Bonney and the Korean American poet Myung Mi Kim bring together the hortatory rhetoric of poetry, its calls to come together, with the vanishing spaces that they name "commons." Far from a nostalgic return to a world without capital's enclosures, their poetry encompasses a wide range of strategies for energizing a fragmented and precarized social body. At moments, both these poets are explicitly critical of capital, finance, militarization, and neoliberal politics. Often, however, they explore vulnerability more obliquely. For Bonney and Kim, poetic imagination is one place to look for global solidarity, for a "new social ecology," and for collective agency.[42] These poets revalue poetry as the medium through which a collective takes shape, or, as Kim puts it, as a "provisional location" designed "to mobilize the notion of our responsibility to one another in social space."[43] As a racialized and financialized global capitalism forecloses the possibilities for sociality and solidarity in dramatic ways, Bonney and Kim explicitly align themselves with poetic traditions, from Whitman and Baudelaire to Ashbery and Rankine, of finding oneself in the midst of a crowd. Confronted with the pressures of adjacency and proximity to others, their poetry creates the literary equivalent of a commons: a shared "meditative space," to recall Rankine's phrase, that subverts the hierarchies of power reproduced in other forms of discourse.[44]

Although the language and syntax they use are quite different, the notion of the commons developed in both shares certain qualities.[45] Neither poet lays out a thematic program or a set of slogans for social solidarity or collective political subjectivity. David Harvey underscores this proleptic or anticipatory commons, emphasizing that "the common is not, therefore, something extant once upon a time that has since been lost, but something that, like the urban commons, is continuously being produced. The problem is that it is just as continuously being enclosed and appropriated by capital in its commodified and monetary form."[46] In a formulation that recalls Harvey's, Kim states that a commons is illegible within the "totalizing power of language that serves the prevailing systems and demands of coherence."[47] Within this language, it is a blank space: "_____, a word that cannot be translated: it suggests, 'what belongs to the people.'"[48] Bonney and Kim both fend off a sentimental, affective call to the commons as the return to an idealized precapitalist condition. To do so, the commons appears only through the operations performed on and by the poem. While Bonney's *The Commons* attacks and interrupts the languages of banking and credit, Kim's poetry focuses on war, displacement, and problems of translation.

Bonney's *The Commons* (2011) represents a contemporary version of the poetic curse that hectors, blames, eviscerates, scorns, hates, and condemns.[49] At the same time, his poems perform a kind of gleaning, gathering together lyric songs and popular ballads with a range of other linguistic materials. Bonney's invectives, written after the world financial crisis of 2008 and during the riots in London in 2011, target global finance for its reduction of language, thought, and people to blanks and gasps:

> Meanwhile, in the fast world of banking
> they are thinking in blocks of sound

blank ones
reduced to little knots
of hair & teeth
we were speaking
like any gasping swine.[50]

For those who think in blank "blocks of sound," the voices of the precarious are audible only as "gasping swine." To find another language for precarity, and to create a counter-discourse to that of financial capitalism, Bonney reaches back into the archives of English poetry and song. *The Commons* is a patchwork of citations, from the traditional English song "The Cuckoo Bird" to Rimbaud's "L'Orgie Parisienne"; from The Velvet Underground's "Heroin" to Frantz Fanon's *The Wretched of the Earth*; and from a Hackney Council Housing Benefit Form to Shelley's *Prometheus Unbound*. These references are not disguised, but linked, along with YouTube clips and Bonney's own performances, on Bonney's blog, where the poem was first published. In an author's note, Bonney explains that *The Commons* is written to subvert the official language of neoliberal globalization, which identifies the precarious subject of history as a "zombie":

> The work was originally subtitled "A Narrative/Diagram of the Class Struggle," wherein voices from contemporary uprisings blend into the Paris Commune, into October 1917, into the execution of Charles 1, and on into superstitions, fantasies of crazed fairies and supernatural bandits //// all clambering up from their hidden places in history, getting ready to storm the Cities of the Rich //// to the bourgeois eye they may look like zombies, to us they are sparrows, cuckoos, pirates & sirens //// the cracked melodies of ancient folk songs, cracking the windows of Piccadilly //// or, as a contemporary Greek proverb has it, "smashing up the present because they come from the future."[51]

Instead of "zombies" or "gasping swine," Bonney has the resistance to globalization take the form of figures recuperated from songs and ballads: "sparrows, cuckoos, pirates & sirens."[52]

The material disappearance of the commons is registered in dialectical fashion by the collected remnants of older poems, the "cracked melodies of ancient folk songs," and the silent, invisible groups of people they memorialize. By bundling together these estovers of poetic fragments and titles of songs, Bonney's *Commons* reminds us that the high status of poetry in Anglophone literature in the mid-sixteenth century coincides almost exactly with the English enclosure movements begun by the dissolution of the monasteries in 1536.[53] The rhetoric of lament acknowledges the foreclosure of a collective struggle, even as it insists on the adjacency of others:

> moan, now
> on his white bones
> his intolerable name.
> He is the man or woman
> sitting beside you,
> bitter & false & snapped
> inside every nation
> such hawks & hounds, such ravens
> o bitter statistics
> the cuckoo is a pretty bird[54]

Into the space of the absent commons slip the folk songs and figures that serve as so many indices of revolutionary activity. These include the "cuckoo," which, from Jacobite minstrelsy to Wordsworthian balladry, appears to announce a spring that cannot yet be seen or imagined. Many of these anonymous songs, such as "The Cuckoo Bird" or "The Three Ravens," predate the earliest significant period of privatization in the modern capitalist world-system, the passing into law of the enclosure of the commons in the early seventeenth century. They represent much more than "a sentimental space, purely/some kind of folk song."[55] They also provide a crucial reminder that the current period of neoliberalism, financial capitalism, and endless war is a late moment in a four-hundred-year cycle of economic regulation and deregulation.[56]

Bonney's poetry searches for a relation between a revolutionary poetic language and a revolutionary political subject. The "intolerable name" of precarious life—the global "we" of the contemporary period, the "man or woman/sitting beside you"—cannot be explicitly summoned within the poem:

> Cold/blows[57] the future
> ballads of the
> -blank-
> my true love[58]

While the poem retains the poetic address to "my true love," the addressee of the "future ballad" appears as a prolepsis, a "blank" that will be filled in later. Perhaps the "blank" is also a musical rest, a withholding of sound or word, a single beat that calls attention to the absence of what might fill it. "The sun has been disconnected," Bonney writes elsewhere:

both electricity and poetic inspiration—one traditional symbol of which is the "sun"—have been cut off because of poor credit.[59] Nor can the "windows of Piccadilly" be cracked simply by gleaning bits of song and juxtaposing them, rewriting *The Waste Land* during a different moment of crisis in the modern world-system. In Bonney's poem, there is little to suggest that a viable position exists outside the "prepared vocab" of neoliberalism:

> history is those who sit
> inside their prepared vocab,
> the comfortable ones,
> the executioner, especially,
> never utters an articulate sound
> quietly gets on with his work.[60]

Even as the poet screams "slaughter the fascist BNP," much of *The Commons* is specifically about the complicity and continuity between the language of the poem and the language of power.[61]

Bonney's poetry launches an explicit critique of the language of neoliberal globalization. But his poems do more than interrupt the circulation of neoliberal discourse. They also perform, in a version of poetic commoning, a recombination of linguistic registers, literary sources, and heterogeneous lexicons. *The Commons* can be understood as an "anti-discourse," to borrow Christian Lotz's term, that frees words to exist in hitherto unknown relations to each other. Lotz writes,

> if it is true that poetic speech inhibits and "brackets" the primary
> function of language in our everyday world, such as conversation,
> information, narration, description, and performative tasks, then it is
> easier to see how poetry not only releases words out of their ordinary
> connections, but also introduces and builds up new relations.[62]

Lotz builds on Karlheinz Stierle's effort to describe what is "exceptional" about lyric poetry in particular: "[Lyric] is not its own literary genre, but a specific mode . . . that signifies the transgression of discursive schema."[63] The analyses by Stierle and Lotz of lyric as "transgression" and "anti-discourse" are part of a venerable critical tendency to mark the identity of lyric as paradoxical, dialectical, excessive, or simply contradictory: the lyric is "a hesitation between the sound and sense"[64]; "a reciprocal catastrophe of sound and sense"[65]; "a dialectical play of ritual and fictional phenomena"[66]; "some secret pursuit of music . . . in the reserve of Discourse"[67]; "a verbal message whose aesthetic function is its dominant"[68]; "a formal practice that keeps in view the linguistic code and the otherness of the material medium of language to all that humans do with it—refer, represent, express, narrate, imitate, communicate, think, reason, theorize, philosophize."[69] These definitions share an understanding of European lyric as a kind of "wrenching away" from what it tries to express,[70] or from "sense."[71]

Bonney dramatizes such an alienation or othering of poetry from its own language. He does this not by foregrounding the materiality of the "aesthetic function" but rather by documenting the poem's own fraught composition, its own making and unmaking:

> the 'reverie' is a
> stop, oppressive line
> "is this is that"
> like a mystical shudder?
> yeh, that's hideous.
> anyway, false, as I was saying[72]

Bonney's hesitation to define reverie or cuckoo or sea or moon relies on a tactic of incessant interruption and self-reference. The appearance of "as I was saying" and of the related phrase "ok, say that again" is one of countless moments of self-recognition, self-criticism, and self-revision documented by the poem.[73] Other lines remind the poet to insert material that will signal the presence of a contemporary poem: "*-archaic pop reference here-*," "*-archaic credit reference here-*," "*favorite epoch here*," "insert hope & love," "insert world of banking."[74] Holding "the voice of our political poets" up to scrutiny, Bonney finds no room for a straightforward "flip discount menace" that poets might once have hoped to use against "the hounds of capital."[75] A certain rhetorical promiscuity dominates the poem: the times, Bonney suggests, require all of the poet's rhetorical dexterity. Even as it reflects on the limitations of the power of its address, *The Commons* sustains a relatively direct, colloquial style.[76] And even as the poem distances its audience with self-critical reflections on its own making, *The Commons* invites the same audience into the poem with its calls to riot and revolution, as well as its cries and laments.

As *The Commons* rages, blames, and excoriates, the time-scale of precarious lives—a transnational "we" that is radically uncertain, constantly vulnerable to interruption, forced to sign weekly or even daily contracts for labor—is revalued as a poetic and political strategy for insurrection. While Bonney criticizes the Situationist directive to "just, like, détourne yourself," something like a détournement, or a wrenching of words from their habitual meanings, ultimately occurs by the time the poem ends.[77] Despite its anxieties about "discount menace," *The Commons* takes up, at moments, positions of pure antagonism—"HAIL SHIT"[78]—that occupy forms of lyric address ("hail to thee, blithe Spirit!").[79] In this manner, Bonney activates "music love abstraction/the twisted branches/at the centre of our lives," all of which "ignite on interruption."[80] Within the incendiary lyricism of *The Commons*, a "we" emerges as those who, by virtue of their precarity, possess the imaginative capacity to seize and interrupt the categories with which they are classified and silenced:

> & we, with our downturned mouths
> are maidens,
> our credit ratings threaded with flowers.
> & we are bleating,
> & we are fucking immense
> shrieking with gibes and curses -[81]

This "we" can only be declared by the poet when the tropes of pastoral are revealed as interwoven with, or "threaded" through, the financialized subject of the speculative economy.

The plural "we" flashes forth in Bonney as a revolutionary subject in the process of being made, of scattering, and of reforming. Bonney's work coincides with riots in the streets of London and with revolutions in the squares of Tunisia, Egypt, the United States, and Turkey, among other sites of protest. In contrast, Myung Mi Kim's *Commons* (2002), written in the United States during the post-9/11 surge of U.S. territorial expansion and military occupation, avoids almost entirely thematic representations of a collectivity, desiring instead to "activate" language's ability "to call into question, to disclose, to make common."[82] As this quotation makes clear, the commons to which the title refers does not exist in the past, susceptible to recovery, but remains to be "made." The fact that Bonney and Kim share a title is more than a matter of coincidence. In both, the making of the commons occurs through a hortatory form that searches for a language of the precarious beyond the "prepared vocab" available. With Kim, however, this hortatory form is anatomized and radicalized through a rigorous attention to the smallest particles of language; to the possibilities of translating between languages; to the discrepant ways that English and Korean index material processes of war, poverty, and displacement; and, finally, to the potential for the poem to make a space for multiple languages while denaturalizing the precedence of a monolithic global English.

A professor at SUNY Buffalo, one of the institutional homes for experimental poets and critics in the United States, the Korean-born Kim investigates the links between destabilizing language and disrupting political or economic structures. She shares with the U.S. avant-garde traditions of L=A=N=G=U=A=G=E poetry an interest in finding the places where referential and nonreferential functions of language jostle against each other.[83] But such a general description of Kim's work threatens to erase its documentation and performance of collective suffering and violence under racial capitalism. It might be more precise to say, with Joseph Jonghyun Jeon, that her collections, from *Under Flag* (1991) and *The Bounty* (1996) to *Commons* (2002) and *Penury* (2009), make visible "issues of historical violence, immigration, and diaspora" by framing them "through linguistic rather than social lenses."[84] This use of language as the lens through which to encounter history makes Kim's work undeniably elusive, difficult, and austere. The first section of *Commons*, "Exordium," begins with the following passage: "In what way names were applied to things. Filtration. Not every word that has been applied, still exists. Through proliferation and differentiation. Airborn. Here, this speck and this speck you missed." Many of the elements of Kim's defamiliarizing syntax and compositional procedure are already present here. The short paragraph opens with a reference to Adamic naming, as though to draw attention to its own place at the beginning of the book as well. Next, the word "filtration" could be a metaphor for the "way names were applied to things," or it could be an example of a name applied to a thing; the word creates two divergent tracks for interpretation. "Proliferation," "airborn," and "speck" all pick up on the "filtration system," but "differentiation" keeps active the linguistic references in the first and third sentences. It is possible, then, that "proliferation and differentiation" name the processes by which words that have been applied to things in the past cease to "exist." Finally, "missed" supplies a third binding agent by virtue of its vowel and consonant sounds, which recall "exists" as well as the short "i" sounds in proliferation and differentiation.

As this fragment suggests, Kim defamiliarizes and disrupts a reader's acquired ability to discover meaning in a poem by describing how the units of the poem interact. To prevent an attitude of absorption in the text, Kim also includes meta-commentary on the writing of the poem itself. This self-consciousness is present throughout *Commons*, but it is especially prevalent in the final section, a paratactic series of notes about her poetic process entitled, "Pollen Fossil Record." Here, Kim explains that "*commons* elides multiple sites: reading and text making, discourses and disciplines, documents and documenting. Fluctuating. Proceeding by fragment, by increment. Through proposition, parataxis, contingency—approximating

nerve, line, song."[85] The poems cobble together disparate sources from
which Kim gleans a single sound, word, phrase, or sometimes a large paragraph. These sources are not given, but they include bald, declarative statements from what would seem to be counterinsurgency manuals; single
letters or diphthongs; travel narratives; Da Vinci's notebooks; definitions
of fairly obscure words, such as "periplus" or "muo"; songs and lyric poems
from both English and Korean traditions; and quotations from the news.
Although these programmatic lines from "Pollen Fossil Record" ostensibly
describe the book, they also resemble closely, in their own form, the poetry
in the preceding sections. "Pollen Fossil Record" is both a key to the rest
of the text and an extension of it. Commoning, in Kim's terms, involves a
method of "elision" by which incommensurate discourses are conjoined or
by which poetry cohabits space with its "others."[86]

    Kim's poems are crowded with elements that resist easy explanations for
their simultaneous presence in the poem. Such a fractious assemblage
makes it hard to identify a "we," even as a metaphor for the heterogeneous
materials in the poem. Instead, Kim's poetry prepares the ground for a
genuine "we" by exposing the false universality and the politically produced coherence of existing discourses. Against this, Kim writes that
poetry has the ability to grasp the "'particularizable' prosody of one's living."[87] The specific "prosody of living" that Kim dissects and reconstructs
through poetry is not prised from BNP and global finance, as in Bonney's
work, but from a globalized English language riven by differential forms of
material suffering and expulsion: "What *is* English now, in the face of mass
global migrations, ecological degradations, shifts and upheavals in identifi-
cations of gender and labor? . . . How to make plural the written and spoken. . . ."[88] Kim's "commons" designates the linguistic space for a "plural"
English, an English that "belongs to the people" linked together by the
shared experiences of global precarity.[89]

    To examine the possibilities for a "plural" English, Kim constructs
incomplete or deliberately thwarted translations from Korean to English
song and back. Frequently in *Commons*, the ghost of a quatrain will appear,
as in the poem marked "405":

Little flower,
What day is it
The light stops at glum
O'clock and f[90]

At first, "little flower" might be read as an apostrophe to the flower. The
second line could then be the question addressed to it. One thinks here of

William Blake's line "Little lamb who made thee" and of the habit certain poems have of apostrophizing the nonhuman. In Kim's poem, the third line supports and elaborates this reading, but then takes a sharp turn from it in the final word, "glum," which, in light of the fourth line, seems to have been substituted for a specific hour. This unexpected adjective, given additional emphasis at the end of a line, casts doubt over the interpretation of the previous two lines: "What day is it" might be a question the speaker poses to herself; "Little flower" might be a description rather than an address. Lines one and two may have no necessary relation at all. The temptation to grant a certain poetic license in the fourth line—"glum / O'clock" as some dreary hour—disappears with the single syllable *f.* If "f" stands for "forte," an indication of volume on a musical score, then the reader is given an instruction for how to voice the poem—a self-conscious move that comes as a jolt after the way the initial lines set up a scene. Just as likely, however, "f" introduces an unrelated, nonsignifying sound into the poem, and the flickering scene deteriorates further.

I read this passage as a draft of a "bad" translation, allowed to retain its ventures and soundings (*f*) as well as its "mistakes" (glum). At the same time, the passage clearly borrows from a ballad-like form: Kim notes in "Pollen Fossil Record" that she juxtaposes a fourteenth-century Korean *sijo* and "an alliterative English poem from about the same time" and "translates" them simultaneously. She explains her procedure and its stakes in the global:

> It is not the actual translation or even the state of translatability between the two texts that is intriguing but the possibilities for transcribing what occurs in the transversal between the two languages (and, by extension, between the two "nations," their mutually implicated histories of colonization, political conflicts, and so on). What is the recombinant energy created between languages (geopolitical economies, cultural representations, concepts of community)?[91]

To render this transversal legible, to explore "how 'English' is made and disseminated," Kim reduces her lyrics to the barest vowels, consonants, and diphthongs, those units of language that, when thrust together, create "recombinant energy." This is the level on which we might locate her own hortatory poetics, her exhortations to build "concepts of community" "between languages." While creating a dissonant music out of translations-in-process, Kim's poetry presents the activities of translation and transliteration as one of the poetic means by which racialization, differentiation, and dehumanization can be transcribed.

Kim's poems about the romanization of Korean into English, or the representation of Korean using a Latin script, make her practice and critique clearer. The second section of the book, "Lamenta," stages what Kim calls a "rehearsal of listening" in which she raises the questions "Whose ears are at work? Where does the authority of romanizing reside? How might it be entered into otherwise?"[92] For Kim, a pluralized English—an English spoken by a conjectural "we" created by colonization, war, dislocation, environmental destruction—becomes apparent through a process of mishearing and its consecration in writing. The resulting poem is not nonsense, but rather the denaturalization of a single authoritative position from which sense can be made.[93] Poem 506 of "Lamenta" generates one of Kim's "transversal" translations:[94]

$$\frac{ap}{ac}$$

Pock

ji-wuat-dah   erased
jil-eu-dah   shouted

Regarded among penury
Numb pie mum pie

jip-sae-gi   ji-pah-raeng-e   :   show here

Look at that noise!
Numb pie mum pie[95]

Here, the structure of the poem is reduced to a set of notes and enunciations, carefully arranged on the page.[96] The first set of letters, "ap" and "ac," sets up an initial test for the word "pock," offering different ways "pock" might be heard. Then, the slight mishearing of two words in Korean brings "erased" and "shouted" into imaginative proximity. Similar words pertaining to lack and amplitude, "penury" and "noise," are both heard as the same thing in English; the phrases "regarded among penury" and "look at that noise!" become "numb pie mum pie." Poem 506 presents a drama of garbling and partial legibility, exploring what happens when two phrases in Korean and two phrases in English are transliterated.

Kim's poetry undermines the authority of a single position from which English and Korean sounds might be turned into a romanized form and mutually understood. As one of Kim's "practices in transliteration," poem 506 opens a gap between "standard romanization" and "what [I] might be said to be hearing."[97] The notion of a commons, in this particular case, refers to the room within transliteration to mishear, or to hear multiple things at once. But the poem does more than this. As the "illegible" comes into speech, the elements of a scene scramble into view, although the details of this scene are limited to a set of verbs: to erase, to shout, to show. The "recombinant energy" generated by transliterating these verbs—the "commoning" of sounds together—is one way for the poem to reveal a precarious global subject in the grip of exigency, first shown poor, then seen shouting.

Bonney and Kim generate a poetics that resists privatization and a "totalizing" global English, respectively. I do not wish to minimize the differences between the two, especially since Kim's work makes a unique intervention within processes of racial ascription by undermining the authority of the listener, the translator, and the romanizer. Bonney's incendiary lines, meanwhile, are conducive to modes of performance and to poetry readings in a way that Kim's textual experiments are not: it would be hard to capture in speech the large blank spaces or the brackets, ratios, colons, and ideograms that appear on many of Kim's pages. Reading them side-by-side, however, adds to critical thinking in global studies, which, over the last two decades, has revisited notions of the commons in the face of precarity, scarcity, commodification, and privatization. As Peter Linebaugh argues, the commons not only demarcates a physical space for grazing, fishing, irrigation, or the gathering of firewood. It also designates a set of lost words, activities, and relations once tied to that space. Linebaugh writes, "The widow's estovers of common is thus the phrase that leads us to a completely different world, a world of use values."[98] Confronted with the necessity of representing a commons in the absence of a language for it, Bonney and Kim write a kind of hypothetical poem that refuses to settle into a completed shape on the page. Calling attention to the process by which the poem is composed, they transcribe the decisions, hesitations, and mistakes that generate the interruptive, recombinant energy of a language of the precarious.

Whitman's capacious free verse had stretched open the poem to contain the multitude of voices and varieties of difference in a union of states: "O friend, whoe'er you are . . . let us go." Bonney replaces Whitman's confident exhortation to the "friend" with a blank space where the subject of the poem, and of a future commons, might be: "the future / ballads of the / -blank- / my true love." This chapter concludes with a limit case of the poetic call, one in which cohabitation seems all but unimaginable. The Kashmiri American Agha Shahid Ali is a poet whose conditions of life are inconceivable except as part of the contemporary contestation over Kash-mir by India and Pakistan. Ali's poetry cannot refer directly to a "we" or "us," since there is no extant national social body that can be explicitly summoned or exhorted to fight for freedom. Ali's ghazals must instead summon into existence a cosmopolitan Kashmiri subject, if "cosmopoli-tan" is understood here in a wounded rather than celebratory sense, as I explore later. The poetic manifestation of the "Kashmiri American" requires both the tight strictures and the wild juxtapositions of the ghazal form itself. Ali's ghazal "Tonight" juxtaposes multiple and competing "calls" to group-belonging, sectarianism, and cultural affiliation around literary and sacred texts. Its hortatory voices, when forced to cohabit within the form of the ghazal, ultimately dissolve the putative sovereignty of the poetic "I" into acts of dependency and prayer.

From the first poems in his career, Agha Shahid Ali remarks on his dis-comfort at filling his poetry with explicitly political themes. An early pal-inode concludes, "please mutilate / my wounded poetry hands // i will not write again."[99] "History broke the back // of poetry," he writes in "After the Partition of India."[100] Ali was born in 1949 in New Delhi, two years after the partition of India. In the United States, where he lived until his death from a brain tumor in December 2001, he referred to himself as a "Kashmiri-American" and a "triple exile."[101] As Aamir Mufti explains, to call oneself Kashmiri American is to make

> a gesture of solidarity with the ongoing Kashmiri struggle for *āzādi*
> that emerged in 1990—*āzādi* is an overcoded signifier in the Kashmiri
> context, a first level of whose meanings could be limned simply as
> freedom or independence—and a repudiation both of the Indian state's
> savage and ongoing repression of the Kashmiri Muslim population
> and of the equally callous and stupid manipulation of the Kashmiri
> struggle by the Pakistani state, which facilitated a violent global jihad
> in Kashmir that not only fractured Kashmiri society along Hindu-
> Muslim lines but has now rebounded on the Pakistani state and society
> themselves.[102]

Referring to himself as a "national poet" rather than a "nationalist" poet,[103] Ali makes it clear that his form of a global poetics is not enacted through political invective, but rather through something like a performa-tive spell: "If one writes in free verse—and one should—to subvert West-ern civilization, surely one should write in forms to save oneself *from* Western civilization?"[104]

Ali finds this form in the ancient Arabic, Persian, and Urdu ghazal, which first emerges during the seventh century. The ghazal is among the most restrictive of poetic designs: it contains at least five discrete couplets whose second lines (after the first couplet) share both an end rhyme (*radīf*) and internal rhyme (*qafia*). Each line generally has the same number of syllables, and the final couplet references the poet's name or nickname. Ali translated the Urdu ghazals of the Pakistani poet Faiz Ahmed Faiz; collected, and often criticized, Anglophone attempts at the ghazal; and wrote many of his own ghazals. As Ali often stresses in his comments on the ghazal, the ghazal ignores—indeed, militates against—a thematic narrative or a unified progression that culminates in the last couplet.[105] Instead, a single word ramifies across the entire poem, deferring a single meaning or connotation.[106] The couplets hold together by virtue of "a classical exactness" that "underscores a profound cultural connectedness."[107] In this sense, the ghazal depends on a pattern of expectation and surprise, as well as on a kind of dislocation.[108] Taking stock of Ali's cross-cultural influences, Jahan Ramazani describes the ghazal's other potential uses: "Ghazalified, modernist syncretism, hardly a disabling imperial influence, functions for Ali as a counterweight to tyrannies closer to 'home'—the religious and nationalist absolutisms that have ravaged Kashmir."[109] By their inclusion, cross-cultural references and inclusions can generate commentary on "tyrannies closer to 'home'" at the same time that the poem, through its elaborate formal mirrorings, resists unity and narrative progression.

Ali's "Tonight," from his final book, *Call Me Ishmael Tonight* (2003), bristles with the poetry of others, recalling the form's classical incorporation of certain stock phrases and images. Here are the first three stanzas:

Where are you now? Who lies beneath your spell tonight?
Whom else from rapture's road will you expel tonight?

Those "Fabrics of Cashmere—" "to make Me beautiful—"
"Trinket"—to gem —"Me to adorn—How tell"—tonight?

I beg for haven: Prisons, let open your gates—
A refugee from Belief seeks a cell tonight.[110]

The opening of the poem, with its reference to "rapture's road," recalls the first surah of the Qur'an. In the sixth verse of the Surah Al-Fatihah, the servant prays God to "guide us to the straight path," which is described in the next verse as "the path of those upon whom you have bestowed favor, not of those who have evoked [Your] anger or of those who are stray."[111]

The other citations are from Laurence Hope's popular 1906 poem "Kashmiri Song" and from Emily Dickinson's poem "I am ashamed—I hide—/What right have I—to be a Bride—"[112] As Dina Al-Kassim suggests, Ali creates a dense network of references that resist, by virtue of their irreducible specificity, "the impulse to globalize [the poem] as world lit."[113] At the same time, these jostling religious and poetic traditions attain a formal coherence of sound.[114] They are linked by the repeated final syllables, the penultimate rhymes in the second line of each couplet (on "-el"), and a certain overlapping in what Ali calls "mood."[115]

The multiplying cultural references in the ghazal—the poem's catholic taste includes everything from Dickinson's dashes to Job's despair to Melville's opening line from *Moby-Dick*—are not themselves sufficient marks of a global "we," as though their syncretism would form an alternative locus of belonging in and of itself. Indeed, they seem to bend the poem toward the opposite orientation, reminding us of the ineluctable localism that persists under globalization and prohibiting a hierarchical ordering of traditions. This specificity of reference, which makes it unlikely any single reader would pick up on every allusion, is nevertheless compatible with a certain kind of cosmopolitan aesthetics. Its cosmopolitanism is not so much that of the erudite reader and world traveler, but rather that of Edward Said, who offers an alternative definition. In a lecture on Freud and the "non-European," Said calls the "essence of the cosmopolitan" a "troubled, disabling, destabilizing secular wound" that cannot be healed "through dispensing palliatives such as tolerance and compassion."[116] He concludes the lecture by asking, "Can so utterly indecisive and so deeply undetermined a history ever *be* written? In what language, and with what sort of vocabulary?"[117] "Tonight" attempts to write this history of Said's cosmopolitan, or of Ali's Kashmiri American, who is defined not through belonging to a certain exiled group, but through the critique of that belonging.

This wounding critique is translated into poetic language as a series of calls and cries. The poem depends on the rhetoric of exhortation and on scenes of supplication pulled from clashing beliefs and traditions. As "Tonight" progresses, a set of paradoxes appears, embedded in the language of repeated exhortations. Beginning this destabilizing process, the paradoxes in "Tonight" are metaphors for the ghazal itself. First, the ghazal is the prison that, paradoxically, provides the only freedom from belief: "I beg for haven: Prisons, let open your gates—/A refugee from Belief seeks a cell tonight."[118] Or it is a mughal ceiling, in which the image of the individual self multiplies: "Mughal ceilings, let your mirrored convexities/multiply me at once under your spell tonight."[119] Perhaps most significantly, however, Ali identifies the ghazal's repeating final word with the cry of the gazelle, a pun that may double as an etymology: "The hunt is over, and I hear the Call to Prayer/fade into that of the wounded gazelle tonight."[120] Call turning into cry: many of the couplets begin with a summons and end with a sob, flickering between exhortation and pain, supplication and pity.

The ghazal's wound is its incomplete synthesis of its many references, its blasphemous convocation of the profane and the sacred, of Dickinson and Melville, of Job and Hussayn Ibn Ali. Yet this wound, which appears as suffering and especially as weeping, does not necessarily leave the poet with the dubious resources of individual autonomy as the alternative to dogmatic faith or xenophobic nationalism. Ali writes the cosmopolitan by slowly abdicating poetic authority, undermining the sovereignty of the singular voice. This strategy appears first in a particularly witty couplet: "*Lord*, cried out the idols, *Don't let us be broken;/Only we can convert the infidel tonight.*"[121] Here the ghazal reverses the scene of iconoclasm, so that the idols—many of which were indeed broken during the violence in Kashmir—cry out for their own preservation. At the end of the poem, the cry of the wounded ghazal, or gazelle, becomes the cry of God himself. A weeping divinity concludes the poem: "And I, Shahid, only am escaped to tell thee—/God sobs in my arms. Call me Ishmael tonight."[122] Whereas the earlier couplet has idols beg for their own preservation, here the ultimate source of poetic authority and of the word—God—is reduced to a cry, the poetic voice to a plea. Standing in for the principle of authorship, divine omnipotence merges with the poetic "call me." There is a parallel here at the level of poetic making: through the relinquishment of control over the form, the ghazal invites the poet to fill it, only to multiply the self in its lexical mirrors. By adhering strictly to the ghazal form, both the word and the poem are reduced—or exalted—to exhortation: come fill me, share me, call me Ishmael, the unwanted son who is sent away. The cry of the wounded ghazal is the poetic voice that cracks—the God, or "I," that puts aside omnipotence, individualism, autonomy, immunity, and sovereignty in favor of exhortation.

The song of Kashmir, or of Ishmael, is quite evidently not the same as the song of the open road. In Ali's "Tonight," there is no "certainty of others," in the Whitmanian sense. There is, of course, no certainty of Kashmiri national belonging in that way.[123] It is tempting to claim that Ali conjures an exilic crowd through a version of parataxis in which literary and religious texts are laid side-by-side in compulsive cohabitation. Yet the multiculturalism of its many references does not explain the poem's repeated insistence on the ecstatic call, nor does it help to account for the

poem's reversals of agency, its pleading idols, and its sobbing God.[124]
Through supplications, prayers, pleas, and calls, Ali emphasizes poetically
that the alternative to absorption in violent communitarianisms does not
have to be a "Westernized," secular individualism. The ghazal does not at
all culminate in the formal artifactuality that so often fulfills and satisfies
the poetic search for self-knowledge and the mark of the knowing poet.
Cutting in the opposite direction instead, the ghazal casts its spells of self-
release, in which each couplet presents an exercise at the "limits of the
autonomy of the will," to borrow Allen Grossman's evocative phrase.[125]
Vitiating the autonomy of the poetic will, Ali's poem substitutes the rhap-
sody of its limitations. Its witty paradoxes perform the double work of an
estranging and transporting desire. They distance the poet from belief
while detaching him from the self, arguing against the need to substitute
one kind of sovereignty for another.

For the poets in this chapter, the difficulties of exhorting a collective
require poetic innovations that elude and critique existing forms of belonging and identity. I began with Bonney, whose English ballads extend a
robust tradition of denouncing enclosure movements. Refashioned as the
vehicles for a proleptic revolutionary subject and a protean rhetorical performance, they are well suited for decrying contemporary "new enclosures" of financial capitalism. Kim's version of commoning takes place in
what she calls the "recombinant energy" of translating Korean and English
texts in such a way as to reveal their mutual imbrication in global processes.
I concluded with Ali, whose Kashmiri American ghazal assembles the rebel
personae of a cross-cultural commons (Ishmael, Emily Dickinson, heretics,
an abject God)—all to point away from both a facile global cosmopolitanism and a violent battle over national belonging. All three poets confront
transformations of subjectivity in the modern period: masses of displaced,
colonized, exiled, and racialized communities whose narratives and whose
representations of their own experience are often treated as illegible, inex-
pert, or inaudible. Their work nevertheless calls a globalized "we" into
existence, though not into direct view: as Kim writes, poetry is a kind of
"thinking towards what doesn't already exist."[126] In the process, they also
make it clear how sharply this poetic "we" diverges from philosophical
accounts of a global ethics that rely on the language of obligation, as well
as liberal, universalist accounts of a "we" that elide difference. The recep-
tivity to others—whether as gleaned bits of song or mishearings of pho-
nemes—is presented neither as a claim of obligation nor as a casual
assumption of solidarity, but rather as a desire and a longed-for possibility,
the possibility that the "cohabitation" of the commons might take a visible,

aesthetic form. Bonney, Kim, and Ali thread a global ethics not of alterity, but of a galvanizing proximity through the figures, formal conventions, and linguistic remnants of Anglophone, Korean, and Urdu poetic sources.

The non- or anti-sovereignty of Ali's poetic voice leads directly into the themes of the final chapter, which shifts the examination of precarity from the rhetorical power of the voice to the topos of the distant view. Confronted with the finality of the Anthropocene, poets who write at the intersection of global finance, race, and ecology adapt the conventions of the prospect poem. Historically, the prospect poem has been one of the poetic subgenres most directly tied to a rhetorical position of global dominance and spectatorial mastery. The modern and contemporary renewal of the prospect poem constitutes an effort to think from within and to gaze beyond the finality of the catastrophic present. The view from the top of the hill, long associated with the most imperial visions of the poetic "I," is paradoxically occupied by the precarious global subject. In this process of flattening the heights, poets found the agency of a global subject not in an infinite otherness, but in an unelected nearness.

CHAPTER 4

The No-Prospect Poem

Poetic Views of the Anthropocene

The remaking of nature and the recognition of anthropogenic climate change are subjects intuitively suited to poetry, which has rarely posited a strong separation of the human from the natural. The poetic embedding of human life in an ecological web takes diverse poetic forms in English, from Coleridge's conversation poems and Clare's invectives against land enclosure to the critical histories of regional U.S. environments by C. S. Giscombe and C. D. Wright to the imbrications of global capital and ecology I trace in this chapter. Poetry's particular modes of perception and its fictions of personhood depend on a well-developed ecological sense. Steph Burt describes how "one of the standard ways to write a very personal, and yet figurative, 'lyrical' poem, was to stand in a place and let the place stand for the person, the outward geography for the inner life."[1] Margaret Ronda adds that, for ecocritically minded poets, this substitution of outward geography for inner life makes a political and ethical claim on the poet. She writes that "this sense of an unbearable responsibility that somehow must be borne is central to the psychic operations of these poems, to their forms of defacement, and to the destructive potential they evoke."[2] Already implied or assumed in the process of making poetry, then, is the human making of the world. Yet the current era appears as an unwelcome fulfill-ment of poetry's most aggrandized promises: "There is no place or living thing that we haven't changed," writes Jedediah Purdy.[3] In the contempo-rary period, this intimacy creates a formal problem for poets who continue to write while acknowledging that the human making of the world has created irreversible destruction and ecological catastrophe.

The periodizing term "Anthropocene" recognizes the myriad number of ways in which human activity has fundamentally changed the environ-ment. The word has an early twentieth-century provenance in the work of Aleksei Pavlov, though the concept of a "Human" or "Anthropozoic" epoch appears already in the mid-nineteenth century.[4] Paul J. Crutzen and Eugene F. Stoermer popularized the Anthropocene as a concept in an essay published in 2000. For them, anthropogenic climate change begins with industrialization and specifically with the refinement of the steam engine.[5] Other scientists, such as Simon L. Lewis and Mark A. Maslin, date the onset of the Anthropocene to the early seventeenth century, while acknowledging that industrial-type production occurred thousands of years earlier.[6] Dating the Anthropocene to 1610, as Lewis and Maslin do, stresses the particular damage wrought by global capitalism. In *Capitalism in the Web of Life* (2015), Jason Moore writes

> If the destructive character of capitalism's world-ecological revolutions has widely registered—the "what" and the "why" of capitalism-in-nature—there has been far too little investigation of *how* humans have made modernity through successive, radical reconfigurations of all nature. *How* capitalism has worked *through*, rather than *upon* nature, makes all the difference.[7]

Moore's distinction between "through" and "upon" emphasizes that nature is not a pristine landscape destroyed by capitalism. Such a concep-tion of nature would encourage a nostalgic impulse toward conservation rather than the radical interventions needed to disentangle the logic of capital from the destruction of the planet. Like Timothy Mitchell, whose *Rule of Experts* (2002) critically examines social scientific assumptions about nature and nonhuman forms of agency, Moore argues that nature has been both victim and vehicle of the expansion of capital.

The Anthropocene does much more than orient our attention to human complicity in climate change, however. The adoption of the term accom-panies dramatic shifts in both historical and scientific inquiry, epistemo-logical changes that are tied into post-1970s globalization and that occupy an indispensable place in a book about global poetry. For scientists, the

92   *The No-Prospect Poem*

epistemological rupture marked by the Anthropocene forces us to reconceive classical ecological thinking. While the "ecological" posits a relation between humans and their environment, the Anthropocene must be understood within the "earth system" thinking inaugurated in the 1980s and 1990s. Earth system science brings together human and natural history, "the integrated and holistic concept of the earth as a total ecosystem or ecosphere." Although the notion of a "humanized Earth" has long existed, Clive Hamilton and Jacques Grineveld argue that the Anthropocene belongs to the science of Earth as "a complex system beyond the sum of its parts."[8] If we follow Hamilton and Grinevald, a poetics of the Anthropocene would question the existence of an external vantage point from which human consciousness might understand nonhuman processes.

This chapter ranges widely across the global poetics of the Anthropocene. If the verse, or *versus*, of poetry once represented the turning of the plow, now perhaps the emblems for the poetic line are the furrows created by fracking, oil drilling, and mineral extraction.[9] Focusing on the Anthropocene also means including poems that grapple with the ongoing political and economic devastations of the transatlantic slave trade and the damage to the environment wrought by financial speculation and underdevelopment. Poetry of the Anthropocene confronts the fact of direct human responsibility in global processes. Yet the poetic forms in this chapter avoid reproducing the same rhetorical or didactic strategies as other kinds of writing about the Anthropocene. As Heather Davis and Étienne Turpin argue more generally, the value of turning to art's encounter with climate change lies in its "non-moral form of address that offers a range of discursive, visual, and sensual strategies that are not confined by the regimes of scientific objectivity, political moralism, or psychological depression."[10] This chapter discovers that, to bring the Anthropocene into a specifically poetic language, poets have returned to and revised the form of the prospect poem. By doing so, they both acknowledge human culpability and call upon the human to take a certain distance from the world. Moreover, prospecting, as a way of telling the future when the future seems dramatically foreclosed, falls to the most precarious populations rather than the experts or global financial elites. Since the prospect looks outward instead of inward, even as prospects in general are in serious doubt, it serves as an apt figure for the final chapter of this book.

Narrative genres, such as those that form the category of cli-fi, or climate fiction, have been instrumental in making climate change legible. Confronting what he calls the "slow violence" of ecological catastrophe, Rob Nixon identifies a challenge to literary representation created by "the pervasive but elusive violence of delayed effects."[11] For Nixon, narrative and story-driven literary forms are necessary for the analysis of globalization because they grant visibility to that which eludes the evental, sensational nature of media. The narrative genres he studies, including the picaresque and the fairy tale, address the question of what unique capabilities literature might have to add to the study of globalization. According to Nixon, literary narratives make visible slow violence, bringing it into the public eye. At the same time, the task of representing large-scale, anonymous catastrophe fundamentally alters the genres used to represent it.[12] Nixon asks,

> how can we convert into image and narrative the disasters that are
> slow moving and long in the making, disasters that are anonymous and
> that star nobody, disasters that are attritional and of indifferent inter-
> est to the sensation-driven technologies of our image-world?[13]

Nixon traces the reciprocal process that follows from this question, in which the conversion into narrative both alters a literary genre and brings to light a hidden dimension of the global.

Though much poetry embraces a narrative component, storytelling is not the paramount function of the poetry in this book. Indeed, a significant strand of contemporary poetry is riddled with doubt about its ability to represent and redress the global effects of climate change and the role of the human in creating ecological devastation. In Maureen McLane's *Miz N* (2016), a poem titled "Palinode" criticizes the poet for her distant stance. The tone of the poem is deceptively light:

> Just like you
> to lean on a lyre
> float in a meadow
> when the cracking world
> needs action, facts[14]

The poet ventriloquizes someone who might excoriate her for not acting. The general question is easy to imagine: why write poetry at all in a time of disaster? But the deliberate reductiveness of the poet's position, a cliché of a Romantic dreamer, is matched by the reductiveness of what is said to be necessary: the importance of action or facts. The limited set of possibilities listed for both sides opens up a relation between the two and distances the poet from the voice speaking. On one side, there is a caricature of the poet's disdain for the world; on the other, there is a caricature of the activist's call to the world. McLane's "Palinode" does not indict the poet, but rather opens up anew the question of whether poetry can or should make anything happen in a world cracked by human beings.

Leaning on a lyre and floating in a meadow: both activities suggest the wayward gaze of the Romantic poet, cast either onto the immediate surroundings (Wordsworth's daffodils) or onto the sublime heights (Shelley's Mont Blanc). Poetry has a conventional form ready at hand for capturing "the long emergencies of slow violence": the prospect poem. In the prospect poem, we find the co-emergence of a revised poetic subgenre and a vision of global ecology missing from both social scientific works and other aesthetic forms. True to its name, the prospect poem both acknowledges the attenuated (figurative) prospects for life on earth and the literal sights the poet glimpses in the distance. Like the ode, the prospect poem has long been the property of antiquarians or literary historians. I argue here that it takes its place among the other varieties of poetry in this book as a central form for the poetic making of the global.

The prospect poem is one of the special genres in which contemporary literature grapples with the ecological changes wrought by human beings. In keeping with the other kinds of poetry that appear in this book, however, the prospect poem is unlike inherently story- or narrative-driven forms. As a structure or subgenre of poetry, the prospect poem has a long history. Its uses, traditionally, have been to consolidate mastery over the environment by surveying all that lies within the vision of the gazing poet. This tradition, which I trace later in greater detail, has its fissures and contradictions, as in certain Romantic poems that shuttle between awe and suspicion of the power of the poet's gaze. The structure of the prospect poem evinces a tension between the knowledge that a future for the planet has been irremediably destroyed and a call to work within the conditions of the present. What poetry brings to the devastating knowledge of anthropogenic climate change is more than a lament, although elegiac tones are common. These poems are not only full of obligation and responsibility. They also foreground an untimely rhetoric of elating and sustaining.

The task of the prospect poem in the contemporary period is to complicate the idea that, by acknowledging a certain separation from the world, the poet is somehow guilty or complicit in its continued destruction. In the past, certain strands of Anglophone poetry have been all too ready to anthropomorphize the world, a process that poetic devices from prosopopoeia to the pathetic fallacy have long enabled or assumed. Indeed, the vision of human separation from the world that we find in prospect poetry is precisely what both poetry and the Anthropocene have both rendered nearly unthinkable. As Lewis and Maslin write, "Past scientific discoveries have tended to shift perceptions away from a view of humanity as occupying the center of the Universe . . . adopting the Anthropocene may reverse this trend by asserting that humans are not passive observers of Earth's functioning."[15] In the past, this separation was placed frequently in the service of mastery over a domain. Today the danger of a detached expertise certainly remains. One of the places we hear this mastery is in the loud silence at the end of Keats's sonnet "On First Looking into Chapman's Homer" (1816), when the conquistadors on the boat first glimpse the long history of violence they are about to set into motion.

Standing alongside the historical-poetic figures of the sixteenth-century conquistador, the eighteenth-century surveyor, and the nineteenth-century wanderer, however, new figures are appearing on the top of the hill. The prospect affords them the interpretive authority over processes described as too complex for common understanding and therefore as better left to the experts. Taking control over the description of the view, the contemporary prospect poet speaks from the paradoxical position of being included in what she sees, yet removed from its immediacy.[16] As a result, the prospect poem often employs various contortions of time, creating a tension within a genre that, in its past iterations, has not always been receptive to a politics from below. We find in the contemporary prospect poem a dynamic contestation of form that manifests itself in an emphasis on sensing the world via an unusual relationship to temporality, one represented by the singer, the worker, and the dead. The prospect poem positions itself, quite believably, as singing after the world has ended. It is one of the poetic forms in which, as Roy Scranton puts it, we learn to die in the Anthropocene.[17]

The word "prospect" combines topography and temporality, as indeed the subgenre of the prospect poem also tends to do. Contemporary poets are forced to navigate the finality and irreversibility of human-created climate change. As Ronda writes, "What is distinctive, perhaps, about the planetary anthropogenic *poiesis* of the Anthropocene is both its irreversibility and its seemingly endless capacity to unmake."[18] In full view of environmental catastrophes, of endless wars, of the devastating migrations produced by the agricultural policies of the Global North, and of the precariousness of life induced by neoliberal global capitalism, contemporary poetry finds itself confronted with what Hannah Arendt presciently named "the finality of a last judgment," an "unredeemably stupid fatality."[19] This poetic subject expresses the absence of recourse and the limits of mitigation: that which may no longer be prevented or undone. At the same time, the poem insists on life and song under these conditions. A strong tradition of contemporary poetry in the late twentieth and early twenty-first centuries once again takes as its occupation the persistent question of a line of modern English-writing poetry running from Walt Whitman through Allen Ginsberg and Adrienne Rich to Language Writing and New Narrative—namely, what might be the links between poetic form and the imagination of a revolutionary political agency? This chapter considers how poems and lyrical prose by J. H. Prynne, Kofi Awoonor, Natasha Trethewey, and Juliana Spahr examine the prospects for a global subject in the light of finality.

The continued exploitation of resources depends, of course, on downplaying or effacing the role of human contributions to climate change, and so there is a considerable danger in suggesting that the prospect poet celebrates a distance from the world. In the abstract, this disassociation has the potential to be a delusion or a compensatory device to ameliorate the feeling that "the world is too much with us." Equally problematic are the distances from which Western "aid," "democracy," or "civilization" scans the prospects for its interventions. Part of what I argue, therefore, is that a global politics is rethought by means of the prospect poem: not an ethics based on theological Otherness, whether of object or of human, but a politics of ecological adjacency. The prospect poem depends neither on a sublime encounter with the inhuman terrors of an alien world nor on the domestication of nature as adjunct to the human. The prospect poem represents instead an attempt to find a human distance in which right action might be conceivable, in which human needs and subjectivities might be decentered, and in which the array of global facts might appear from the perspective of those most damaged by them. In the prospect poem, the poet undertakes a difficult task: to recognize the inextricability of human making from the devastated landscape she surveys while using poetic rhetoric to sing an adequate distance from the world.

The prospect poem acknowledges the poet's distance: he or she is on a hill, separated from the action and the facts. And yet the prospect poem also certifies the poet's role as one that is much more than floating over a meadow. Distance, in the prospect poem, does not have to mean complicity. Indeed, complicity in the processes of anthropogenic climate change is perhaps more likely to take the forms of direct involvement. The prospect poem complicates what human intervention in the "cracking world" entails by focusing on something other than action or facts. Attempting to remove oneself poetically from the scene—adopting, in effect, the maligned role of the spectator or bystander—carries with it a possible agency as well as a risk of irrelevance or defeatism. The prospect from the hill might involve feeling overwhelmed, but it does not necessarily invoke paralysis, to use the distinction that Judith Butler draws when discussing suffering observed at a distance.[20]

Although the writers in this chapter are usually grouped in quite distinct and separate poetic traditions, a recognition of precariousness, or the forms of life and labor shaped by global capitalism in the late twentieth and early twenty-first centuries, unites their work. Recalling and revising the tradition of the loco-descriptive poem and the prospect poem, Prynne, Awoonor, Trethewey, and Spahr use the hill as an imaginative location for staging the dilemmas of the putative "global citizen" examined at length in Chapter 2. In literary criticism of the last decade, spatial metaphors for ethics have shifted from verticality to horizontality: the dominance of Levinasian alterity, which would posit the "height" of the Other as its radical difference, has given way to new formulations of a global politics of adjacency or laterality, seared by the struggles of indigenous groups and populations under regimes of settler colonialism.[21] From hills in England, Ghana, and New Orleans, the view of poetry stretches out laterally to accommodate global suffering, inequality, and the lives of others, who, however far or close, shape the contours, the possibilities and dangers, of the poem's immediate vicinity. Far from offering spectatorial mastery to the poet, however, the hill is transformed into the ground and habitation of precarious life. The hill thus makes visible an alternative trajectory of contemporary subjectivity in which the poem's "I" emerges from and is shaped by the collective immiseration of global capitalism.

Anglophone poetry has a long history of employing the language of topographical description to generate particular modes of thinking and seeing. Seventeenth- and eighteenth-century prospect poems typically ascend the hill to assume a position of superior knowledge granted by the privileges of gender and class.[22] The conventions of the prospect poem are, from the start, clearly politicized: the topographical poem in English begins in the middle of the political crisis of the Civil War. M. H. Abrams and Geoffrey Galt Harpham trace a history of prospect poetry that, starting with John Denham's *Cooper's Hill* (1642; 1655), includes "historical, political, or moral reflections that are associated with the scene or suggested by its details."[23] More specifically, Denham's poem examines and enacts the king's right to land.[24] A description of the Thames serves as the vehicle for a poetics and a politics of moderation: the river, like the poem and the monarchy, runs "though deep, yet clear, though gentle, yet not dull, / Strong without rage, without o'erflowing full."[25] The poem concludes with a double warning against oppressing subjects and against granting too many concessions to "popular sway."[26] In this way, the prospect poem contains a pronounced tendency toward celebrating values and toward restoring social order. The abstraction of morals from topography continues in Thomas Gray's "Ode on a Distant Prospect of Eton College" (1742), when a carefully arranged procession of allegorical figures—from Anger, Fear, and Shame to Death, Poverty, and Age—menaces the schoolchildren observed by the speaker in the "vale of years beneath."[27] The conclusion of the poem brings a universal moral, that "all are men / Condemned alike to groan."[28]

These "masculine, objective, and disinterested" prospects are, Jennifer Keith shows, complicated by their "reliance on figures of the feminine."[29] Writing in and against this genealogy, poetry by Anne Finch and Jean Adams captures a gendered "alienation from the landscape" that mirrors their "legal-economic alienation from the land."[30] Rather than inhabiting a dominating presence over the land, some prospect poems by women in the eighteenth century turn to fugitive states of reverie and dream instead. Finch's "A Nocturnal Reverie" (1713) describes the repose and harmony that reign while "tyrant man" is asleep. The daylight prospect and its masculine conventions, the poem suggests, exclude a relation between women and landscape. In Finch's couplets, the feminist discourse of the nighttime prospect does not serve as a complement for the male tradition, but as a way of transcending it by working through paradoxes of revelation and occlusion, sight and feeling, speech and silence, inside and outside:

> When a sedate content the spirit feels,
> And no fierce light disturbs, while it reveals,
> But silent musings urge the mind to seek
> Something too high for syllables to speak;
> Till the free soul to a compos'dness charmed,
> Finding the elements of rage disarmed,
> O'er all below a solemn quiet grown,
> Joys in th' inferior world and thinks it like her own . . .[31]

Also making use of an oneiric mode, the working-class poet Jean Adams begins her poem "A Dream, or the Type of the Rising Sun" (1734) with a flight from the body entirely: "Loosed from its bonds my spirit fled away, / And left behind its moving tent of clay."[32] This fantasy of liberation becomes the imaginary condition for the critique of a society governed by "natural" values of Duty, Fortitude, Honor, and Interest. Half a century later, the perch on Charlotte Smith's *Beachy Head* (1807) provides the setting for a critique of beauty that acknowledges and condemns the violence of global processes: the speaker compares the beauty of the sun, common to all, with the beauty of minerals extracted through slave labor.[33]

By the time John Keats writes his early poem "I stood tiptoe upon a little hill" (1817), the prospect unfolds not so much outside as inside the poem's language itself, which, while focusing intently on the foreground, makes visible a panoramic vista of Latinate and Anglo-Saxon vocabularies. "A filbert hedge with wildbriar overtwined/and clumps of woodbine taking the soft wind/upon their summer thrones"[34]: here Keats spins "w" and "i" around each other in various permutations of sound until the lines seem to fade slightly into slower, or perhaps more distant, "n's" and "o's." Neither a platform for a vision of universal suffering and the passage of time nor a site for the critique of empire, the Keatsian prospect poem is a mode of description linked to the variety, and hence the irreducible particularity, of words and things. Increasingly, the poet is drawn into the prospect, rather than sharply distinguished as a spectator. This paradox of embeddedness and removal characterizes a modernist experiment in the topographical mode: H. D.'s "Oread" (1914). In that poem, considered one of the key texts of Imagism, the mountain-dwelling speaker casts a spell over the sea to "whirl up." With its dramatic verbs placed at the beginning of each line and its language that intercalates the features of the mountain (pines, fir) with those of the sea (rocks, pools), the poem transforms its own metaphorical field even as it performatively asserts its magical control over the landscape below. H. D.'s poem thus represents a certain modern terminus for the prospect poem. The poem draws on the Romantic imbrication of spectator and landscape, the celebration of poetic powers, and the reinvention of classical references. But "Oread" also continues the eighteenth-century counter-tradition of women poets abjuring their economic alienation from the right to land and overcoming their literary alienation from the right to the prospect poem itself.

This brief account is not meant to cover the history of a vast subgenre of Anglophone poetry, but rather to emphasize the deep literary-historical memory behind the topographical sites that contemporary poetry reworks to stage a precarious globality. The hill, in particular, is a paradigmatic topos for the global because it brings about the recognition that the local is connected to the far removed. While the sheer cliffs of the sublime, theorized by Burke and Kant and dramatized by Wordsworth and Shelley, have been examined by contemporary critics from Slavoj Žižek to Doris Sommer, the view from the hill is, in contemporary poetry, an alternative site for a global ethics and politics. Although the height of the hill could suggest either "totality" or "infinity"—the mastery over others or the responsibility to them—the verticality of this poetic tradition is paradoxically what allows its opposite, a flattened adjacency, to take form.[35] In this way, prospect poems question both the transcendent, communitarian ethics of difference and the neocolonial presumptions of universalism. Such poems are peculiarly receptive to the precariousness of labor; the finality of the death of a social world under capitalism; and the global development that serves as an alibi for racism and mass murder. The hill is not an obstacle, nor is it a monument to individual power or to the hidden power of a supra-individual spirit. Rather, the hill provides the footing for a particularly contemporary subject-position, beckoned to contemplate suffering at a distance.[36] The sights one sees from a hill are inflected by remote suffering, just as, for instance, the ordinary lives of Chinese and Jamaican workers are inextricable from the state-supported multinational corporations that control the special economic zones and export processing zones.[37] Stuart Hall describes this "tricky version of the 'local'" as that which "has been thoroughly reshaped by 'the global' and operates largely within its logic."[38] In short, the hill renders visible, through the poem, the precarious subjectivities shaped by twentieth-century ideologies of modernization and neoliberalism.

Poets bring together the immediate, local globality of the hill with an aspect of precariousness, perceived as finality. There are intimations of this association between topography and loss in early twentieth-century poetry. In Rilke's "Eighth Elegy," the experience of the hill becomes a paradigmatic experience of departure:

> Who has twisted us around like this, so that
> no matter what we do, we are in the posture
> of someone going away? Just as, upon
> the farthest hill, which shows him his whole valley
> one last time, he turns, stops, lingers—,
> so we live here, forever taking leave.[39]

In his simile, Rilke compares a chronic, everyday sense of loss with a moment of looking back. Rilke's leave-taking is ontological, frozen in its perpetual recurrence like a Bernini statue. It is that sculptural sense, also present in Eliot's later poems, of movement within stillness that grants the finality of the poem a certain luminous universality. It is paired at the same time with a lack of agency—"Who has twisted us around like this?"—and thus a kind of perpetual bewilderment at being in this state. Here, daily life is figured as the pause at the top of hill, the backward glance over what or who has been left—but that glance has been extended, as it were, to take up all the time that remains in a life.

For Walter Benjamin, writing at the same time, it is not the gaze from the hill, or the climb to the top, so much as it is the rapid movement down-hill that, paradoxically, provides an emblem of irrevocability or finality. Benjamin's short, poetic meditations in his collection of narrative minia-tures from 1923, *Denkbilder*, might be considered prose poems in the line of Baudelaire, Rimbaud, and Valéry. "Downhill" anchors its analysis of *Erschütterung*, or shock, a central term for Benjamin, in Marcel Proust's sudden realization that his grandmother is permanently absent. Benjamin draws an analogy between Proust's physical movement of bending over to remove his shoes and the posture of the hill-walker as he descends. "Who knows," Benjamin wonders about the stumble downhill, "whether these are thoughts that shock him, or the rough ground? His body has become a kaleidoscope that brings before him at every step the changing figures of truth."[40] While the figure of the human kaleidoscope might be familiar from Baudelaire's description of the *flâneur*, Benjamin's shattering descent into truth carries the sense not only of walking downhill, but, metaphori-cally, of a general downturn, a *katabasis*.[41]

Benjamin's prismatic "Downhill" brings together the topos of the hill with a phenomenological experience of time, memory, and perception that has its origin in the shock of an ending. The brush with irrevocability— here, in the figure of the grandmother's death—comes home as an unseat-ing of the subject, surrounded by a *tableau vivant* that changes shape at every step. Here the landscape is not stable enough to appear below as an object of the gaze. The descent down the hill surrounds the subject with the truth, but the truth is given in constantly changing forms. Rather than being paralyzing or stultifying, the sense of finality in Benjamin and Proust is creative and generative, if somewhat breathtaking in the variety of the figures it produces. Employing poetic language to explore finality, Rilke and Benjamin both create scenes of personal leave-taking, in which a medi-tation on catastrophe is rooted in an individual's departure: the nameless figure in Rilke's elegy, the grandmother's death in Benjamin's miniature.

In English-language poetry after the 1970s, the poetic hill tends to focalize collective experiences of exploitation and immiseration instead. My case studies below are the British poet J. H. Prynne, the Ghanaian poet Kofi Awoonor, and the U.S. poets Natasha Trethewey and Juliana Spahr. All these poets manipulate the form of the prospect poem to investigate global ecological damage. In different ways, they trouble or unseat the vertical gaze of the poetic "I." In the process, they capture the violence of capital and of colonization without representing it only on the level of theme or content. These poets have varying political affiliations, poetic genealogies, and personal histories: Prynne is a reclusive U.K. experimental poet who recently gave his first interview; Awoonor was the Ghanaian ambassador to Brazil, Cuba, and the United Nations; Trethewey has been the U.S. poet laureate; Spahr is the coeditor of Commune Editions, a Marxist press in Oakland. These poets share a perception that contemporary global capitalism cuts across and revises the international division of labor marked by "North" and "South." Since my concern throughout this book is to explore the way that poets add to a critical global studies, I bring these poets together here as a cross-section or snapshot of contemporary poetry that reckons with the Anthropocene by working within the rhetoric and topos of the prospect.

Prynne's *The White Stones* (1969), written at the dawning of U.S.-driven financialization, is shaped by a sense of subjects entrapped, collectively, by the forces of global capital and ecological destruction. Some of the titles of the poems point in this direction: "Airport Poem: Ethics of Survival," "Oil," "The Glacial Question, Unsolved," "Song in Sight of the World," "Star Damage at Home," "Starvation/Dream." When we turn to these poems for a description of what the titles suggest, however, the subject slips quickly away:

> In the matter of ice, the invasions
> were partial, so that the frost
> was a beautiful head
>   the sky cloudy
> and the day packed into the crystal
> as the thrust slowed and we come to
> a stand, along the coast of Norfolk.[42]

These opening lines, from "The Glacial Question, Unsolved," enact the ecological process that Burt describes, bringing "geography" and "inner life" together.[43] But Prynne disguises any hinges between the person and the place. We cannot disentangle, syntactically, the "we" who arrive, in line 6, from the "invasions" and "thrust" of the glaciers. To account for this constant ambiguity in *The White Stones*, Keston Sutherland has described Prynne as creating a "new figure for human existence at the far extreme of its mortal potential." Sutherland continues by examining Prynne's political commitment to an expanded materialism, which "would be radicalized to include among its objects of speculative dialectical analysis the relations of *natural* production, from deglaciation to the North

Atlantic turbine."[44] Prynne's concern, as Jason Moore might say, is to uncover the ways that capitalism works "through" nature.

Yet this sense remains deliberately understated, present more as a precipitate of Prynne's startling syntactical leaps than as any explicit argument or set of figures. In "Concerning Quality, Again," Prynne explains this avoidance of transparency, offering a brief palinode:

> We *have* no mark for our dependence, I would
> not want to add a little red spot to the wrist of
> the man in the newsreel, the car passing the lights.
> I draw blood whenever I open my stupid mouth[45]

The difficulty of the poems is necessary because Prynne believes that language is complicit in world-historical violence; language is one of the means by which humans destroy the world. The task for Prynne is to write despite the knowledge that any position the poet might take will draw blood: what poetry can possibly emerge from this contradiction? Prynne's avant-garde poetics requires a focus on the shifts in perspective that the poems undertake as a process of "depersonalization."[46] These shifts in perspective turn the poems into complex versions of the prospect poem. "Thoughts on the Esterházy Court Uniform" begins in a recognizably loco-descriptive mode:

> I walk on up the hill, in the warm
> sun and we do not return, the place is
> entirely musical. No person can live there
> & what is similar is the deeper resource, the
> now hidden purpose. I refer directly to my
> own need, since to advance in the now fresh &
> sprouting world must take on some musical
> sense. Literally, the grace & hesitation of
> modal descent, the rhyme unbearable, the
> coming down through the prepared delay and
> once again we are there, beholding the
> complete elation of our end.[47]

From its first line, which cues the poetic figures of the hill, the ascent, and the sun, Prynne's poem is shaped by themes that are both clearly poetic and fundamentally global: the impossibility of return; the permanence of exile ("no person can live there"); and the potential of aesthetic experience (here, music) to provide a way of understanding the destitution of a social world.

The globality of the poem accumulates force through a constellation of related terms. "Exile," "migration," "sovereign," "constant loss," "displacement," "stranger," and "home" all feature prominently in the poem, but they are detached from each other and from any specific context. Still, these words provide important clues to the politics of the prospect poem. Prynne writes from the hill, and from a position at Cambridge University, in a language that he distrusts, a global English that "draws blood." Under these conditions, and keeping in mind his position as a white, male poet from the United Kingdom, his method cannot be to adopt a position of direct witnessing or, more generally, of representing directly the processes in which he too is enmeshed. Climbing the hill, in other words, does not provide a vantage point, but, paradoxically, removes a vantage point—or what the poem calls, tellingly, a "sovereign point." The emphasis on music, the form of art that most eschews representation, might seem to provide an escape from this complicity. By the end of the poem, the concepts of suffering, duration, and abstraction are linked together in something that approximates a plea: "With such/patience maybe we can listen to the rain/without always thinking about rain." Or perhaps it is a prayer, since "the sacred resides in this." Yet the poem denies a strong reparative reading, and insists that music only makes loss legible to us, "since it is how we most/deeply recognize the home we may not/have."

As Prynne charts the process of climbing and descending, suffering and bearing, beholding and listening, the poem seems increasingly unable to maintain, through its poetic devices, the meaning of these paired movements: "my life slips into music &/increasingly I cannot take much more of this." The unbearableness of "this," which presumably refers to the process of writing itself, becomes most vivid at the end of each line, where attention to a poem is usually most heightened, but where, in this poem, the final words of each line are almost universally slight and monosyllabic. The poem revises attention by drawing us constantly to the beginning of each line rather than the end, where meaning accumulates through words such as "purpose," "need," "world," "sense," "descent," "coming down," "again," and, perhaps unexpectedly, "elation." Most of the caesurae in the poem also occur near the beginning of the line. If the end of the poetic line can serve as an outlook—a place to pause, take stock of what has come, and glimpse what might come next—Prynne's lines challenge this reading of enjambment. Distinctions between a word such as "the" and a word such as "descent" dissolve. Prefiguring the relation between syntactical forms and political formations that would orient much of Language writing in the 1970s and 1980s, Prynne's arrangement disrupts normative patterns of movement through syntax. More importantly, however, it deemphasizes the masterly skill of the individual poet's genius, traditionally manifest in a careful decision about where to end the line.

By trespassing against the line, Prynne's poem arguably enacts some kind of defeat over finality and especially the idea that this finality, in the mimetic guise of enjambment, might be under the poet's control.[48] Yet it remains unclear why this process would be felt as "elation." "Elation," from the Latin *effere*, "to elevate or rise," concludes this part of the poem with a complicated synthesis of affect, perception, space, and time. Having descended, we are carried upward again, in emotion but also in sight, as what we behold now changes to be the hill that had been underfoot. By changing the object of the gaze from the local prospect to the hill itself, Prynne builds into the poem a retrospective moment that is also emblematic of a certain feeling of life at the dawn of the first global age. The total inability to go back, the planetary destruction of the "fresh and sprouting world" that accompanies late capitalism—"no person can live there"!—, and the very prospect of our "end" are accompanied by "elation." The language of the poem, even as it surges again and again toward the recognition of finality, is overdetermined and ambiguous, caught within the etymological lift of wonder that "elation" contains, that accompanies an act of "beholding," and that uncovers where the "sacred" "resides."

Prynne's poetic excursion denies the singular, sovereign point of the hill, which also means arranging the language of the poem to approximate music. In an echo of Adorno, music provides the poet with a negative image of home. The Ghanaian poet Kofi Awoonor's poetic method bears a surface resemblance to Prynne's, since both are, in some sense, collage artists. The formal resemblance ends here, though, since the necessity of sustaining song in unpropitious conditions emerges from a post-independence Ghana, not a United Kingdom on the edge of neoliberalism. The poet in Awoonor's *The House by the Sea* (1978) speaks from within a position that is figured differently: as posthumous, or perhaps post-lyric, if we draw on the association between lyric and song. The "house by the sea" refers to the Ussher Fort prison in Ghana where Awoonor spent a year. Having returned to Ghana on sabbatical from his U.S. teaching position at Stony Brook, Awoonor was arrested on December 31, 1975.[49] The *New York Times* covered the arrest; prominent U.S. poets, including Stanley Kunitz and Louis Simpson, rushed to protest it.[50] *The House by the Sea*, which comprises poems written before and during imprisonment, is structured in two parts, "Before the Journey . . ." and "Homecoming." In the latter section, Awoonor includes the date and "Ussher Fort" with the poem. A long poem,

"The Wayfarer Comes Home," concludes the book with a taut juxtaposition between two sounds that the poet hears from his cell. There are gunshots—"Even here in my cell / in the house of Ussher / I hear the guns"—and birdcalls—"Then I heard a wren / in the morning of the alley sun / Sing." The allusions to Edgar Allan Poe's story and, perhaps, to T. S. Eliot's *Four Quartets* suggest horror, desire, and memory as inseparable themes of the book. But, as concluding sounds that the poet hears, they also prophesy liberation in the final collapse of the house/prison and in the diurnal call of the bird. The task of the book as a whole is to work toward freedom, though this project requires the poet to acknowledge his incarceration in Ghana as the perspective from which he returns to one of the origins of the transatlantic slave trade.

Many of the poems in *The House by the Sea* begin inside the urgency of a confession or soliloquy, with phrases such as "once more I bleed," "now a pattern of the Christians' cross," and "here I lie." The deictic markers "now" and "here" are common, but they quickly give way to fragments of memory. "Poem" shifts, Proust-like, from perception to memory in two lines: "the bluejays mated under my window / summer of 72 in Kalamazoo." In the unexpected movement to a year prior, and to a different location, the poem nods to Poundian modernist collage, and particularly to the Pisan Cantos, written in a very different prison cell. Another immediate relation, however, is to the poetics of dailiness in Awoonor's U.S. contemporaries, including Bernadette Mayer and Alice Notley. Mayer and Notley situate their critique of the everyday inside gendered labor and childcare. Awoonor's diaristic memories of friends, lovers, and travels read more like notes than unified poems, and yet a surging music links the fragments together, gesturing toward an external ordering beyond the constellation of thoughts, perhaps in the Ewe dirges that Awoonor translated in *Guardians of the Sacred Word*. As Teju Cole notes, in a tribute to Awoonor's poetry written after his death, "From that Ewe tradition came the feeling for elegy, which he applied with seriousness and dark irony to the serial crises of post-independence Ghana. The Ewe language also gave his poetry strong musical cadences, so that even when the meaning was opaque, the lines were fluent."[51]

As with Prynne, Awoonor climbs the hill only to question the existence of a vantage point; his prospect is, paradoxically, prospectless. Near the middle of the book, a cascading series of poems accelerates the juxtapositions of Awoonor's memories of places and people. A rhapsodic voice emerges here alongside the mournful, lamenting spirit. While most of these poems are short, self-contained bursts, "Sequences" is a longer medi-

tation in seven short parts. Part 6 locates the beginning and the end of
poetry on the hill:

> Where my song ends
> let me start
> on the hill
> near arcs of light
> the memory of death
> I died once on 90W
> of a winter and
>   greed.
> They saw the faces
> of my children in the Sea
> dead Africans in the passageway
> before abolition
> among us my children
> retrievable shell in my sea
> at home now where
> I once sang of the land
>   where my children live
>   like the sea.[52]

Awoonor surveys the collective death of millions of slaves by announc-
ing the impossibility of representing it in song ("where my song ends"). He
writes from a position inside the social exclusion and political death that
the speaker of the poem lives. In a letter to Martin Tucker, who, in addi-
tion to Kwame Dawes, has written extensively on Awoonor's poetry,
Awoonor describes the "unification" and "fusion" of the "public impulse"
with "individual and existential energy."[53] Yet the public impulse and the
individual energy are rendered here in negative fashion. The form of
Awoonor's poem figures this conjuncture of communal and personal in
sound, line, and rhetoric, from the exhortation ("let me start") to the constant slippage or identification between metaphorical death ("I died once")
and literal murder ("dead Africans in the passageway"). The repeated
monosyllables of the first four lines allow the poem to begin in a processional manner, recalling the Ewe dirges and laments that Awoonor translated and analyzed.[54] While the poem initially adopts a loco-descriptive
mode, albeit the paradoxical one of this posthumous prospect, the fifth
line, "the memory of death," shatters the syntax of the first sentence as it
unfurls and introduces the means by which the subsequent lines might be
extended and sustained. This catalyst for the continuation of the poem is

precisely the "memory" of death in the Middle Passage, lived or experienced by the prison song as the condition for the individual voice ("I died once").

While Prynne's poetry shuttles between perspectives, Awoonor's starts by negating the very existence of perspective. This version of a black Atlantic prospect poem enacts "the refusal of standpoint," to adapt the terms that Fred Moten uses in his investigation of blackness and ontology.[55] Awoonor's imprisoned poet remains "in the hold of the [slave] ship," asking, "what would it be . . . to think from no standpoint: to think outside the desire for a standpoint?"[56] One consequence is that the vehicle of the simile in the poem, "like the sea," has an uncertain tenor. Do the children live "like the sea," embodying both freedom and the memory of the Middle Passage? Or did the poet once sing of "the land" in the same way that he sang of the sea? It seems more likely that the presence of the sea in the poem contains a force that defeats attempts to locate it precisely. Moreover, with the speaker dead, the temporality of the poem unhinges, so that his children are indistinguishable from his ancestors. The dead faces of children appear on the surface of the sea (as seen by the ambiguous and untraceable pronoun "they"), and the sea is inseparable from how the children live in the present and on the land. The sea links past and present, setting the poem itself adrift in both senses of prospect, spatial and temporal.

The fusion of collective memory with the individual gaze from the hill can best be registered, for Awoonor, as a posthumous perspective: he traces, with telegraphic precision, continuities between incarceration, exclusion from political and social life, and the Middle Passage. Such a position is especially difficult to contemplate after Awoonor's tragic shooting death in 2013 while attending the Storymoja Hay Literary Festival in Nairobi. In a poem entitled "Homecoming," the poet insists that the hill is an alternative to death:

> So I reject death now
>   as counterproductive
>   terminal and deadly
> I chose the hills
>   & the sea nearby.[57]

Instead of choosing "life," the poet chooses "the hills" and "the sea." This choice makes sense when we understand the hills and the sea as places of social life, not merely survival, existence, being, or "bare life." As Awoonor makes clear in "Sequences," the hill and the sea are the (non-)

standpoint and the (no-)prospect for those who confront, as the speaker does, the mass grave of the Atlantic and the faces of the dead on its surface. The kind of sociality that "hill" and "sea" represent opposes a universalizing, white, European "life." In this way, the prospect for life recalls Édouard Glissant's image of life shared in the "open boat," which he derives from the closed hold of the slave ship.[58] The difference between the two is that the former requires a poetics, an act of imagination, in order that the atrocity of the latter become more than a sealed history of an exceptional crime.

Prynne's *The White Stones* (1969) and Awoonor's *The House by the Sea* (1978) are separated from contemporary Anglophone poetry by nearly half a century of U.S.-led globalization. During this period, U.S. monetarist policies designed to curb domestic inflation destroy American manufacturing industries and send non-OPEC Third World nations spiraling into debt.[59] Contemporary poetry tracks these changes thematically as well as formally, so that Natasha Trethewey's *Beyond Katrina: A Meditation on the Mississippi Gulf Coast* (2010) and Juliana Spahr's *That Winter the Wolf Came* (2015) refer explicitly to the global circulation of capital, labor, and natural resources. Trethewey maps the "new geography of production" after the 1970s by examining the long, intertwined histories of Gulf Coast ecology, economics, and labor. Offering one model for what a critical global aesthetics might look like, *Beyond Katrina* uncovers the cataclysmic history of Mississippi Gulf Coast development that begins in the 1950s, preparing the way for the 2005 hurricane. "The story of the coast," she writes, "has been a story of urban development driven by economic factors and a much-less-than-needed awareness or consideration of the effects of such development on the environment."[60] Trethewey's particular version of a "poetics of relation" captures the "slow violence" of ecological damage to the Gulf Coast, but only by adopting a form that juxtaposes poetry and prose: Trethewey combines personal memoir, short poetry, and sociological research.[61] In her prosimetric form, meditative reflections are generally set alongside interviews and reportage. Yet the prospect from the hill, where the damage and the repair work are most acutely visible, contaminates the poles of this separation and disrupts the sustained narrative with the rhythms of poetry.

Beyond Katrina begins with an account of the book's composition over two decades, from a journal entry about Hurricane Camille entitled *Natural Disaster* in 1991 to a poetry collection, *Native Guard*, in 2006. What begins, in a poem entitled "Theories of Time and Space," as an existential or metaphysical *nostos*, a journey home, becomes a factual impossibility, the erasure of the poet's home by Katrina. Trethewey writes, "After Katrina the words I had looked to for their figurative values gave way to the reality they came to represent. For me the poem no longer meant what it had before—even as the words remained the same."[62] Sections of the book, including "Pilgrim," "Providence," "Liturgy," "Congregation," and "Benediction," relocate the metaphysical within the loss of the real. Titling her chapters in this way, Trethewey points to the erasure of a political narrative of the development of the coast and its replacement by spurious metaphysical justifications. The work of the book is to think through this reduction, reasserting the political and economic by reinscribing the metaphysical. To do so requires undoing some of the strictures of narrative form, interpolating poetry, for instance, or allowing poetic rhythms to eat away at the linearity of narrative discourse.

The collapse of signification from figurative to real also involves a change in value. It is no accident that Trethewey uses a term favored by Marx here, and a term taken from political economy more generally. The value of the Gulf Coast, Trethewey insists, conflates literary value and labor value. The loss of figurative value in language—the timeless lament of homesickness—makes room for the insistence on labor value in her analysis—the very real sense of the work that the unmaking and remaking of the coast entails. Trethewey constantly stresses the economic stakes of the stories that are told, writing, "This is not the first time that economic decisions have instigated the overlaying of a new narrative on the Gulf Coast, reinscribing it—transforming it."[63] As she goes on to show, in many cases the contested stories that are told after devastation, the "rebuilding" of the coast, exacerbate the damage done by the storm. The revision of the poem thus parallels the work of "revising" the coast: rebuilding, but also destroying, erasing, occluding, misrepresenting. She draws a parallel between poiesis and underdevelopment, the making, unmaking, and remaking of book and of coast. *Beyond Katrina* is a cautionary tale for accounts of globalization, an investigation of the difficulty of revising narratives of economic development: "I was going back to read the narrative I thought was there—one in which gambling and the gaming industry, responsible for so much recent land and economic development on the coast, was a new arrival, not something already ingrained in the culture of the place."[64] Trethewey's writing and revision of the poems in the book self-consciously mirror the disaster and rebuilding of the Gulf Coast after Katrina. A form of pessimism or critique operates throughout Trethewey's book, as she uncovers the rapacity with which the "rebuilding" of the coast continues the damage done by the "natural disaster," which had in turn continued the damage inflicted on the coast since the 1920s.

To revise the narrative of Gulf Coast development, Trethewey turns to the stories of immigrants to the coast, from Eastern Europeans who came in the 1890s to restaurant and casino workers who arrived in the 1990s. Trethewey's brother, Joe, provides an individual locus for the rippling effects of the storm through the catastrophic conditions imposed on labor and everyday life. At one point, his perspective from a hill allows the poetic energies of Trethewey's poetry to break into her prose analysis:

> He got a job directing traffic, standing on the highway waving a flag. He got a job removing debris, clearing the roadways, sorting through the remnants of life before Katrina. He stood in line for a check. He got a job cleaning the beach. He got a job as a watcher, scanning the white and glaring sand for debris that would clog the machines that cleaned the beach. He told me they were looking for chicken bones, scattered there from the warehouses, and for the carcasses of animals. On a quarter tank of gas, he drove to Mobile for supplies. He bought candles and flashlights, food and water, medicine for his grandmother, and beer. He drank with his friends. They drank and looked at the destruction and rubbed their heads and drank some more. He drank on the porch in the evenings by himself. He sat watching the trucks go by on Highway 49. He found a hill where his cell phone worked and called to say, "Everything is gone."[65]

The passage does not only track a progression of jobs, but also an accumulation and overlapping of types of labor, so that the person cleaning the beach has a job watching for the things that might clog the machines that clean the beach. Joe performs emotional or affective labor as well, aiding his grandmother and commiserating with friends. But the passage, which culminates in a view from the hill, has a structure that reinforces and complicates the vision of labor after the storm. Trethewey's anaphora, the repetition of similar phrases at the beginning of sentences, is pivotal to the analysis that the passage undertakes: the anaphora sets different temporalities of globalization in counterpoint, conjuring a homologous grammar of finality. Read in this way, the repetition of the sentences captures the contingent rhythms of labor in the wake of cataclysm. The gerund phrases in apposition with each "job" emphasize the endless and ongoing tasks of repairing the coast and maintaining basic life supplies.

This reading, however, insists on a strict correspondence between the paratactic structure of Trethewey's poetic prose and the indeterminate

rhythms of contingent labor. Alternatively, we might also see this passage
as shattering the possibilities of narrativity and representation. In that case,
Trethewey's writing contains the trace or manifestation, rather than the
successful accomplishment, of making the temporality of syntax represent
a total social world and the self-examination of a poetic speaker. If the
former is "gone" and the latter is radically precarious, then the figurative
value of Trethewey's prose gives way to a critique of homologies between
language and world. In *Beyond Katrina*, poiesis becomes dissociated from
its meaning of fictional making and is connected instead to the incessant
maintenance of collective life. Resembling what Lauren Berlant describes
as "lateral agency," this maintenance is situated in the flattening, encompassing view of the worker who must take multiple jobs to survive and
whose efforts at self-survival ensure the minimal, if absolutely necessary,
persistence of an environment in which others might live as well.[66] Whereas
the poet in Gray's eighteenth-century topographical lyric adopts the
monitory gaze of middle age, Joe shares his condition with those around
and below him: there is no prospect at all. These nonprospective subjects
include Trethewey herself, who concludes the chapter by superimposing
a vision of the coast from the plane and a song by Bessie Smith, "*I went
and stood up on some high old lonesome hill, then looked down on the place I used
to live.*"[67]

Prynne, Awoonor, and Trethewey are linked by a shared sense of writing poetry during the end of the world. Not only do their vistas open onto
unlivable, bleak, and devastated landscapes, but the imperial position
granted to the poet—one of superior knowledge of personal and historical
time or receptive intimacy with the natural world—is no longer the position adopted by the speaker. The singularity of the vantage point on the
hill is brought into question, multiplied in Prynne, denied in Awoonor,
and rendered precarious in Trethewey. The global elite are not the ones
who make the ascent. Instead, the global poet climbs the hill and sings the
lyric. The sense of finality shared by these poets takes on different aspects:
for Prynne, the incipient semioticization of capital ("No person can live
there"); for Awoonor, the creation of a global cosmopolitanism with racism and genocide at its core ("dead Africans in the passageway"); and for
Trethewey, the precariousness of life in the face of ecological devastation
("everything is gone"). In each case, the totalizing vision of earlier prospect
poetry is relocated in the situated standpoint of a precarious subject. The
view from this new Parnassus is of dead slaves, seen from the vantage point
of contemporary labor conditions that are equivalent to new forms of slavery, conceding people and planet to a neoliberal consensus over growth

and agility. The view is of the inescapable place where, in poetry, the agency of a global subject must be negotiated locally within the conditions of finality that the human has produced.

For these poets, the prospect is a literal one, a view from a hill. Other poets, however, constantly attempt to hold in one thought the faraway and the near, which creates a kind of notional prospect poem. Though the poet-speaker is not situated on an actual hill, the imbrication of the personal and the global comes about through the creation of a putative space that can contain the two in the poet's consciousness. Such a notional prospect poetry emerges from the charged spaces of revolutionary political consciousness. Perhaps the most visible of these spaces in the twenty-first century has been the square, from Tahrir to Zuccotti to Maidan. In his analysis of Egyptian "poetry of revolt" in Tahrir Square in January 2011, Elliott Colla sees "the uncertainty of this revolutionary performance" as pointing to the aggrandized potential of poetry during revolution. Alluding to the work of analytic philosopher J. L. Austin, Colla writes, "When philosophers speak of 'doing things with words,' they also remind us that the success of the locutionary act is tied to the conditions in which it is performed. This is another way of saying that any speech act is highly contingent. . . . Success, if it is to occur, happens only in the doing of it."[68] Colla looks at the manner in which poetry not only ornaments but makes revolution, even if this making is always contingent and uncertain in its outcome. This poetry is evental in nature: its conditions are emergent and its appearance necessarily ephemeral. But there is also poetry that, like Trethewey's, thickens the temporality of the single event, disaster, or moment of revolt, underscoring the long processes of globalization that enmesh the revolutionary actor and make possible the moment of struggle. This poetry makes its music from critique, not the efficacy of direct action. Extending and complicating the analysis of the prospect poems in this chapter, I turn now to poetry that finds the view from the hill already written within the structure of song itself.

The first poem from Juliana Spahr's *That Winter the Wolf Came* (2015), "Transitory, Momentary," takes place in an occupied square, though it begins with the circulations of geese and ends with the circulations of oil. Spahr makes a direct connection between the lyre and the cracks in the ground. She begins, however, with a disclaimer that "what I have to offer here is nothing revolutionary. . . . It is just an observation, a small observation that sometimes art can hold the oil wars and all that they mean and might yet mean within."[69] Spahr makes the intimacies of the love song continuous with the effects of oil production and circulation: "For what is epiphanic song if it doesn't spill out and over the many that are pulled from intimacies by oil's circulations?" Her question comes in the middle of a prose poem that meditates on multiple forms of circulation: on Brent geese; the blend of crude oil named after them; the actions of police shooting gas into a park occupied by protestors, who find ways of regrouping; and the raising of a child. Between these lines, the poem contemplates the timeliness of song: "In this time, the time of the oil wars, there are many reasons that singers give for being so lost." Spahr uncovers the conditions for song by cataloguing the lives that circulate with oil:

> The truckers, the sailors and deckhands, the assembly line workers, those who maintain the pipelines, those who drive support in the caravans that escort the tankers, the fertilizers, the thousands of interlocking plastic parts, the workers who move two hundred miles and live in a dorm near a factory, alone, those on the ships who spend fifty weeks circulating with the oil unable to talk to each other because of no shared language and so are left only with two weeks in each year where they can experience the tongue in meaningful conversation. A life that is only circulations.[70]

Combining multiple scales on which things and people circulate, Spahr writes the kind of critical global analysis more commonly found today in anthropology, social theory, or documentary film. The inclusion of the labor force that drives oil production is necessary here: if the poem does not exactly sing, it adumbrates the conditions under which the desire for song continues to be felt. The poem does more than reveal these conditions, however.

"Transitory, Momentary" brings together discrepant flows, circulations that have various associations with the global economy, from branding (the Brent geese and the Brent crude oil) to causality (the workers whose lives are uprooted by the movement of the oil). Through parataxis, Spahr's poem creates its own circulating rhythms. These rhythms are not meant to be reparative, compensatory, or salvific, however. The particular song that triggers these thoughts, in the poem, is sung in the occupied park to a child as the protestors form a human barricade. The singer has no illusions that her losses, and those created by the circulations, will have any obvious remediation. Nor is there anything other than these losses, which fill the space of the poem: "Back there, someone might possibly be singing to a child, singing the epiphanic song that alludes to losing the moment of tongue on clit or cock over and over because the child cannot be comforted, because the singer knows only loss."[71] If there is a role for song here, it is to be found in the curious word "sustaining." Spahr writes, "They had gambled in a sense on a question of sustaining. They had agreed to exist from now on with a shadow."[72] To sustain a note, in music, is to hold a note for an extended period of time; to sustain a life, in Spahr's poem, is to continue to live under brutally unpropitious conditions. Spahr takes "sustainability" away from its central place in neoliberal discourse and instead associates it with revolutionary forms of living under constant loss.

"Transitory, Momentary" is metapoetic: the poem investigates the conditions under which poems are sung. The stanzas and the refrain of the popular love song are mapped onto the circulations of oil and the clearing of the occupied square. To put it more generally, the schemes of poetry—say, seven stanzas with one-word refrains in each—trope and reconfigure the geopolitical situation. But *That Winter the Wolf Came* does not linger in the metapoetic; it also provides an exemplary form of a sustaining song. Later in the book, Spahr composes a love song for the Anthropocene. The poem, "Calling You Here," begins by nodding toward the ballad or country song, with the repetition of several conditionals:

> if you were a snowy plover, you'd be surface feeding
> if you were a northern pintail, you'd be continually whistling
> if you were a magnificent frigate, you'd be flamboyantly displaying
> you'd know what you'd need
> if you were a laughing gull
> or a red-breasted merganser
> if you were this moment, this world[73]

The poem appropriates and runs variations on the Texas country singer Butch Hancock's "If You Were a Bluebird," which Spahr credits in her acknowledgments. Enacting the poiesis that "Transitory, Momentary" theorizes, this longing is situated in the specific circumstances of human dominance over other species. Giving form to this deviation from the normative ballad stanza, Spahr appropriates and then distorts the original text. The regular stanzas, rhymes, and rhythms of Hancock's song are stretched, spread out: the shortest line is four syllables, and the longest is nineteen syllables; rhymes are present, but not in a repeated scheme; and the lines interrupt syntax unpredictably ("but still we are together extremely wide tidal zone"). The flexing of Hancock's form creates a poem in which the standard modes of sustaining (line, rhyme, stanza) are contingent and uncertain.

More than the imaginative leap to transforming one's being, common to children's songs and folk songs, the poem longs for a nondestructive relationship between the human and the nonhuman. Chastened by the impossibility of such a relationship, it necessarily takes the conditional form of "if you were a. . . ." "Calling You Here" thus uses the "minor," the popular song, to "feel enormity," the separation of species and the damage propagated by the human, as well as the desire to take the place of something outside the human. Timothy Morton has described this desire in more deterministic terms, as the inevitable confrontation with a history outside the human. The current period marks

> the beginning of the end of the world, not as a decisive apocalypse or closure, but as the opening of a far more uncanny historicity, in which humans realize we are living on after the end of the world, that is, of a coherent text. . . . A good translation of Anthropocene is *There is no outside-human text.*[74]

Poetry writes through the impossibility of the "outside-human text," but the terms in which it does so are not only those of the psychologically uncanny. Spahr's outside-the-human text takes the wishful form of the common conditional and the poetic address: Spahr addresses the putatively universal species, "you," to imagine the perspectives of the threatened species. The image of relation between the human and the human-wrecked world is not idealized, but already contaminated by the actions of the human, so that "you are not a clean rain/and you are not pristine."

I place Spahr's work in the lineage of the contemporary prospect poems in this chapter despite that fact that no topos of the hill appears directly in the text. The hill is rather a certain orientation toward the political, a name for the perspective from which the ecological coalition in the poem might be glimpsed. The ecological relation called for by the poem is a political one that involves an alliance, not an uncritical assumption of universality or "flat ontology." Spahr imagines the speaker of the poem making common cause against a "them": "if we were a pygmy scaly-tailed flying squirrel, we'd swing down and bite them./if we were an oryx, we'd use our horns against them/if we were an explosive, we'd explode alongside them."[75] The fantasy here is one of reprisal and redress, rather than relief or immunity from disaster. To describe the "we" that might fight back, Spahr uses the governing trope of "spreading," which also describes her formal expansions of Hancock's song: "if we came together our reasons be spreading/our waters, our lands."[76] The vision of spreading needs a rhetorical equivalent in the poem, a gesture of inclusion that does not reinforce dominant epistemologies or forms of naming. And so it is by making recourse to the call—rather than the catalogue—that "Calling You Here" complicates the prospect tradition as well. The poem proceeds from the conditional to the hortatory and ends with an epiphanic, or ecstatic, call to be "here." The deictic "here" is always double, gesturing both outside the text to the fictional location of the poet and directly to the text on the page. For this reason, "calling you here" means that the call occurs within the ambit of the poem. In other words, the call that cannot yet take place in the world finds its habitation in the dynamic process of the poem's own unfolding.

The twenty-first-century prospect poem takes the standpoint of the dead, exploited, surplus, endangered, and embattled—that is, the viewpoint of those who have not counted as part of the human "species." Trethewey's brother, Joe, and Spahr's anonymous, singing lovers are placed in a poetic subgenre associated with mastery of a domain; yet their prospect uncovers the human damage of the Anthropocene and the sustaining alliances forged within it. The unimaginable relation that Spahr calls into the here and now of the poem might be surprising, given other calls to minimize the agency of the human and to adopt an object-oriented or posthuman stance in the era of the Anthropocene. But the prospect poem has always been particularly concerned with the possibilities for and limits to lateral relations with others. How do these relations emerge from their theorization and become legible to us? The poetic vehicle for this flashing up cannot be conceptualized or directly thematized, but is rather prospective, proleptic, anticipatory, or otherwise situated in the register of the call to come.

Coda

Near the beginning of *Three Poems* (1972), John Ashbery writes,

> I'm sorry—in staring too long out over this elaborate view one begins
> to forget that one is looking inside, taking in the familiar interior
> which has always been there, reciting the only alphabet one knows. To
> escape in either direction is impossible outside the frost of a dream, and
> it is just this major enchantment that gave us life to begin with, life for
> each other. Therefore I hold you. But life holds us, and is unknowable.[1]

This passage is a defense of poetry in global terms. After beginning with
a characteristically breezy, offhand apology, the poem first claims that the
view of a certain "elaborate" external prospect might cause us to forget that
the "alphabet" of poetry comes from limning a "familiar interior." Then
the poem moves inward, to the realm of "dream" and "enchantment," as a
contrast to the description of the outside prospect with which the passage
begins. But this movement inside brings us into the domain of relationality
with another person, not solipsism, and Ashbery proceeds to build the
poetic address into an embrace. The poem then moves back outward to a

sense of being held together by "unknowable" forces. Ashbery's "I" constitutes a global subject to the extent that his subjectivity, like the poem itself,
comprises such forces. The poem inverts the imperial gaze of its sovereign,
white, U.S. male poetic speaker, who determines that the "elaborate view"
before him is one of immanent rather than eminent domain, at one with
the "major enchantment" that brings "life for each other." This view
requires both active care and the acknowledgment of precarity: the depen-
dence upon unseen forces that exceed our forms of knowing. The poem is
built through a dialectical movement in which the address to and care for
the other's welfare is transformed into an enchanted sense of being grasped
by the world, an ecstatic process of encountering the unknowable in the
alphabet of the known.

Ashbery's ethical and oneiric language in *Three Poems* stands at an oblique
angle to the brutality of the early 1970s—the dawning of our current
"global age," as Martin Albrow names it in his eponymous study.[2] And yet
the precise meaning, political valence, and general usefulness of "global" as
a term to describe this period remain unsettled and subject to intense
debate. This book has turned to contemporary Anglophone poets, writing
from a variety of positions in the world economy, for a reconsideration of
what "global" signifies and for the terms, keywords, and concepts we might
use to grasp it. As the work of these poets suggests, a reappraisal of the
global also requires a reassessment of the literary historical forms of poetry
in English. Ashbery's example is an outlier when placed next to the more
explicit test cases in the rest of this book. Nevertheless, the curious seman-
tic field of "The New Spirit" makes sense when its global conditions are
restored and its dynamic movement through these conditions is made
explicit. The discovery of a vast distanciation of time and space gives way to
its mirroring within the self, which in turn leads to the creation of a political
and ethical relation to those in unexpected proximity ("life for each other").
The interdisciplinary critique of global capitalism is an ally, not a foe, to a
poetic criticism attentive to form and literary history. It is to the advantage
of both that the rigorous unmasking of capitalist exploitation and the nuanced
unfolding of poetic texts continue to be undertaken in concert.

The previous chapters attempt to open a shared space between the two
disciplines to uncover a mutually constitutive relation between globalization and Anglophone poetry. I have proceeded with the axiomatic belief
that the development of modern Anglophone poetic modes, subgenres,
and forms is inseparable from the development of global capitalism. Landscape poetry and the ode, lyric poetry, hortatory poetry, and prospect
poems: these overlapping poetic categories are born, or born global, from

the legal and political enclosures that drive the early modern expansions of the capitalist world-system.[3] They are marked in their contemporary forms by the precariousness and exclusions that accompany the elimination of spaces of the commons, the extraction of surplus value from labor, the erasure of reproductive labor, and the racism devised to justify it all. This means, however, that Anglophone poems have also served as theaters in which poets forge global subjectivities, exhort collectivities, sing past the limits of representation, imagine the beauty of resistance, and make visible the shifting systems of exclusionary politics. I have located some of these histories in a contemporary resurgence during capitalism's crisis of overaccumulation, arguing that poets hope to make good on their accumulated power while revisiting their conventions in dialectical relation to the new conditions of capitalist exploitation.

This book has focused on poets who write in English and on a few poets in translation. A majority of the poets in the previous chapters live in the United States or the United Kingdom and teach in academic institutions. Quite obviously, I do not attempt here a comprehensive, multicultural congress of world literature. Indeed, as I hope to have made clear, the book joins the ongoing critique of celebratory notions of a "one-world" global polity and encyclopedic ambitions of world literature.[4] Writing in English is a global act in a different sense: by doing so, a poet opens herself to charges of complicity with the hegemonic spread of the language through military occupation, scientific research, publishing, and commerce. The forms of poetry written in English register and complicate this geopoliticization of the language. To conclude, then, I reflect briefly on the tensions or problems for poets writing about globalization in English—namely, that the spread of English itself has been inseparable from the violence of the global and has abetted its propagation. In this brief coda, I turn from Ashbery, whose perspective is situated within the U.S. metropole, to the Iranian American poet Solmaz Sharif, whose poetry maneuvers within an English shaped by its use in military invasion and occupation.

In her debut poetry collection, *Look* (2016), Solmaz Sharif writes about the Iran-Iraq War, the twenty-first-century U.S. invasion and occupation of Iraq, and the detainment of prisoners in Guantanamo Bay. The language that Sharif uses in her poetry bears the impress both of Anglophone poetic genres and of an English irrevocably altered by its use in U.S.–led wars and military occupations in the Middle East. The book begins with an epigraph pulled from the 2007 U.S. Department of Defense *Dictionary of Military and Associated Terms*. As defined there, the word "look" means "in mine warfare, a period during which a mine circuit is receptive of an influence."[5]

Describing the process of composing *Look*, Sharif writes, "It started as a rewrite of the dictionary, and wanting to redefine the terms to reveal the truth beneath the terms. It then evolved into revealing those terms as a part of our lives everywhere, daily in the U.S."[6]

In Sharif's work, the notion of a "global English" takes on a strange new sense, one that diverges from the ways in which that term is commonly understood. As Emily Brown Coolidge Toker points out, "globalized English" and "global Englishes" refer to distinct phenomena. The former suggests the standardization of English across the globe, while the latter "recognizes multiple distinct and fluid (but mutually intelligible) dialects or strands of English adapted to the specific locale and usage of a given population."[7] Sharif tracks how common English words, presented in her work in all capital letters, are weaponized through the revisions of a military dictionary. Her poetry provides one example of how the poet can draw attention to that process by writing within the complex linguistic space it opens up. A global English, as it manifests in Sharif's poetry, refers not to the commodification of English as a global facilitator for business deals and scientific research, nor to the localized indigenization of English, but rather to the overlapping of the language of territorial occupation and remote drone warfare with forms of poetic intimacy and address.[8]

Endless wars, torture, and detainment define, as much as anything else in these chapters, the making of the global by the United States. Understood in David Harvey's terms as the interlocking "territorial and capitalistic logics of power," the new U.S. imperialism is closely related to the other facets of globalization I have examined previously. As a solution to the crisis of overaccumulation that begins in the 1970s, the counterinsurgencies in Iraq, Afghanistan, and now Syria are "profitable uses" for surplus capital.[9] Arrighi has shown that periods of financial expansion, as opposed to periods of commodity production, rely on territorial expansion and war as sources for investment of excess capital.[10] In a detailed analysis, Timothy Mitchell argues that the roots of U.S. militarism in Iraq and the Middle East are traceable to financial deals that secured the return of dollars to the United States in the 1970s:

> As the producer states gradually forced the major oil companies to share with them more of the profits from oil, increasing quantities of sterling and dollars flowed to the Middle East. To maintain the balance of payments and the viability of the international financial system, Britain and the United States needed a mechanism for these currency flows to be returned. This was especially a problem for the US, since the value of the dollar was fixed in relation to gold, and pro-

vided the basis for the Bretton Woods financial system. Arms were particularly suited to this task of financial recycling, for their acquisition was not limited by their usefulness.[11]

Far from the inevitable product of conflicting belief systems, counterinsurgencies, occupations, and weapons deals are the current theater for the making of global capitalism by the United States. The economic analysis matters here not only because it more accurately represents the determining force behind the brutality of the early twenty-first century, but also because it explains how the everyday economic constraints on a U.S. citizen depend on the violence of military occupation.

To capture this particular form of globality brought on by territorial expansion as a solution to capital overaccumulation, Sharif intertwines the military dictionary with the legal genre of the contract and the poetic genre of the love poem. The eponymous first poem in *Look* collects the evidence of daily life until the point at which separate incidents, genres, and allusions overlap, words and images become overdetermined, and love, politics, war, and poetry share the same linguistic spaces:

> It matters what you call a thing: *Exquisite* a lover called me. *Exquisite.*

> Whereas *Well, if I were from your culture, living in this country,* said the man outside the 2004 Republican National Convention, *I would put up with that for this country;*

> Whereas I felt the need to clarify: *You would put up with* TORTURE, *you mean,* and he proclaimed: *Yes;*

> Whereas what is your life;

> Whereas years after they LOOK down from their jets and declare my mother's abadan block PROBABLY DESTROYED, we walked by the villas, the faces of buildings torn off into dioramas, and recorded it on a handheld camcorder;

> Whereas it could take as long as 16 seconds between the trigger pulled in Las Vegas and the Hellfire missile landing in Mazar-e-Sharif, after which they will ask *Did we hit a child? No. A dog.* they will answer themselves;[12]

The poem's structure plays with the scheme of anaphora. Anaphora works in general by accumulation, producing a fiction of totality, as in Walt Whitman's catalogues, or an incantatory state, as in Allen Ginsberg's "Howl." The point is not to create a false equivalence through poetic structure. Instead, the anaphora in "Look" uncovers the existing relations between the language used to make things happen—primarily, to kill and torture—and the intimacies of poetic and literary language. Rather than recalling Whitman or Ginsberg, perhaps the two most famous U.S. poetic practitioners of anaphora, Solmaz's anaphora makes us think of juridical pronouncement or contractual obligation. All the lines of the poem, except for the first one and the last four, begin with "whereas." In legal documents, "whereas" sets up a foundation of evidence or a series of subcontracts. The counterinsurgency, Laleh Khalili argues, is characterized by such an "insistence on legality of action," which "goes hand in hand with the will to improve that is inherent to liberal imperial invasions, occupations, and confinements."[13] By the end of the poem, Sharif resituates "looking" in the scene of love. The military meaning of the word cannot be erased or overcome, however. "Looking" becomes instead an uneasy metaphysical conceit linking the time lapse between trigger and missile hit to the ephemerality of love: "Let me LOOK at you in a light that takes years to get here." Sharif's point is not to conflate the lover and the target, but to show how constant wars militarize English and to uncover the permanent effects that militarized English has on everyday life.

The Germanic "look," cognate with the Old Saxon *lokon*, suggests a number of related colloquial phrases—look out or look up, but also look past, overlook. As an imperative, "look" might be the demotic form of "behold," the word that announces a revelation. Looking has its own long poetic and philosophical history, from "ecce homo," the phrase from Pontius Pilate that Nietzsche borrows to encapsulate his philosophical project, to Wallace Stevens's "Thirteen Ways of Looking at a Blackbird" and its modernist experiment in multiperspectival seeing. Rhetorically, "look" functions as both a command and a deictic gesture of pointing at something, an imperative directed at a person or multiple people. Even without pointing to the world, "look" reorients attention within a conversation, as when one says, "Look, what I meant was. . . ." The latter usage has the vague flavor of impatience: "look" interrupts a conversation to correct it or to stop it altogether. In all these instances, "look" implies an audience or companion, exhorted to see without being told how they should see.

Sharif translates the interpersonal address created by the command "look" into the structure of a contract as indicated by the repetition of the contractual word "whereas." The poem also conjures one of the more specific manifestations of contractual obligation: a will. While the poetic epitaph, which often contains an act of bequeathing, has found its exponents in a line of critics from Johnson to Wordsworth to Geoffrey Hartman, the poetic testament is at once more capacious and less poetic than the epitaph.

Not just a form of tomb writing, the testament blurs the line between poetic and juridical discourse. Whether testaments written in poetic form or poems written with the purpose of testaments, the will and the poem seem to share a common impulse, one that exceeds memorialization or monumentality. Crucial to the context for the poetic genre, from François Villon's *Le Testament* (1461) to Sharif's contemporary version, is the prospect of immediate death. The connection between look and testament comes through the act of witnessing, an act that Sharif places into question.

What happens, then, when the language of the poem, as well as the generic heritage of the testament poem, is not at all the property of the poet to give away? In this case, the testament records what has been taken away from the poet. A possible poetic precursor for Sharif, Adrienne Rich, cautions in "North American Time" that "everything we write/will be used against us/or against those we love."[14] Rich's choice of verb leaves no room for a language that escapes the contested ground of its use: "will," not "might" or "can." As her example, Rich describes "one line typed twenty years ago" that "can be blazed on a wall in spraypaint." Rich writes against complacency, arguing for vigilance in the context of ceaseless appropriation. Her sobering vision of the political ambiguity of poetic language informs this reading of Sharif's book. In Sharif's case, the language is an English pulled from the pages of the military dictionary. If one definition of global English is a standardization of the language that "facilitates communication around the world," the global English of the military dictionary facilitates U.S. military violence and territorial grabs.[15] By its nature, this English language does not belong to Sharif's poetic speaker, even though it uses the same words that "standard" English does, and is in fact weaponized to kill the family described in the poem.

Sharif's poetry joins a growing corpus of poetry collections that use existing texts to critique U.S. militarization. Rob Halpern's *Music for Porn* (2012) and *Common Place* (2015) manipulate found texts, including autopsies, to examine the eroticization of the detainee. Sara Uribe's *Antígona González* (2016) uses various texts of and about Sophocles's *Antigone* in its investigation of disappeared Mexican bodies. Srikanth Reddy's *Voyager* (2011) selectively erases text from the memoirs of Kurt Waldheim, UN secretary general and former Wehrmacht officer. In the end, however, Sharif's work is perhaps most like Ali's. The lines or verse paragraphs of "Look" resemble those of a ghazal, held together by mood or related images rather than unified theme. Both Sharif and Ali write poetry as an exilic practice, from the standpoint of those who are prevented, in different ways, from having the right to Anglophone poetry. They write nevertheless from the heart of U.S. empire: the terms of the Anglophone love poem and the terms of the military dictionary are perhaps not so far removed after all. Sharif's process is to reveal the connection between the two. She defamiliarizes the language of the love poem by associating it with contemporary warfare at the same time that she relocates the weaponized English of the military dictionary in the intimacy of the lover's look.

Sharif's work offers a critical analysis and transformation of what it means to write poetry in English during a period in which a military dictionary is actively refashioning what English words mean and do. The 2007 *Dictionary of Military and Associated Terms* presents as its primary criterion for inclusion the "inadequate coverage in a standard, commonly accepted dictionary, e.g. by Merriam-Webster."[16] Yet the *DOD Dictionary* goes beyond its stated goal of becoming a supplement to standard dictionaries. As Khalili argues with respect to counterinsurgency manuals, the redefinition of common words in military contexts is a strategy by which ostensibly liberal regimes pursue illiberal occupations.[17] Sharif shows how this process pervades culture and literature more generally: the traditions and tropes of Anglophone love poetry, her work suggests, are inseparable today from their militarization by an English redefined to serve drone warfare and military dictionaries. To understand poetry like Sharif's, this book has argued for a broader scope for poetry criticism, one that brings together global studies and the analysis of poetic form. In Sharif's case, the specific work that her poetry does is to prevent the language from becoming ceded entirely to the cultures of U.S. military occupation, maintaining the possibility that language can continue to be transformed. Rich warns that poetic language is complicit in exploitation and oppression—which means that it has the power, at the same time, to call into question the settled decisions of who has the mandate to interpret, create, and transform global processes.

The belief that has guided my writing throughout the book is that poetry cannot be read in isolation from the political economy, anthropology, and sociologies of global capitalism. My aim has been to bring out the ways in which the structures and literary histories of English-language poetry are themselves necessary contributions to understanding how contemporary globalization was made and continues to be made. The enduring notion that poetry is rarefied and exceptional speech, remote from the crisis of capital accumulation that defines the contemporary, helps to produce and to normalize the kinds of subjectivity that continue to prop up global capitalism. The academic and professional privatization of U.S. poetry, in particular, has often occurred through the ejection, suppression, or mystification of those elements of the poem that have a global politics of race, gender, and class. The result has been an enclosure movement around English-language poetry, rendering it the property of those who, under the current system, are already granted full citizenship and full rights.

Yet beyond these boundaries, poetry from Cairo to Calais to Ferguson is most recognizable today as an artistic tactic for anti-capitalist, anti-racist, and political struggle. It is forged in public occasions of revolution, protest, and social vulnerability. Poems are recited, discussed, and evaluated by those who are excluded from national belonging and social provision, who lack "the right to have rights," as Arendt famously puts it. The poems here participate in that process in their own distinct ways: they diagnose complex and exploitative global systems by reimagining literary forms. They are not policy recommendations, which belong to the practice of global development, but neither are they limited to being diagnostic tools. At a moment when globalization has quite evidently failed to benefit the populations of those countries that created it, let alone the populations of those countries that have been expelled from political participation in shaping it, these poems claim a place between critical thought and action, renewing the conditions under which their readers might be moved to remake the global present.

ACKNOWLEDGMENTS

This book would not have been written without the support and intellectual companionship of my colleagues and students at Clemson University. Erin Goss read the manuscript and gave invaluable advice. Michael LeMahieu provided an important suggestion for the organization of the book and feedback on several chapters. Brian McGrath generously offered dialogue and criticism at every point. Angela Naimou helped me conceptualize the book's argument as a whole. I have been fortunate to work and think alongside Raquel Anido, Susanna Ashton, Garry Bertholf, Nic Brown, Cameron Bushnell, David Coombs, Camille Cooper, Jonathan Beecher Field, Gabriel Hankins, Cynthia Haynes, Jan Rune Holmevik, Steve Katz, Chenjerai Kumanyika, Saadiqa Kumanyika, Andrew Lemons, Kimberly Manganelli, Steve Marx, Amy Monaghan, Sean Morey, Keith Morris, Lee Morrissey, Elizabeth Rivlin, Aga Skrodzka, Will Stockton, Pauline de Tholozany, Rhondda Thomas, Michelle Ty, and Jillian Weise. I also thank staff and former staff members Shannon Baldwin, Brennan Beck, Susan Chastain, Keri Crist-Wagner, Emily McKinney, Aleesa Millet, Jessica Owens, Beverly Pressley, and Zaria Washington.

At the University of Virginia, Jahan Ramazani shared his insatiable love of poetry with me. His capacious, catholic sensibilities have kept me thinking constantly about the relation between the style and politics of poetic criticism. Elizabeth Fowler and Victor Luftig offered invaluable advice and support. Josiah Luftig offered his own poetry in Galway. I thank Talbot Brewer for his intellectual companionship. Many of the ideas that grew into this book were first developed while teaching Global Development Studies alongside Richard Handler. I was fortunate to be in conversation with other faculty at UVA: Stephen Cushman, David Edmunds, Jessica Feldman, Rita Felski, Jennifer Greeson, J. Paul Hunter, Krishan Kumar, Katharine Maus, Jerome McGann, John Parker, Caroline Rody, Marlon Ross, Sandhya Shukla, Lisa Russ Spaar, Herbert Tucker, and Cynthia Wall. I thank the English department staff, including Sarah Colvin, Randy

Swift, and June Webb. This book benefited from a Faculty Senate Fellowship and research and travel grants from the Department of English and the Society of Fellows.

I thank my friends and colleagues from a semester guest teaching at the National University of Ireland-Galway, especially Daniel Carey, Muireann O'Cinneide, Lionel Pilkington, Sean Ryder, Elizabeth Tilley, and Justin Tonra. The book was finished during two summers of teaching at Deep Springs College. I thank David Neidorf, Amity Wilczek, and the members of the community for their hospitality.

My gratitude to Jorie Graham and Peter Sacks at Harvard University for their teaching began well before this book and continues after it. Thanks to those who have shaped this book: Benjamin Bateman, Stéphane Bouquet, Marijeta Bozovic, Angèle Cristin, Kathryn Crim, Shaun Cullen, Amy De'Ath, Michael Dowdy, Tim Duffy, Laura Goldblatt, Jonathan Eburne, Amy Elias, Harris Feinsod, Marta Figlerowicz, Gloria Fisk, Anne-Lise François, Roland Greene, Rob Halpern, Lenora Hanson, Matthew Hart, Stephen Macekura, Sean O'Brien, Marie Ostby, Giulio Pertile, André Pesic, Siobhan Phillips, Hilary Plum, Marie de Quatrebarbes, Margaret Ronda, Zach Savich, Nathan Suhr-Sytsma, Dorothy Wang, and Andrew Zawacki. Late-night talks with Robert Stilling provided ballast and inspiration. I thank Rachel Galvin for reading the entire manuscript and Joshua Kotin and Shirley Wong for reading sections of it.

Thanks to friends: Elizabeth Baxa, Julia Bozer, Adam Brock, Jason Canavan, Sarah D'Adamo, Alexander Davis, Emily Galvin, Julia Jarcho, Kira Manser, Sarah Matalone, Jessie Modi, Brighde Mullins, Annie Musgrove, Jennifer Nelson, Laura Nelson, Tom and Kristen Rock, Jocelyn Spaar, Jordan Taylor, Jia Tolentino, Raine Trainor, Amara Warren, Stephanie de Wolfe, and Caroline Zavakos. I thank Cody Carvel and Richard Re for their humor and deep understanding. I thank Katie Peterson for teaching me and for teaching with me. A special place in this book must be kept for Jennifer Wicke, whose advice and wisdom over the past ten years have shaped my life in indelible ways.

I am deeply grateful to my two readers: Gillian White, whose attention to multiple points in the argument has made this a much better book, and an anonymous second reader, whose helpful criticism sharpened the historical focus. Tom Lay at Fordham University Press believed in the book from the beginning. Many thanks to Eric Newman and my copy editor, Aldene Fredenburg, for their help and expertise.

A portion of the introduction was published in *ASAP/Journal* in a forum on "Global Poetics." An excerpt from Chapter 1 appeared in "Materialisms," a special issue of *symplokē*, guest edited by Marta Figlerowicz, Padma D. Maitland, and Christopher P. Miller. A section of Chapter 3 was published by *Cultural Critique*. Part of Chapter 4 was originally published in the *minnesota review* in a special focus section, "Emergent Precarities and Lateral Aesthetics," edited by Benjamin Bateman and Elizabeth Adan.

I am grateful to Youngsuk Suh for the cover photo.

I thank my father, Walt; my mother, Janet; and my sister, Aubrey, for their gentleness, enthusiasm, and curiosity. I thank Sean Flood, Susan Hunter, Ward Shaumburg, and Pamela, Richard, and Lauren Turner for their support. There is no way to thank Lindsay Turner for imagination and for love.

1. There is an analogous danger with the broader term "poetics," which, Mary Gallagher argues, "is traditionally linked to broadly Western theories of representation, fiction, imagination, aesthetics, literariness, form, meaning, etc., theories that seldom, if ever, reflect on their own ethnocentricity or on their possibly (contextually) limited validity"; Gallagher, "Poetics, Ethics, and Globalization," in *World Writing: Poetics, Ethics, Globalization*, ed. Mary Gallagher (Toronto: University of Toronto Press, 2008), 5.

2. In her concluding essay for *The Cambridge History of American Poetry*, Steph Burt questions "how we narrate—or fail to narrate—the procession of poets that leads up to our own day." Burt calls for a "pluralist" version of literary history that points to the impossibility of telling "one story" about any period of U.S. poetry; Burt, "American Poetry at the End of the Millennium," in *The Cambridge History of American Poetry*, ed. Alfred Bendixen and Stephanie Burt (Cambridge: Cambridge University Press, 2015), 1162–63. For a nineteenth- and early twentieth-century history of the diverse uses and receptions of U.S. poetry, see Joan Shelley Rubin, *Songs of Ourselves: The Uses of Poetry in America* (Cambridge, Mass.: Harvard University Press, 2007).

3. For analyses of capitalism in earlier historical periods, I have relied on the work of Janet Abu-Lughod, Giovanni Arrighi, C. A. Bayly, Fernand Braudel, Robert Brenner, Christopher Hill, Peter Linebaugh, Immanuel Wallerstein, and R. Bin Wong. While acknowledging that globalization is a process that includes colonization and that stretches back to the formation of the capitalist world-system around 1500, it is still possible, and necessary, to mark the "*differentia specifica* of today's globalization," as Jasper Bernes puts it; Bernes, "Logistics, Counterlogistics, and the Communist Prospect," *Endnotes*, accessed June 10, 2017, https://endnotes.org.uk/issues/3/en/jasper -bernes-logistics-counterlogistics-and-the-communist-prospect. The distinctive conditions of post-1970 globalization can be traced to the floating of the dollar in 1971 and the abolition of U.S. controls on finance capital in 1975; see Saskia Sassen, "Global Finance and Its Institutional Spaces," in *Oxford Handbook of the Sociology of Finance*, ed. Karin Knorr Cetina and Alex

Preda (Oxford: Oxford University Press, 2012), 16; Timothy Mitchell, *Carbon Democracy: Political Power in the Age of Oil* (New York: Verso, 2011), 187; Joshua Clover, *Riot, Strike, Riot: The New Era of Uprisings* (New York: Verso, 2016), 170; Greta Krippner, *Capitalizing on Crisis: The Political Origins of the Rise of Finance* (Cambridge, Mass.: Harvard University Press, 2011), 52; Leo Panitch and Sam Gindin, *The Making of Global Capitalism: The Political Economy of American Empire* (New York: Verso, 2012), 196. Vijay Prashad identifies at least four specific factors: "the disarticulation of Northern Fordism, the emergence of satellite and undersea cable technology, the containerization of ships, and other technological shifts that enabled firms to take advantage of differential wage rates"; Prashad, *The Poorer Nations: A Possible History of the Global South* (New York: Verso, 2012), 5. More generally, the "unprecedentedness" of contemporary globalization "consists precisely in the fact that it is a *world-system* that is also, uniquely and for the first time, a *world* system"; Warwick Research Collective, *Combined and Uneven Development: Towards a New Theory of World-Literature* (Liverpool: Liverpool University Press, 2015), 8.

4. Michael Davidson, "Introduction: American Poetry, 2000–2009," *Contemporary Literature* 52 (2011): 600; Bernes, "Logistics, Counterlogistics, and the Communist Prospect."

5. Critics have attended to the absence of race from accounts of twentieth-century poetry. Timothy Yu shows how the formation of U.S. poetic avant-gardes is inseparable from an awareness of race: "Although movements such as the Harlem Renaissance offered earlier examples of racialized avant-gardes, I argue that after 1970 the question of race became central to the constitution of *any* American avant-garde, as writers and artists became increasingly aware of how their social locations inflected their aesthetics"; Yu, *Race and the Avant-Garde: Experimental and Asian American Poetry Since 1965* (Stanford, Calif.: Stanford University Press, 2009), 2. Nevertheless, as Dorothy Wang argues, this close relation between the avant-garde and race has not been accompanied by equal attention to poetry by racialized persons, which "no matter the aesthetic style, is almost always read as secondary to the larger (and more 'primary') fields and forms of English-language poetry and poetics—whether the lyric, prosody, rhetorical tropes, the notion of the 'avant-garde'—categories all too often presumed to be universal, overarching, and implicitly 'racially unmarked'"; Wang, *Thinking Its Presence: Form, Race, and Subjectivity in Contemporary Asian American Poetry* (Stanford, Calif.: Stanford University Press, 2013), xx. See also Cathy Park Hong's "Delusions of Whiteness in the Avant-Garde," which begins with the sentence "To encounter the history of avant-garde poetry is to encounter a racist tradition"; Hong, "Delusions of Whiteness in the Avant-Garde," *Lana Turner*, accessed Febru-

ary 18, 2016, http://www.lanaturnerjournal.com/7/delusions-of-whiteness-in-the-avant-garde. This book draws on the work of Yu, Wang, Hong, and others who question the erasure of racialized subjects from poetry criticism. I look at poets who situate race within the networks of global capitalism, from Claudia Rankine, whom I read as analyzing transcolonial forms of exploitation in the United States, France, and Algeria, to Trethewey, who historicizes Hurricane Katrina in the context of the economic development of the Mississippi Gulf Coast.

6. Christopher Nealon, *The Matter of Capital: Poetry and Crisis in the American Century* (Cambridge, Mass.: Harvard University Press, 2011), 3. Nealon argues, and I agree with him, that the criticism produced in the 1970s and 1980s is characterized by the "refusal to think about the role of capital" (7). Whereas Nealon emphasizes that "the workings of capitalism are a central subject matter of twentieth-century American poetry in English," I offer an analysis of the formal shapes and poetic structures that, I hope to show, have been reinvigorated in the present (1).

7. Charles Altieri and Marjorie Perloff, who have written some of the most influential histories of contemporary poetry, begin their accounts with early twentieth-century modernist poetry (and, in Perloff's case, important nineteenth-century precursor poets such as Arthur Rimbaud). In Altieri's recent work, late twentieth-century poets compose responses to modernist struggles with poetic rhetoric and the social values it models or makes visible. He writes that "because these poets realized that they could not continue maintaining the sharp modernist distinctions between poetry and rhetoric that enabled them to subsume social into spiritual problems, they tried to reformulate their strategies to elaborate new ways for poetry to take social responsibility"; Altieri, *The Art of Twentieth-Century American Poetry: Modernism and After* (Malden, Mass.: Blackwell, 2006), 3. Perloff, in her *Poetics of Indeterminacy*, uncovers a tradition of poetry, from Rimbaud and Stein to Cage and Ashbery, in which "the symbolic evocations generated by words on the page are no longer grounded in a coherent discourse, so that it becomes impossible to decide which of these associations are relevant and which are not"; Perloff, *The Poetics of Indeterminacy: Rimbaud to Cage* (Princeton, N.J.: Princeton University Press, 1981), 18. My book tells a different story about poetry since 1970, one that does not begin with individual poets or with a periodization based on breaks from or continuities with modernist aesthetics. By placing global conditions at the center of each chapter, I claim that a strong tradition of Anglophone poetry from the 1970s to the present is best understood when situated within historical capitalism.

8. See Jacob Edmond, *A Common Strangeness: Contemporary Poetry, Cross-Cultural Encounter, Comparative Literature* (New York: Fordham University

Press, 2012); Harris Feinsod, *The Poetry of the Americas: From Good Neighbors to Countercultures* (Oxford: Oxford University Press, 2017); Rachel Galvin, *News of War: Civilian Poetry 1936–1945* (Oxford: Oxford University Press, 2017); Matthew Hart, *Nations of Nothing But Poetry: Modernism, Transnationalism, and Synthetic Vernacular Writing* (New York: Oxford University Press, 2010); Jahan Ramazani, *A Transnational Poetics* (Chicago: University of Chicago Press, 2009); Anthony Reed, *Freedom Time: The Poetics and Politics of Black Experimental Writing* (Baltimore: Johns Hopkins University Press, 2016); Wang, *Thinking*; Yu, *Race*.

   9. See Emily Apter, *Against World Literature: On the Politics of Untranslatability* (New York: Verso, 2013); Elizabeth Anker, *Fictions of Dignity: Embodying Human Rights in World Literature* (Ithaca, N.Y.: Cornell University Press, 2012); David Damrosch, *What Is World Literature?* (Princeton, N.J.: Princeton University Press, 2003); Taylor A. Eggan, "Regionalizing the Planet: Horizons of the Introverted Novel at World Literature's End," *PMLA* 131 (2016): 1299–1315; Eric Hayot, *On Literary Worlds* (New York: Oxford University Press, 2012); Paul Jay, *Global Matters: The Transnational Turn in Literary Studies* (Ithaca, N.Y.: Cornell University Press, 2010); Aamir Mufti, *Forget English! Orientalisms and World Literature* (Cambridge, Mass.: Harvard University Press, 2016).

   10. Lisa Lowe, *The Intimacies of Four Continents* (Durham, N.C.: Duke University Press, 2015), 2. Saidiya Hartman provides an exemplary formulation of this critique in *Scenes of Subjection* (1997), her study of "the forms of violence and domination enabled by the recognition of humanity, licensed by the invocation of rights, and justified on the grounds of liberty and freedom"; Hartman, *Scenes of Subjection: Terror, Slavery, and Self-Making in Nineteenth-Century America* (Oxford: Oxford University Press, 1997), 6. The critique of liberalism has occupied a central place in postcolonial theory. For Dipesh Chakrabarty, "European thought is at once indispensable and inadequate in helping us think through the experiences of political modernity in non-Western nations, and provincializing Europe becomes the task of exploring how this thought . . . may be renewed from and for the margins"; Chakrabarty, *Provincializing Europe* (Princeton, N.J.: Princeton University Press, 2000), 16. For a global feminist critique along the same lines, see Gayatri Chakravorty Spivak, *An Aesthetic Education in the Age of Globalization* (Cambridge, Mass.: Harvard University Press, 2012), 123. For social scientific perspectives on liberal modernity, see James Ferguson, *Global Shadows: Africa in the Neoliberal World Order* (Durham, N.C.: Duke University Press, 2006), and Mitchell, *Carbon Democracy*. For a capacious overview of the history of development, see Stephen Macekura, *Of Limits and Growth* (Cambridge: Cambridge University Press, 2015).

11. In their essay "The University and the Undercommons," Fred Moten and Stefano Harney write that "to enter this space [of the undercommons] is to inhabit the ruptural and enraptured disclosure of the commons that fugitive enlightenment enacts, the criminal, matricidal, queer, in the cistern, on the stroll of the stolen life, the life stolen by enlightenment and stolen back, where the commons gives refuge, where the refuge gives commons"; Moten and Harney, "The University and the Undercommons: Seven Theses," *Social Text* 22 (2004): 103.

12. Lowe, *Intimacies*, 3.

13. For flow, see Stuart Alexander Rockefeller, "Flow," *Current Anthropology* 52 (2011): 557–78. A strong critique of leveling terms such as flow can be found in Ferguson, *Global Shadows*. For work on hybridity in poetry and an overview of the term in postcolonial theory, see Ramazani, *The Hybrid Muse: Postcolonial Poetry in English* (Chicago: University of Chicago Press, 2001). For scape, see Arjun Appadurai, "Disjuncture and Difference in the Global Cultural Economy," *Public Culture* 2 (1990): 1–24.

14. See Radhika Desai, *Geopolitical Economy: After US Hegemony, Globalization, and Empire* (London: Pluto, 2013); David Harvey, *A Brief History of Neoliberalism* (Oxford: Oxford University Press, 2007); Mitchell, *Carbon Democracy*; Kristin Ross, *Communal Luxury: The Political Imaginary of the Paris Commune* (New York: Verso, 2015); Sassen, *Expulsions: Brutality and Complexity in the Global Economy* (Cambridge, Mass.: Harvard University Press, 2014).

15. Rob Nixon, *Slow Violence and the Environmentalism of the Poor* (Cambridge, Mass.: Harvard University Press, 2011).

16. Khaled Furani's *Silencing the Sea: Secular Rhythms in Palestinian Poetry* (Stanford, Calif.: Stanford University Press, 2012), and Michael Dowdy's *Broken Souths: Latina/o Poetic Responses to Neoliberalism and Globalization* (Tucson: University of Arizona Press, 2013) bring a global perspective to post-1945 and contemporary traditions of Palestinian and Latina/o poetry. Both books are less interested in an account of poetry that describes its transnational circulation or cross-cultural hybridity than in an analysis of global forces and conditions (of occupation, marginalization, underdevelopment, financialization) as they shape poetic innovation. Multiple other recent and forthcoming books read poetry in light of specific aspects of global capitalist structures. Amy De'Ath examines "the capitalist production of abstract identity qualities" by looking at contemporary "feminized poetry"; De'Ath, "Unsociable Poetry: Antagonism and Abstraction in Contemporary Feminized Poetics" (unpublished Ph.D. diss., Simon Fraser University, 2017). Both De'Ath and Jasper Bernes show how the historical framework of deindustrialization shapes the forms of contemporary poetry. In Bernes's case, poets also contribute to the developments in industry through the commodification of art "as an activity

that can be turned into waged labor"; Bernes, *The Work of Art in the Age of Deindustrialization* (Stanford, Calif.: Stanford University Press, 2017), 1. Lindsay Turner recasts poiesis as a type of work, with particular attention to reproductive labor and to contemporary U.S. poetry; Turner, *Poetry's Work: Labor and Poiesis, 1950–Present* (unpublished Ph.D. diss., University of Virginia, 2017). Turning to the distinct ecological phase of the Great Acceleration, Margaret Ronda looks to contemporary American poetry for its responses; Ronda, *Remainders: American Poetry at Nature's End* (Stanford, Calif.: Stanford University Press, 2017). A manuscript in progress by Marijeta Bozovic introduces Russian poets engaged in rethinking the relation between poetry and politics after the end of the U.S.S.R.; Bozovic, *Avant-Garde Post-: Radical Poetics After the Soviet Union* (forthcoming).

17. Reed, *Freedom Time*, 3.

18. Panitch and Gindin, *Making of Global Capitalism*.

19. Krippner, *Capitalizing*, 59–60.

20. Prashad, *Poorer Nations*, 88.

21. Jay, *Global Matters*.

22. Anthony Giddens, *The Consequences of Modernity* (Stanford, Calif.: Stanford University Press, 1990), 64.

23. Hilary E. Kahn, "Introduction," in *Framing the Global: Entry Points for Research*, ed. Hilary E. Kahn (Bloomington: Indiana University Press, 2014), 6.

24. D. A. Powell, "Long Night Full Moon," *poets.org*, accessed August 26, 2017, https://www.poets.org/poetsorg/poem/long-night-full-moon.

25. Timothy Morton, *The Ecological Thought* (Cambridge, Mass.: Harvard University Press, 2010).

26. For background on these earlier conceptions of the global, see David Held and Anthony McGrew, "The End of the Old Order? Globalization and the Prospects for World Order," *Review of International Studies* 24 (1998): 219–43, and Roland Robertson, *Globalization: Social Theory and Global Culture* (London: Sage, 1992).

27. Panitch and Gindin, *Making of Global Capitalism*, 174.

28. Sassen, *Expulsions*, 118.

29. Fernand Braudel, *The Wheels of Commerce*, vol. 2, *Civilization and Capitalism: 15th–18th Century*, trans. Siân Reynolds (Berkeley: University of California Press, 1992), 230.

30. Giovanni Arrighi, *The Long Twentieth Century* (London: Verso, 2010); Donald MacKenzie, *An Engine, Not a Camera: How Financial Models Shape Markets* (Cambridge, Mass.: MIT Press, 2006), 12. For a study of cultural texts and the financialized economy, see Annie McClanahan, *Dead Pledges: Debt, Crisis, and Twenty-First-Century Culture* (Stanford, Calif.: Stanford University Press, 2016).

31. Appadurai, *Banking on Words: The Failure of Language in the Age of Derivative Finance* (Chicago: University of Chicago Press, 2015).

32. Nealon, *Matter of Capital*, 23–24.

33. Harvey, *Brief History*, 2.

34. Panitch and Gindin, *Making of Global Capitalism*, 97.

35. Jodi Melamed, *Represent and Destroy: Rationalizing Violence in the New Racial Capitalism* (Minneapolis: University of Minnesota Press, 2011), 146.

36. Tejaswini Ganti, "Neoliberalism," *Annual Review of Anthropology* 43 (2014): 90.

37. Hartman, *Scenes*, 62.

38. Virginia Jackson, *Dickinson's Misery: A Theory of Lyric Reading* (Princeton, N.J.: Princeton University Press, 2005), 8.

39. Jonathan Culler, *Theory of the Lyric* (Cambridge, Mass.: Harvard University Press, 2015), 138.

40. Geoffrey Hartman and Daniel T. O'Hara, eds., *The Geoffrey Hartman Reader* (New York: Fordham University Press, 2004), 63.

41. Moten, *In the Break: The Aesthetics of the Black Radical Tradition* (Minneapolis: University of Minnesota Press, 2003), 38–39.

42. As K. Aarons argues, "Far from disappearing with the 13th amendment, or even in the post–civil rights period, afropessimists argue that the formal traits of the slave relation were reproduced and kept alive through the perpetuation of a form of social and civil death that continues to *materially* and *symbolically* locate the Black body 'outside Humanity'"; Aarons, "No Selves to Abolish: Afropessimism, Anti-Politics, and the End of the World," *Mute*, accessed August 26, 2017, http://www.metamute.org/editorial/articles/no-selves-to-abolish-afropessimism-anti-politics-and-end-world.

43. Danez Smith, *[INSERT] BOY* (Portland, Ore.: YesYes, 2014), 93.

44. Ibid., 93.

45. Ibid., 108.

46. See "Forum: Global Poetics" *ASAP/Journal* 1, no. 3 (September 2016): 365–88.

47. Sarah Brouillette and David Thomas are among those who call literary critics to attend more closely to "the mediating factor of the nature of the production of culture." They argue that "an emphasis on literature's production and on the contexts for its end uses forces us, at least, to see capitalist restructuring in response to crises as something that is in literature from the ground up, rather than something the work reflects in its themes or its complex mix of stylistic features and innovations"; Barbara Harlow, Sarah Brouillette, David Thomas, Maria Elisa Cevasco, Joshua Clover, and David Damrosch, "First Responses," *Comparative Literature Studies* 53 (2016): 511. Nathan Suhr-Sytsma underscores the political stakes of attending to "cultural gatekeepers like editors": "When these gatekeepers are based in the former

imperial capital, literary struggles for recognition can become proxies for political aspirations, as postcolonial poets strive to overcome the structural inequalities inherited from colonialism"; Suhr-Sytsma, "Publishing Postcolonial Poetry," in *The Cambridge Companion to Postcolonial Poetry* (Cambridge: Cambridge University Press, 2016), 237.

48. Melamed's *Represent and Destroy* concisely articulates the problem in its title.

1. STOLEN LANDSCAPES: THE INVESTMENTS OF THE ODE AND THE POLITICS OF LAND

1. Susan Stewart, "Lyric Possession," *Critical Inquiry* 22 (1995): 34.

2. Habib Tengour, *Exile Is My Trade: A Habib Tengour Reader*, trans. Pierre Joris (Boston: Black Widow, 2012), 259.

3. Michael Levien, "Regimes of Dispossession: From Steel Towns to Special Economic Zones," *Development and Change* 44 (2013): 381.

4. Levien, "From Primitive Accumulation to Regimes of Dispossession," *Economic and Political Weekly* 50 (2015): 147.

5. Saskia Sassen, *Expulsions: Brutality and Complexity in the Global Economy* (Cambridge, Mass.: Harvard University Press, 2014), 3.

6. Mike Davis, *Planet of Slums* (New York: Verso, 2006), 16–17.

7. Vijay Prashad, *The Poorer Nations: A Possible History of the Global South* (New York: Verso, 2012), 62.

8. Amy Chazkel and David Serlin, "Editors' Introduction," *Radical History Review* 109 (2010): 1.

9. Michael Komorowski, "Public Verse and Property: Marvell's 'Horatian Ode' and the Ownership of Politics," *ELH* 79 (2012): 330.

10. "The 'ghost estate' was a powerful political symbol because it linked the abstract machinations of capital to the level of everyday reality. But for these same reasons, the 'ghost estate' became a potent tool in the service of neoliberal ideology, by linking the narrative of 'excess' to the individual 'consumer'"; Cian O'Callaghan, Mark Boyle, and Rob Kitchin, "Post-Politics, Crisis, and Ireland's Ghost Estates," *Political Geography* 42 (2014): 131.

11. As David Harvey writes, "The violent neoliberal attacks on the rights and power of organized labor that, from Chile to Britain, began in the 1970s are now being augmented by a draconian global austerity plan that, from California to Greece, entails losses in asset values, rights, and entitlements for the mass of the population, coupled with the predatory absorption of hitherto marginalized populations into capitalism's dynamics . . . every major initiative to solve the problem of global poverty since 1945 has insisted on exclusive use of the means—capital accumulation and market exchange—that produce relative and sometimes absolute pov-

erty"; Harvey, "The Future of The Commons," *Radical History Review* 109 (2010): 107.

12. Paula Meehan, *Painting Rain* (Winston-Salem, N.C.: Wake Forest University Press, 2009), 13.

13. Rob Nixon, *Slow Violence and the Environmentalism of the Poor* (Cambridge, Mass.: Harvard University Press, 2011), 19.

14. Harvey, *The Enigma of Capital and the Crises of Capitalism* (London: Profile, 2010), 244.

15. Ian Baucom, "Found Drowned: The Irish Atlantic," *Nineteenth-Century Contexts* 22 (2000): 113.

16. Fernand Braudel, *The Mediterranean and the Mediterranean World in the Age of Philip II*, trans. Siân Reynolds (Berkeley: University of California Press, 1995), 373.

17. Ibid., 374.

18. Mary O'Malley, *Asylum Road* (Cliffs of Moher, Ireland: Salmon, 2001), 61.

19. Greta Krippner, *Capitalizing on Crisis: The Political Origins of the Rise of Finance* (Cambridge, Mass.: Harvard University Press, 2011), 60.

20. Rob Kitchin, Rory Hearne, and Cian O'Callaghan, "Housing in Ireland: From Crisis to Crisis," *NIRSA Working Paper Series* 77 (2015): 12.

21. Ibid.

22. Ibid., 14.

23. "By pushing for maximum commercial returns, NAMA is working against those looking for an affordable and secure home. It is continuing the speculative-asset approach to housing that fueled the crisis. This promotes residential property as a commodity rather than a social good. In this sense, NAMA is facilitating a massive transfer of wealth created by the Irish people to foreign and domestic investors"; ibid., 17.

24. Sarah Clancy, *The Truth and Other Stories* (Cliffs of Moher, Ireland: Salmon, 2014), 15.

25. Adrienne Rich, *Later Poems: Selected and New, 1971–2012* (New York: W. W. Norton, 2013), 247.

26. Seamus Heaney, "'Place and Displacement': Recent Poetry from Northern Ireland," *Wordsworth Circle* 16 (1985): 49.

27. Ibid., 53.

28. Ibid., 50–51.

29. Ibid., 56.

30. Heaney, "Banks of a Canal," *Guardian*, accessed August 15, 2016, https://www.theguardian.com/books/2014/oct/03/seamus-heaney-last-poem-national-gallery-ireland-anthology.

31. Braudel, *Mediterranean*, 70–75.

32. Ibid., 75.

33. John Keats, *The Complete Poems* (New York: Penguin, 1988), 369.

34. Sassen, *Expulsions*, 121.

35. Giovanni Arrighi, *The Long Twentieth Century* (London: Verso, 2010), 318.

36. Ibid., 326.

37. Ibid., 334.

38. Arjun Appadurai, *Banking on Words: The Failure of Language in the Age of Derivative Finance* (Chicago: University of Chicago Press, 2015), 147.

39. Franco "Bifo" Berardi, *The Uprising: On Poetry and Finance* (Los Angeles: Semiotext(e), 2012), 86.

40. Appadurai, *Banking*, 138.

41. Jasper Bernes, *The Work of Art in the Age of Deindustrialization* (Stanford, Calif.: Stanford University Press, 2017), 24.

42. See Keston Sutherland, "Blocks: Form Since the Crash," accessed May 20, 2017, https://archive.org/details/BlocksSeminarAtNYU13Novem ber2015.

43. Cowper's abolitionist politics are discussed in Karen O'Brien, "'Still at Home': Cowper's Domestic Empires," in *Early Romantics: Perspectives in British Poetry from Pope to Wordsworth*, ed. Thomas Woodman (London: Macmillan, 1998), 134–47; Joanne Tong, "'Pity for the Poor Africans': William Cowper and the Limits of Abolitionist Affect," in *Affect and Abolition in the Anglo-Atlantic, 1770–1830*, ed. Stephen Ahern (Burlington, Vt.: Ashgate, 2013); and Marcus Wood, *Slavery, Empathy, and Pornography* (Oxford: Oxford University Press, 2002).

44. Prominent exceptions come to mind immediately, from Robert Lowell's "For the Union Dead" (1964) to Frank O'Hara's many odes and from Alice Notley's "At Night the States" (1988) to Sharon Olds's *Odes* (2016). A partial list of contemporary odes includes "Filter OD," in Sean Bonney's *Blade Pitch Control Unit* (Cambridge: Salt Press, 2005); the four odes by Marianne Morris, Josh Stanley, Luke Roberts, and Sophie Robinson, in *Untitled Colossal Parlour Odes* (Cambridge: Bad Press, 2010); "Lunar Fork Ode," in Francesca Lisette's *Teens* (Cambridge: Mountain Press, 2012); Jennifer Cooke's *not suitable for domestic sublimation* (London: Contraband, 2012); "Again Ode," "Ode Farage," and "Having Coke with You," in Joe Luna's *Astroturf* (Brighton: Hi Zero, 2012).

45. Of the two main strands of classical odes, the Pindaric has become associated with ecstasy and the Horatian with tranquility and meditation. Gregory Nagy calls the Pindaric ode a "public poetic testimony"; Nagy, *Pindar's Homer: The Lyric Possession of an Epic Past* (Baltimore: Johns Hopkins University Press, 1990), 113. He notes that the victory odes, or "epinikia,"

possessed a certain "transcendent occasionality": "Though each of Pindar's victory odes was an occasional composition, centering on a single performance, each containing details grounded in the historical realities of the time and place of performance, still each of these victory odes aimed at translating its occasion into a Panhellenic event, a thing of beauty that could be replayed by and for all Hellenes for all time to come"; ibid., 114.

46. Qtd. in Norman Maclean, "From Action to Image: Theories of the Lyric in the Eighteenth Century," in *Critics and Criticism: Ancient and Modern*, ed. R. S. Crane (Chicago: Chicago University Press, 1952), 427. Maclean's essay, written in 1952, is still one of the indispensable histories of the ode: in Maclean's genealogy, "the late eighteenth century turned the minor lyric to the tender, and the tender is generally personal, as the personal is generally contradicted by any sign of premeditation"; ibid., 457.

47. Helen Vendler, *The Odes of John Keats* (Cambridge, Mass.: Harvard University Press, 1985), 46. Vendler describes the Keatsian ode as "a network of combinatorial powers engaged in a constantly shifting set of relations"; ibid., 10.

48. "Ode," in *Princeton Encyclopedia of Poetry and Poetics*, ed. Roland Greene (Princeton, N.J.: Princeton University Press, 2012), 971.

49. M. H. Abrams, "Structure and Style in the Greater Romantic Lyric," in *From Sensibility to Romanticism: Essays Presented to Frederick A. Pottle*, ed. Frederick W. Hilles and Harold Bloom (New York: Oxford University Press, 1965), 201.

50. See the Cleanth Brooks–Douglas Bush debate over Andrew Marvell's "Horatian Ode": Cleanth Brooks, "Criticism and Literary History: Marvell's Horatian Ode," *Sewanee Review* 55 (1947): 199–222, and Douglas Bush, "Marvell's 'Horatian Ode,'" *Sewanee Review* 60 (1952): 363–76.

51. The Russian formalist Yuri Tynianov, in "The Ode as an Oratorical Genre" (Russian original 1927; English trans. 2003), states that "elements of poetic discourse in the ode are used, constructed as if it were an act of oratory"; Tynianov, "The Ode as an Oratorical Genre," *New Literary History* 34 (2003): 567.

52. Abrams, "Structure," 218.

53. Emily Apter, *Against World Literature: On the Politics of Untranslatability* (New York: Verso, 2013), 335.

54. Keats, *Complete Poems*, 349–50.

55. Friedrich Hölderlin, *Selected Verse*, trans. Michael Hamburger (London: Anvil Press Poetry, 1986), 258.

56. W. H. Auden, *Collected Poems*, ed. Edward Mendelson (New York: Vintage, 1991), 540–42.

57. Michael Komorowski's treatment of Andrew Marvell's "Horation Ode" makes that text appear as a precursor for Sutherland's. Komorowski writes, "The ode offers a space for articulating why and how the relative fluidity of property ownership during this time was a primary contingency in any government's hold on power"; Komorowski, "Public Verse," 320.

58. C. D. Wright, "The New American Ode," *Antioch Review* 47 (1989): 289.

59. Clover writes, "The purportedly thoughtless and natural character of riot, lacking reason, organization, and political mediation, is aligned with the racist tradition wherein racialized subjects are figured as natural, animalistic, irrational, immediate"; Clover, *Riot. Strike. Riot: The New Era of Uprisings* (New York: Verso, 2016), 112.

60. Sutherland, "Statement for Revolution and/or Poetry," *Revolution and/or Poetry*, accessed June 8, 2014, https://revolutionandorpoetry.wordpress.com/2013/10/15/keston-sutherlands-statement-for-revolution-andor-poetry/; emphasis in original.

61. Sutherland, *The Odes to TL61P* (London: Enitharmon, 2013), 7.

62. Susan Stewart, "What Praise Poems Are For," *PMLA* 20 (2005): 238. Franco Berardi's claim that poetry marks "the return of the sensuous body of language" and "the language of nonexchangeability" finds a precedent in Stewart's argument and an echo in Sutherland's own definition of poetry as "the communication of energy." For Berardi, poetry is a source of political possibility, a "reopening of the indefinite." In *The Uprising*, Berardi elaborates a theory of poetry as nonexchangeability: "Poetry is language's excess: poetry is what in language cannot be reduced to information, and is not exchangeable, but gives way to a new common ground of understanding, of shared meaning: the creation of a new world." This is a notion of poetry that, in its excesses, resists the logic of austerity. Berardi's general diagnosis is that, since the '80s, "digital financial capitalism" and the war on labor "makes the social body frail at the level of work, while virtualization makes the social body frail at the level of affection." Berardi calls for the reactivation of the social body, the strengthening of affective bonds, and the empowerment of the general intellect through the linguistic excesses and rhythms of poetic language; Berardi, *Uprising*, 128.

63. Sutherland, "Interview with Keston Sutherland," *The White Review*, accessed June 20, 2014, http://www.thewhitereview.org/interviews/interview-with-keston-sutherland/.

64. Writing about contemporary Russian poetry in an essay called, tellingly, "Beyond the Poetics of Privatization," Kirill Medvedev emphasizes a similar "erosion of barriers between different spheres"; Medvedev, "Beyond the Poetics of Privatization," *New Left Review* 82 (2013): 79. By jamming together the voices of "market traders, shop assistants, students, policemen,

photojournalists, nurses, refugees, art critics," the work of Keti Chukhrov, in Medvedev's account, captures "social and gender subjugation, alienation, material frustration, and political disillusionment"; ibid., 81.

65. Sutherland, *Odes*, 18.

66. Karl Marx, *Capital*, vol. 1, *A Critique of Political Economy*, trans. Ben Fowkes (New York: Penguin, 1992), 46.

67. Ibid., 1:47.

68. For reconsiderations of Keats's politics, see Elizabeth Jones, "Writing for the Market: Keats's Odes as Commodities," *Studies in Romanticism* 34 (1995): 343–64, and Jacques Rancière, "The Politics of the Spider," trans. Emily Rohrbach and Emily Sun, *Studies in Romanticism* 50 (2011): 239–50.

69. Keats, *Complete Poems*, 143–44.

70. Sutherland, "Statement."

71. Sutherland, "Interview."

72. Sutherland, *Odes*, 16.

73. Emmanuel Levinas, *Totality and Infinity: An Essay on Exteriority*, trans. Alphonso Lingis (Pittsburgh, Pa.: Duquesne University Press, 1961), 86.

74. See Fredric Jameson's comments in *The Prison House of Language*: "There is a basic Manichaeism of the world of scarcity, and it is scarcity which causes the Other to appear before me as a primal enemy"; Jameson, *The Prison House of Language: A Critical Account of Structuralism and Russian Formalism* (Princeton, N.J.: Princeton University Press, 1975), 69.

75. Judith Butler, "Precarious Life, Vulnerability, and the Ethics of Cohabitation," *Journal of Speculative Philosophy* 26 (2012): 140. Lauren Berlant's notion of "lateral agency" is relevant here for its emphasis on nonsovereignty: "We need to think about agency and personhood not only in inflated terms but also as an activity exercised within spaces of ordinariness that does not always or even usually follow the literalizing logic of visible effectuality, bourgeois dramatics, and lifelong accumulation or self-fashioning"; Berlant, *Cruel Optimism* (Durham, N.C.: Duke University Press, 2011), 99.

76. Anne Boyer, *Garments against Women* (Boise, Idaho: Ahsata, 2015), 1.

77. Ibid., 2.

78. E-mail exchange with Al-Sheikh, May 26, 2014.

79. Poem received by e-mail from the author.

80. Hannah Arendt, *The Origins of Totalitarianism* (New York: Harcourt, Brace, Jovanovich, 1973), 296.

2. LET US GO: LYRIC AND THE TRANSIT OF CITIZENSHIP

1. Roland Greene, "The Lyric," in *The Cambridge History of Literary Criticism*, ed. Glyn P. Norton (Cambridge: Cambridge University Press, 1999), 3:224.

2. Jennifer Ashton, "Labor and the Lyric: The Politics of Self-Expression in Contemporary American Poetry," *American Literary History* 25 (2013): 217.

3. Ibid., 222.

4. Jared Sexton, "The Social Life of Social Death: On Afro-Pessimism and Black Optimism," In*Tensions Journal* 5 (2011): 29.

5. Virginia Jackson and Yopie Prins, eds., *The Lyric Theory Reader* (Baltimore: Johns Hopkins University Press, 2013), 2.

6. Anthony Reed, *Freedom Time: The Poetics and Politics of Black Experimental Writing* (Baltimore: Johns Hopkins University Press, 2016), 5.

7. Evie Shockley, "Race, Reception, and Claudia Rankine's 'American Lyric,'" *Los Angeles Review of Books*, accessed August 25, 2017, https://lareviewofbooks.org/article/reconsidering-claudia-rankines-citizen-an-american-lyric-a-symposium-part-i/#!.

8. Oxford English Dictionary.

9. Immanuel Wallerstein, *The Modern World-System*, vol. 4, *Centrist Liberalism Triumphant* (Berkeley: University of California Press, 2011), 217.

10. See the argument of Peter Schuck and Rogers Smith, qtd. in Peter Spiro, *Beyond Citizenship: American Identity after Globalization* (New York: Oxford University Press, 2008), 14.

11. Ibid.

12. Stuart Hall, "Culture, Community, Nation," *Cultural Studies* 7 (1993): 361.

13. Ibid., 360–61.

14. Ibid., 361.

15. Audre Lorde, *Sister Outsider* (Trumansburg, N.Y.: Crossing, 1984), 115.

16. Jodi Melamed, *Represent and Destroy: Rationalizing Violence in the New Racial Capitalism* (Minneapolis: University of Minnesota Press, 2011), 139.

17. Ibid., 149.

18. In *Neoliberalism as Exception*, Aihwa Ong shows that "the elements that we think of as coming together to create citizenship—rights, entitlements, territoriality, a nation—are becoming disarticulated and rearticulated with forces set into motion by market forces"; Ong, *Neoliberalism as Exception: Mutations in Citizenship and Sovereignty* (Durham, N.C.: Duke University Press, 2005), 6.

19. Atossa Araxia Abrahamian, *The Cosmopolites: The Coming of the Global Citizen* (New York: Columbia University Press, 2016), 144.

20. Claudia Rankine, interview by Sandra Lim, *National Book Foundation*, http://www.nationalbook.org/nba2014_p_rankine_interv.html#.V4FxoY7bDhM.

21. Robert von Hallberg, *American Poetry and Culture 1945–1980* (Cambridge, Mass.: Harvard University Press, 1985), 62.

22. Spiro, *Beyond Citizenship*, 11.

23. Ibid., 13–14.

24. Ibid., 60.

25. Rankine, *Citizen: An American Lyric* (Minneapolis: Graywolf, 2014), 18.

26. Rankine and Alexandra Schwartz, "On Being Seen: An Interview with Claudia Rankine from Ferguson," *New Yorker*; accessed July 21, 2015.

27. Christopher Nealon, *The Matter of Capital: Poetry and Crisis in the American Century* (Cambridge, Mass.: Harvard University Press, 2011), 152.

28. Emma Kimberley, "Politics and Poetics of Fear After 9/11: Claudia Rankine's *Don't Let Me Be Lonely*," *Journal of American Studies* 45 (2011): 782.

29. Kevin Bell, "Unheard Writing in the Climate of Spectacular Noise: Claudia Rankine on TV," *Global South* 3 (2009): 94.

30. Nealon, *Matter of Capital*, 151.

31. Ibid., 152.

32. M. H. Abrams and Geoffrey Galt Harpham, *A Glossary of Literary Terms* (Independence, Ky.: Cengage Learning, 2011), 89.

33. René Wellek, "Genre Theory, the Lyric, and 'Erlebnis,'" in *Festschrift für Richard Alewyn* (Cologne: Böhlau-Verlag, 1967), 412. But cf. Lewis Turco: "Most *lyric* poems are written in the subjective voice"; Turco, *The Book of Forms* (Lebanon, N.H.: University Press of New England, 2000), 120. Turco cites, as does Daniel Albright, T. S. Eliot's essay "The Three Voices of Poetry," in which Eliot distinguishes between "the poet talking to himself— or to nobody," "the poet addressing an audience," and "one imaginary character addressing another imaginary character"; Eliot, *On Poetry and Poets* (New York: Farrar, Straus and Giroux, 2009), 19. Gérard Genette notes that the classical division of genres into lyric, epic, and dramatic is a "retrospective illusion" and that the lyric falls outside the purview of Aristotle's analyses of genre; Genette, *The Architext*, trans. Jane E. Lewin (Berkeley: University of California Press, 1992), 5, 10.

34. Samuel Johnson, *Lives of the English Poets*, ed. George Birkbeck Hill (Oxford: Clarendon, 1945), 3:251.

35. Jonathan Culler, *Theory of the Lyric* (Cambridge, Mass.: Harvard University Press, 2015), 177; italics mine.

36. Angela Naimou, *Salvage Work: U.S. and Caribbean Literatures amid the Debris of Legal Personhood* (New York: Fordham University Press, 2015), 19.

37. Culler follows M. H. Abrams in tracking the shift from a mimetic to an expressive regime; he dates the legitimation of lyric as a genre to 1563 and to Antonio Minturno, the first "to treat lyric as a genre on par with the epic and the dramatic"; Culler, *Theory*, 72. Roughly speaking, then, the modern lyric emerges as a genre precisely at the moment of the creation of the modern world-system, as Immanuel Wallerstein charts it. The "real-world" lyric is very much the lyric of global capitalism. More specifically, the epideictic

acts, anti-discursive figuration, and value-oriented statements legitimate the lyric at the moment of the greatest expansion of capital in the world prior to the current period.

38. Rei Terada, "After the Critique of Lyric," *PMLA* 123 (2008): 196.

39. Ibid., 198.

40. Jonathan Arac, Conclusion, in *Lyric Poetry: Beyond New Criticism*, ed. Chaviva Hošek and Patricia A. Parker (Ithaca, N.Y.: Cornell University Press, 1985), 353.

41. Claudia Rankine and Elizabeth Hoover, "Poet Claudia Rankine on Wounds We Should Not Forget," *Sampsonia Way*, accessed August 24, 2017, http://www.sampsoniaway.org/literary-voices/2010/11/12/poet-claudia-rankine-on-wounds-we-shouldnt-forget/.

42. G. W. F. Hegel, *Aesthetics: Lectures on Fine Arts*, trans. T. M. Knox (Oxford: Oxford University Press, 1975), 1:204.

43. Northrop Frye, *Anatomy of Criticism: Four Essays* (Toronto: University of Toronto Press, 2006), 231.

44. Mark Jeffreys, "Ideologies of Lyric: A Problem of Genre in Contemporary Anglophone Poetics," *PMLA* 110 (1995): 197.

45. Claudia Rankine and Lauren Berlant, "Claudia Rankine," *BOMB Magazine*; https://bombmagazine.org/articles/claudia-rankine, accessed 21 July 2015.

46. John Stuart Mill, "Thoughts on Poetry and its Varieties," *Crayon* 7 (1860): 95.

47. Rankine, *Citizen*, 73.

48. Robert Lowell, *Life Studies and For the Union Dead* (New York: Farrar, Straus and Giroux, 1964), 92.

49. Michelle Clayton, *Poetry in Pieces: César Vallejo and Lyric Modernity* (Berkeley: University of California Press, 2011), 17.

50. Rankine, *Citizen*, 142.

51. Ibid., 71, 72.

52. Wallerstein's examples include French women who, after the Revolution, lose the vote they had had before it, and free blacks in the United States, who find many of the rights they had had in the eighteenth century taken away by nineteenth-century laws.

53. Rankine, *Citizen*, 16.

54. For work on ethics and poetry, see Peter Nicholls, Tim Woods, Xiaojing Zhou, Matthew G. Jenkins, Adam Potkay, Crystal Parikh, John Wrighton, and Rachel Cole. Although several recent books follow a Levinasian model for linking postwar poetry to an ethics of alterity, the ethical approach tends to lack historical specificity. See R. Radhakrishnan's caveat that "the Levinasian model works with an allegorical blitheness that refuses to engage with history and its many lowercase selves and others"; Radhakrishnan, "Theory, Democracy, and the Public Intellectual," *PMLA* 125 (2010): 793.

55. Shockley, "Race."

56. Rankine, *Citizen*, 86.

57. Culler, "Apostrophe," *diacritics* 7 (1977): 59.

58. Angela Hume, "Toward an Anti-Racist Ecopoetics: Waste and Wasting in the Poetry of Claudia Rankine," *Contemporary Literature* 57 (2016): 106.

59. Qtd. in Michael Riffaterre, "Prosopopeia," *Yale French Studies* 69 (1985): 107.

60. Paul de Man, "Autobiography as De-facement," *MLN* 94, no. 5 (1979): 926. See also Michael Riffaterre's reply to de Man in "Prosopopeia."

61. Virginia Jackson, *Dickinson's Misery: A Theory of Lyric Reading* (Princeton, N.J.: Princeton University Press, 2005), 159–60. Jackson writes that "the way in which Dickinson's writing often invites or assumes a reader other than its (often unavailable or out of reach) historical addressee and other than an imaginary, sympathetic eavesdropper or theatrical audience in the distant future, is difficult to characterize, or at least contemporary literary criticism has no language for it."

62. William Waters, *Poetry's Touch: On Lyric Address* (Ithaca, N.Y.: Cornell University Press, 2003), 2.

63. Barbara Johnson, "Apostrophe, Animation, and Abortion," *diacritics* 16 (1986): 34.

64. Ibid., 34.

65. Catherine Zuromskis, "Complicating Images," *Los Angeles Review of Books*, accessed August 26, 2017, https://lareviewofbooks.org/article/reconsidering-claudia-rankines-citizen-an-american-lyric-a-symposium-part-i/.

66. Dave Zirin, *Brazil's Dance with the Devil: The World Cup, the Olympics, and the Right for Democracy* (Chicago: Haymarket, 2014), 166; see also Eduardo Galeano, *Soccer in Sun and Shadow* (New York: Nation, 2013).

67. Rankine, *Citizen*, 122–28.

68. Paul Gilroy writes, "I want to develop the suggestion that cultural historians could take the Atlantic as one single, complex unit of analysis in their discussions of the modern world and use it to produce an explicitly transnational and intercultural perspective"; Gilroy, *The Black Atlantic: Modernity and Double Consciousness* (London: Verso, 1993), 15.

69. Kristin Ross, *Communal Luxury: The Political Imaginary of the Paris Commune* (New York: Verso, 2015), 16.

70. Hume, "Toward an Anti-Racist Ecopoetics," 104.

71. Claudia Rankine, "The Provenance of Beauty: A South Bronx Travelogue (Excerpt)," *Nation*, accessed January 20, 2013, https://www.thenation.com/article/provenance-beauty-south-bronx-travelogue-excerpt/.

72. For a description of the route the bus takes and a review of the production, see Donatella Galella, "(Re)Presenting the South Bronx," *PAJ: A Journal of Performance and Art* 33 (2011): 82–88.

73. Leo Panitch and Sam Gindin, *The Making of Global Capitalism: The Political Economy of American Empire* (New York: Verso, 2012), 165.

74. Rankine, "The Provenance of Beauty: A South Bronx Travelogue (Excerpt)," *Nation*, accessed January 20, 2013, https://www.thenation.com/article/provenance-beauty-south-bronx-travelogue-excerpt/.

75. Roderick Ferguson, "On *Citizen*: Ethics and Method," *Los Angeles Review of Books*, accessed August 26, 2017, https://lareviewofbooks.org/article/reconsidering-claudia-rankines-citizen-an-american-lyric-a-symposium-part-i/.

76. Terada, "After the Critique," 198.

3. THE CROWD TO COME: POETIC EXHORTATIONS FROM BROOKLYN TO KASHMIR

1. Walter Benjamin, *Illuminations*, trans. Harry Zohn (New York: Schocken, 1968), 161.

2. Jonathan Culler, "Apostrophe," *diacritics* 7 (1977): 59.

3. Ariel Bloch and Chana Bloch, trans., *The Song of Songs* (Berkeley: University of California Press, 1995), 105.

4. Aristotle, *Rhetoric*, trans. W. Rhys Roberts (New York: Cosimo, 2010), 35.

5. *Region of Unlikeness* is the title of Graham's 1991 collection of poems.

6. In her work on the "we" in poetry, Bonnie Costello writes against a notion of plurality as "imperial authority or forced consensus," instead suggesting that poetry "often tries to bring into being a particular 'we' that has been obstructed in history"; Costello, "The Plural of Us," *Jacket2*, accessed August 26, 2017, http://jacket2.org/article/plural-us.

7. Walt Whitman, *Complete Poetry and Collected Prose* (New York: Library of America, 1982), 627–28.

8. Ibid., 308.

9. See Helen Vendler's comments on the ethical address of Whitman and Ashbery; Vendler, *Invisible Listeners: Lyric Intimacy in Herbert, Whitman, and Ashbery* (Princeton, N.J.: Princeton University Press, 2005), 4–5.

10. See, however, Nico Israel's reading of Ashbery's use of "globe": "We may want to escape our globalized predicament, but the globe's very dimension 'will not allow it'"; Israel, "Globalization and Contemporary Literature," *Literature Compass* 104 (2004): 1–2.

11. John Ashbery, *Planisphere* (New York: Ecco, 2009), 113.

12. Benjamin, *Illuminations*, 161.

13. Ibid., 177.

14. Ibid.

15. Ibid., 179, 186.

16. Ibid., 189.

17. Ibid., 194.

18. Theodor Adorno, "On Lyric Poetry and Society," in *Notes to Literature*, trans. Shierry Weber Nicholsen, ed. Rolf Tiedemann (New York: Columbia University Press, 1991), 1:39.

19. Ibid., 1:38.

20. Ibid., 1:39.

21. Ibid., 1:42.

22. Robert Kaufman, "Adorno's Social Lyric, and Literary Criticism Today: Poetics, Aesthetics, Modernity," in *The Cambridge Companion to Adorno*, ed. Tom Huhn (Cambridge: Cambridge University Press, 2004), 363.

23. Adorno, "On Lyric Poetry," 1:39.

24. Ibid., 1:44.

25. Benjamin, *Illuminations*, 156.

26. Ibid., 193.

27. Emmanuel Levinas frequently describes the relation to the Other in Judeo-Christian terms of transcendence, height, domination, and revelation: "This presence dominates him who welcomes it, comes from the heights, unforeseen, and consequently teaches its very novelty; . . . the Other is not the incarnation of God, but precisely by his face, in which he is disincarnate, is the manifestation of the height by which God is revealed"; Levinas, *Totality and Infinity: An Essay on Exteriority*, trans. Alphonso Lingis (Pittsburgh, Pa.: Duquesne University Press, 1961), 66, 79.

28. Judith Butler, "Precarious Life, Vulnerability, and the Ethics of Cohabitation," *Journal of Speculative Philosophy* 26 (2012): 145.

29. Lauren Berlant, *Cruel Optimism* (Durham, N.C.: Duke University Press, 2011), 193.

30. Ibid., 192.

31. The 2011 report of the United Nations Conference on Trade and Development states that "the frequent and wide price fluctuations that have been observed in the markets for many commodity groups since 2007, particularly in oil and agricultural markets, have been unprecedented, and in many instances they have no obvious link to changes on the supply side"; *United Nations Conference on Trade and Development Report, 2011* (New York and Geneva: United Nations, 2011), 113.

32. Paulo Virno, *A Grammar of the Multitude*, trans. Isabella Bertoletti, James Cascaito, and Andrea Casson (Los Angeles: Semiotext(e), 2004), 87.

33. Pierre Bourdieu, *Acts of Resistance: Against the Tyranny of the Market*, trans. Richard Nice (Cambridge: Polity, 1998), 97.

34. Saskia Sassen, "Global Cities and Survival Circuits," in *Nannies, Maids, and Sex Workers in the New Economy*, ed. Barbara Ehrenreich and Arlie Russell Hochschild (New York: Henry Holt, 2002), 257, 264.

35. Franco "Bifo" Berardi, *The Uprising: On Poetry and Finance* (Los Angeles: Semiotext(e), 2012), 118.

36. Berlant, *Cruel Optimism*, 270n2.

37. For a concise history of the economics, politics, and culture of neo-liberalism, see Miguel A. Centano and Joseph N. Cohen, "The Arc of Neo-liberalism," *Annual Review of Sociology* 38 (2012): 317–40.

38. Studying the positions of "cautious" and "strong" globalizers, the economist Emma Aisbett identifies several methodological factors that muddle arguments made from empirical data about liberalization, growth, and poverty. She concludes that "the empirical work to date has contributed to a broad acceptance that trade and FDI are growth promoting." Still, she cautions that "much work remains to show which policies can reduce the adjustment costs borne by the poor and maximize the share of the benefits they obtain from globalization"; Aisbett, "Why Are the Critics So Convinced That Globalization is Bad for the Poor?," in *Globalization and Poverty*, ed. Ann Harrison (Chicago: University of Chicago Press, 2007), 67. See the work of Robert H. Wade for a thorough examination of the neoliberal argument that liberalization has reduced inequality and poverty: Wade, "Is Globalization Reducing Poverty and Inequality?" *World Development* 32 (2004): 567–89.

39. In his work with four communities in southwestern Madagascar, Bram Tucker finds the "folk model" of understanding poverty to be "largely incompatible with pro-growth, business, and wealth-generation models common to international development." Tucker concludes that other Western models of development—ones that emphasize modes of production and the importance of local institutions—make a better fit; Tucker, Amber Huff, Tsiazonera, Jaovola Tombo, Patricia Hajasoa, and Charlotte Nagnisaha. "When the Wealthy Are Poor: Poverty Explanations and Local Perspectives in Southwestern Madagascar," *American Anthropologist* 113 (2011): 302.

40. Wade, "The West Remains on Top, Economically and Politically," in *The Global Political Economy of Raúl Prebisch*, ed. Matias E. Margulis (New York: Routledge, 2017), 137.

41. Jonathan Ostry, Prakash Loungani, and Davide Furceri, "Neoliberalism: Oversold?" *Finance and Development* 53 (2016): 41.

42. Berlant, *Cruel Optimism*, 193.

43. Myung Mi Kim, *Commons* (Berkeley: University of California Press, 2002), 111.

44. Claudia Rankine and Elizabeth Hoover, "Poet Claudia Rankine on Wounds We Should Not Forget," *Sampsonia Way*, accessed August 24, 2017, http://www.sampsoniaway.org/literary-voices/2010/11/12/poet-claudia-rankine-on-wounds-we-shouldnt-forget/.

45. In her Nobel Prize–winning research on common-pool resources in Japan, Switzerland, Spain, and the Philippines, the economist Elinor Ostrom criticizes the assumption, popularized by Garrett Hardin in "The Tragedy of the Commons," that the "creation of private property rights . . . is an obvious solution to the problem of degradation"; Ostrom, *Governing the Commons:*

The Evolution of Institutions for Collective Action (Cambridge: Cambridge University Press, 1990), 60.

46. David Harvey, "The Future of The Commons," *Radical History Review* 109 (2010): 106.

47. Kim, *Commons*, 110.

48. Ibid., 109.

49. Other recent books of poetry that employ the lyric to explore similar concerns are Rae Armantrout's *Money Shot* (Middletown, Conn.: Wesleyan University Press, 2012), Ariana Reines's *Mercury* (Albany, N.Y.: Fence, 2011.), Lisa Robertson's *The Men* (Toronto: Book Thug, 2006), and Keston Sutherland's *Hot White Andy* (London: Barque, 2009) and *Odes to TL61P* (London: Enitharmon, 2013).

50. Sean Bonney, *The Commons* (London: Openned, 2011), 6.

51. This description is taken from the home page of Openned Press, found at http://www.openned.com/print/category/sean-bonney.

52. John Bloomberg-Rissman suggests that *The Commons* might be a sonnet sequence, "although its somewhat disjunctive nature allows it to be read straight through as well"; Bloomberg-Rissman, Review of *The Commons*, by Sean Bonney, *Galatea Resurrects*, accessed February 24, 2016, http://galatea resurrection17.blogspot.com/2011/12/commons-by-sean-bonney.html.

53. For a concise history of enclosure movements and the English state, see Christopher L. Hill, *Reformation to Industrial Revolution: A Social and Economic History of Britain, 1530–1780* (New York: Penguin, 1967), 51.

54. Bonney, *Commons*, 11.

55. Ibid., 17.

56. See Giovanni Arrighi, *The Long Twentieth Century* (London: Verso, 2010), 1–26.

57. This slash is not a line break, but rather inserted by Bonney within the line itself.

58. Bonney, *Commons*, 14.

59. Ibid., 6.

60. Ibid., 22.

61. Ibid., 3.

62. Christian Lotz, "Poetry as Anti-Discourse: Formalism, Hermeneutics, and the Poetics of Paul Celan," *Continental Philosophy Review* 44 (2011): 499.

63. Karlheinz Stierle, "Die Identität des Gedichts—Hölderlin als Paradigma," in *Identität (Poetik und Hermeneutik 8)*, ed. Odo Marquard and Karlheinz Stierle (Munich: Wilhelm Fink, 1979), 514; my translation.

64. Paul Valéry, qtd. in Roman Jakobson, "Closing Statement: Linguistics and Poetics," in *Style in Language*, ed. T. A. Sebeok (New York: Wiley and Sons, 1960), 367.

65. Giorgio Agamben, *The End of the Poem*, trans. Daniel Heller-Roazen (Stanford, Calif.: Stanford University Press, 1999), 42.

66. Roland Greene, *Post-Petrarchism: Origins and Innovations of the Western Poetic Sequence* (Princeton, N.J.: Princeton University Press, 1991), 5.

67. Stéphane Mallarmé, qtd. in Philippe Lacoue-Labarthe, *Musica Ficta (Figures of Wagner)*, trans. Felicia McCarren (Stanford, Calif.: Stanford University Press, 1991), 81.

68. Jakobson, *Language in Literature*, ed. Krystyna Pomorska and Stephen Rudy (Cambridge, Mass.: Harvard University Press, 1987), 43.

69. Mutlu Konuk Blasing, *Lyric Poetry: The Pain and the Pleasure of Words* (Princeton, N.J.: Princeton University Press, 2007), 2.

70. Philippe Lacoue-Labarthe, *Poetry as Experience*, trans. Andrea Tarnowski (Stanford, Calif.: Stanford University Press, 1999), 20.

71. Jean-Luc Nancy, *Multiple Arts: The Muses II*, ed. Simon Sparks (Stanford, Calif.: Stanford University Press, 2006), 6.

72. Bonney, *Commons*, 9.

73. Ibid., 3, 11, 18.

74. Ibid., 3, 6, 10, 22, 25.

75. Ibid., 15, 18. As Jacob Edmond argues, "Bonney attends to the way revolutionary writing, if too direct or smooth, can become implicated in the power structures it seeks to overcome"; Edmond, "'Their Echoes Split Us': Sean Bonney Rewrites Baudelaire and Rimbaud," *Jacket2*, accessed February 24, 2016, http://jacket2.org/commentary/%E2%80%9Ctheir-echoes-split -us%E2%80%9D.

76. See Charles Bernstein, ed., *The Politics of Poetic Form: Poetry and Public Policy* (New York: Roof, 1990). In the United States, Steve Benson, Charles Bernstein, Lyn Hejinian, Susan Howe, Bob Perelman, Ron Silliman, and Barrett Watten are a few of the key figures. See also Stephanie Burt, "Sestina! Or the Fate of the Idea of Form," *Modern Philology* 105 (2007): 218–41, for a reading of contemporary American poets as having given up on a relationship between poetic form and political formation.

77. Bonney, *Commons*, 11.

78. Ibid., 26.

79. Percy Bysshe Shelley, *Shelley's Poetry and Prose*, ed. Donald H. Reiman and Neil Fraistat (New York: Norton, 2002), 304.

80. Bonney, *Commons*, 28.

81. Ibid., 6.

82. Kim, *Commons*, 110.

83. Rae Armantrout, in a 1978 essay, perhaps puts it best. She writes, "I use that term [language-oriented writing] but I'm suspicious of it, finally, because it seems to imply division between language and experience,

thought and feeling, inner and outer. The work I like best sees itself and sees the world. It is ambi-centric, if you will"; Armantrout, "Why Don't Women Do Language-Oriented Writing?," in *In the American Tree: Language, Realism, Poetry*, ed. Ron Silliman (Orono, Maine: National Poetry Foundation, 2007), 518–20.

84. Joseph Jonghyun Jeon, "Asian American Poetry," in *The Cambridge History of American Poetry*, ed. Alfred Bendixen and Stephanie Burt (Cambridge: Cambridge University Press, 2015), 998.

85. Kim, *Commons*, 107.

86. In *Poetry and Its Others*, Jahan Ramazani notes that "a poem faces both inward and outward: it enriches itself on its play of euphonies and dissonances within itself and across an array of earlier poems, and it feasts on, digests, and metabolizes linguistic forms of other kinds"; Ramazani, *Poetry and Its Others: News, Prayer, Song, and the Dialogue of Genres* (Chicago: University of Chicago Press, 2014), 6–7.

87. Kim, *Commons*, 111.

88. Ibid., 110. Jeannie Chiu suggests that these "attempts to recover individual and cultural histories" challenge "not only essentialist notions of ethnic and racial identity, but also the transcendent 'I' of conventional lyric poetry"; Chiu, "Identities in Process: The Experimental Poetry of Mei-mei Berssenbrugge and Myung Mi Kim," in *Asian North American Identities: Beyond the Hyphen*, ed. Eleanor Ty and Donald C. Goellnicht (Bloomington: Indiana University Press, 2004), 85.

89. Juliana Spahr argues that Kim's work is part of an "emerging formation of a poetry in English that includes other languages." Refusing associations between identity and language, "Kim returns again and again to question the naturalness of English"; Spahr, "Multilingualism in Contemporary American Poetry," in *The Cambridge History of American Poetry*, ed. Alfred Bendixen and Stephen Burt (Cambridge: Cambridge University Press, 2015), 1130.

90. Kim, *Commons*, 32.

91. Ibid., 110.

92. Ibid., 110.

93. This procedure relies on what Lyn Hejinian describes as the "realism of language": "Content is not imposed from without; rather, it emerges from independent initial points in the language itself"; Silliman, Watten, Benson, Hejinian, Bernstein, and Perelman, "For *Change*," in *In the American Tree*, 470. Charles Bernstein puts it slightly differently, but his point is the same: there is "no logic on which to base the work other than the sense developed ongoing in the actual activity itself"; Silliman, Watten, Benson, Hejinian, Bernstein, and Perelman, "For *Change*," in *In the American Tree*, 471.

94. Each poem in this section is numbered to fit within a span that individual sections introduce (for instance, 406–24).

95. Kim, *Commons*, 52.

96. See also Sarah Dowling's reading of this poem. Dowling situates "Lamenta" within the context of doubling of immigration to the United States between 1970 and 1990, arguing that the poem captures "the new reality inaugurated by the rapid and dramatic increase of Asian immigration to the U.S. Kim does not suggest that the figures she depicts are without legal rights; instead, she demonstrates that inclusion is at once legal reality and a social impossibility"; Dowling, "Interpolation, Coherence, History: The Works of Myung Mi Kim," in *Nests and Strangers: On Asian American Women Poets*, ed. Timothy Yu (Berkeley, Calif.: Kelsey Street Press, 2015), 18.

97. Kim, *Commons*, 110.

98. Peter Linebaugh, *The Magna Carta Manifesto: Liberties and Commons for All* (Berkeley: University of California Press, 2009), 43. In it, Linebaugh traces a history of discommoning and of enclosure, showing the effects of privatization on language, representation, perception, and philosophical ideas of personhood and agency.

99. Agha Shahid Ali, *Bone-Sculpture* (Calcutta: Writer's Workshop, 1972), 28.

100. Ali, *In Memory of Begum Akhtar* (Calcutta: Writer's Workshop, 1979), 28.

101. Qtd. in Shaden Tageldin, "Reversing the Sentence of Impossible Nostalgia: The Poetics of Postcolonial Migration in Sakinna Boukhedenna and Agha Shahid Ali," *Comparative Literature Studies* 40 (2003): 236.

102. Aamir Mufti, *Forget English! Orientalisms and World Literature* (Cambridge, Mass.: Harvard University Press, 2016), 183.

103. Amitav Ghosh, "'The Ghat of the Only World': Agha Shahid Ali in Brooklyn," *Annual of Urdu Studies* 17 (2002): 318.

104. Agha Shahid Ali, ed., *Ravishing DisUnities* (Middletown, Conn.: Wesleyan University Press, 2000), 13.

105. Ibid., 2–3.

106. As Malcolm Woodland puts it, ghazals "do not 'add up' in the way of conventional Western lyrics"; Woodland, "Memory's Homeland: Agha Shahid Ali and the Hybrid Ghazal," *English Studies in Canada* 31 (2005): 266.

107. Ali, *Ravishing DisUnities*, 13.

108. Shaden Tageldin discusses Ali's "impossible nostalgia" and its effects on syntax: the "attempt to link an old 'home' that is no longer home . . . to a new 'home' that never feels quite like home . . . compels [the text] to . . . violently disrupt the syntax of language, identity, geography and temporality"; Tageldin, "Reversing," 234. In David Caplan's analysis, "The farther the

monorhyme moves from its original phrase, the more it suggests exile's omnipresence"; Caplan, *Questions of Possibility: Contemporary Poetry and Poetic Form* (Oxford: Oxford University Press, 2006), 55.

109. Ramazani, *A Transnational Poetics* (Chicago: University of Chicago Press, 2009), 105. Ramazani's argument suggests that the Western modernist/nativist fusions of Ali's ghazal are not necessarily mimetic of a split identity, but rather a "split vision"; Ramazani, *The Hybrid Muse: Postcolonial Poetry in English* (Chicago: University of Chicago Press, 2001), 74.

110. Agha Shahid Ali, *Call Me Ishmael Tonight* (New York: Norton, 2003), 82–83.

111. *The Noble Qur'an*, accessed August 27, 2017, https://quran.com/.

112. Emily Dickinson, *The Poems of Emily Dickinson*, ed. R. W. Franklin (Cambridge, Mass.: Harvard University Press, 1999), 314.

113. Dina Al-Kassim, e-mail to author, April 8, 2013.

114. Stephanie Burt, "Agha Shahid Ali: 'Tonight,'" *Poetry Foundation*, accessed August 27, 2017, https://www.poetryfoundation.org/articles/69597/agha-shahid-ali-tonight.

115. Ali, *Ravishing DisUnities*, 4.

116. Edward Said, *Freud and the Non-European* (New York: Verso, 2004), 54.

117. Said, *Freud*, 55.

118. Ali, *Call Me Ishmael*, 82.

119. Ibid., 82.

120. Ibid., 83.

121. Ibid., 82.

122. Ibid., 83.

123. Mufti writes, "To repeatedly invoke Kashmir in this manner is to invoke a place between nation-states or a place in which two states overlap and their respective sanctioning narratives—the claim to the Indic origin and commonality of all Indian cultures, on the one hand, and a strong-nationalist claim to Muslim distinctiveness from the Hindu-Indic, on the other—have to somehow live together"; Mufti, *Forget English!*, 187. Exploring the relation between Ali's poetry, modernism, and Kashmir, Robert Stilling argues that "Ali sets in motion a series of contrasts marking the interlocking and often discordant co-presences of American, European, Indian, and globalized modernity. . . . Far from postmodern pastiche, the poem grounds its discordant references in material history"; Stilling, "Multicentric Modernism and Postcolonial Poetry," in *The Cambridge Companion to Postcolonial Poetry*, ed. Jahan Ramazani (Cambridge: Cambridge University Press, 2016), 135.

124. I agree here with Mufti's analysis of the figure of the weeping God; Mufti, *Forget English!*, 192. Where Mufti understands the poem to be "a reworking of the mutual relations of polytheistic and monotheistic religious

traditions in the subcontinent," my reading stresses the parallel undermining of the poet's own authority; ibid., 193.

125. Allen Grossman, *The Sighted Singer: Two Works on Poetry for Readers and Writers* (Baltimore: Johns Hopkins University Press, 1991), 209.

126. Lynn Keller, "An Interview with Myung Mi Kim," *Contemporary Literature* 49 (2008): 338.

4. THE NO-PROSPECT POEM: POETIC VIEWS OF THE ANTHROPOCENE

1. Stephanie Burt, *From There: Some Thoughts on Poetry and Place* (Vancouver, B.C.: Ronsdale, 2016), 19.

2. Margaret Ronda, "Anthropogenic Poetics," *minnesota review* 83 (2014): 109.

3. Jedediah Purdy, *After Nature: A Politics for the Anthropocene* (Cambridge, Mass.: Harvard University Press, 2015), 3.

4. Simon L. Lewis and Mark A. Maslin, "Defining the Anthropocene," *Nature* 519 (2015): 173. For precursor concepts, see Clive Hamilton and Jacques Grinevald, "Was the Anthropocene Anticipated?" *Anthropocene Review* 2 (2015): 59–72. These concepts include "Anthropozoic," "Psychozoic," and "Nöosphere." Hamilton and Grinevald argue, however, that "scientists in the 19th and the first half of the 20th centuries did not possess the modern scientific concept of *the Earth system* of which the Anthropocene is an outcome"; ibid., 60–61.

5. Paul J. Crutzen and Eugene F. Stoermer, "The 'Anthropocene,'" *IGBP Global Change Newsletter* 41 (2000): 17.

6. Lewis and Maslin, "Defining the Anthropocene," 175.

7. Jason W. Moore, *Capitalism in the Web of Life* (New York: Verso, 2015), 30.

8. Hamilton, qtd. in Hamilton and Grinevald, "Was the Anthropocene Anticipated?," 67.

9. Kevis Goodman, *Georgic Modernity and British Romanticism: Poetry and the Mediation of History* (Cambridge: Cambridge University Press, 2008), 1.

10. Heather Davis and Étienne Turpin, "Art & Death: Lives Between the Fifth Assessment and the Sixth Extinction," in *Art in the Anthropocene: Encounters among Aesthetics, Politics, Environments and Epistemologies*, ed. Heather Davis and Étienne Turpin (London: Open Humanities, 2015), 4.

11. Rob Nixon, *Slow Violence and the Environmentalism of the Poor* (Cambridge, Mass.: Harvard University Press, 2011), 3.

12. See also Adam Trexler, *Anthropocene Fictions: The Novel in a Time of Climate Change* (Charlottesville: University of Virginia Press, 2015). Trexler argues that "the narrative difficulties of the Anthropocene threaten to rupture the defining features of genre."

13. Nixon, *Slow Violence*, 3.

14. Maureen McLane, *Mz N: The Serial* (New York: Farrar, Straus and Giroux, 2016), 110.

15. Lewis and Maslin, "Defining the Anthropocene," 178.

16. These poets are perhaps theoreticians in the way Jasper Bernes describes the activity of theory: "Theory is a map produced by the lost themselves, offering us the difficult view from within rather than the clarity of the Olympian view from above"; Bernes, "Logistics, Counterlogistics, and the Communist Prospect," *Endnotes*, accessed June 10, 2017, https://endnotes.org .uk/issues/3/en/jasper-bernes-logistics-counterlogistics-and-the-communist -prospect.

17. Roy Scranton, *Learning to Die in the Anthropocene: Reflections on the End of a Civilization* (San Francisco: City Light, 2015), 25. Scranton writes, "The greatest challenge we face is a philosophical one: understanding that this civilization is already dead. The sooner we confront our situation and realize that there is nothing we can do to save ourselves, the sooner we can get down to the difficult task of adapting, with mortal humility, to our new reality."

18. Ronda, "Anthropogenic Poetics," 109.

19. Hannah Arendt, *The Origins of Totalitarianism* (New York: Harcourt, Brace, Jovanovich, 1973), 267. Recent accounts of the postwar period from the perspective of the Global South, such as Vijay Prashad's *The Poorer Nations: A Possible History of the Global South* (New York: Verso, 2012), recover moments in which nations from the South provide clear alternatives to the ideology of neoliberalism.

20. Judith Butler, "Precarious Life, Vulnerability, and the Ethics of Cohabitation," *Journal of Speculative Philosophy* 26 (2012): 136.

21. Emmanuel Levinas, *Totality and Infinity: An Essay on Exteriority*, trans. Alphonso Lingis (Pittsburgh, Pa.: Duquesne University Press, 1961), 86, 171. An ethics of adjacency or laterality appears in works as diverse as Jean-Luc Nancy's *Being Singular Plural* (Stanford, Calif.: Stanford University Press, 2000); Eve Kosofsky Sedgwick's *Touching Feeling: Affect, Pedagogy, Performativity* (Durham, N.C.: Duke University Press, 2003); Lauren Berlant's *Cruel Optimism* (Durham, N.C.: Duke University Press, 2011); and Judith Butler's "Precarious Life, Vulnerability, and the Ethics of Cohabitation." This work joins efforts by Michael Hardt and Antonio Negri (*Multitude: War and Democracy in the Age of Empire* [New York: Penguin, 2004]); Silvia Federici (*Revolution at Point Zero: Housework, Reproduction, and Feminist Struggle* [Oakland, Calif.: PM Press, 2012]); and Peter Linebaugh (*The Magna Carta Manifesto: Liberties and Commons for All* [Berkeley: University of California Press, 2009]) to rethink the commons as a form of resistance to austerity and economic globalization.

22. Ralph Cohen uses the "prospect view" to describe a general practice in which "Augustan poetry converts inherited poetic features or conventions by relating them to scientific spatial assumptions, to philosophical assumptions regarding the acquisition of knowledge by experience, experiment and observation, and to religious assumptions that connect local observation with God's presence in infinity"; Cohen, "The Augustan Mode in English Poetry," *Eighteenth-Century Studies* 1 (1967): 9. Although Cohen notes that the prospect view reinforces, during the Restoration, "the harmonious power of the landed squires as supporters of country and God," his influential article identifies the specific traits of the "Augustan mode" rather than the historical conditions that give rise to this mode.

23. M. H. Abrams and Geoffrey Galt Harpham, *A Glossary of Literary Terms* (Independence, Ky.: Cengage Learning, 2011), 403; see also Timothy Brownlow, "A Molehill for Parnassus: John Clare and Prospect Poetry," *University of Toronto Quarterly* 48 (1978): 23.

24. Jennifer Keith, *Poetry and the Feminine from Behn to Cooper* (Newark: University of Delaware Press, 2005), 83. *Cooper's Hill* shares its combination of royalist panegyrics and topographical description with its contemporary, Edmund Waller's "Upon his Majesty's Repairing of Paul's" (1645).

25. Robert Cummings, ed., *Seventeenth-Century Poetry* (New York: Blackwell, 2006), 355.

26. Ibid., 359.

27. Thomas Gray, *Selected Poems* (London: Bloomsbury, 1997), 607–8.

28. Ibid., 607–8.

29. Keith, *Poetry and the Feminine*, 81.

30. Ibid., 90.

31. Roger Lonsdale, ed., *Eighteenth Century Verse* (Oxford: Oxford University Press, 1984), 107.

32. Ibid., 280.

33. Charlotte Smith, *The Poems of Charlotte Smith* (Oxford: Oxford University Press, 1993), 219.

34. John Keats, *The Complete Poems* (New York: Penguin, 1988), 77.

35. Levinas, *Totality*, 26.

36. In her work on precarious life, Butler examines "times when, in spite of ourselves and quite apart from any intentional act, we are nevertheless solicited by images of distant suffering in ways that compel our concern and move us to act, that is, to voice our objection and register our resistance to such violence through concrete political means"; Butler, "Precarious Life," 135. See also Bruce Robbins, "Blaming the System," in *Immanuel Wallerstein and the Problem of the World: System, Scale, Culture*, ed. David Palumbo-Liu, Bruce Robbins, and Nirvana Tanoukhi (Durham, N.C.: Duke University Press, 2011).

37. Prashad, *Poorer Nations*, 59–60.

38. Stuart Hall, "Culture, Community, Nation," *Cultural Studies* 7 (1993): 354.

39. Rainer Maria Rilke, *Collected Poems*, trans. Stephen Mitchell (New York: Vintage, 1989), 197.

40. Walter Benjamin, *Gesammelte Schriften* (Frankfurt am Main: Suhrkamp Verlag, 1972), 4:408; my translation.

41. Perhaps the relation between the uncertain movement down a hill and philosophical and emotional investigations appears as early as the first sentence of Plato's *Republic* ("I went down to the Piraeus") and of the descents into the underworld of Gilgamesh, Odysseus, and Aeneas.

42. J. H. Prynne, *The White Stones* (New York: New York Review of Books, 2016), 35.

43. Burt, *From There*, 19.

44. Keston Sutherland, "Hilarious Absolute Daybreak," *Glossator* 2 (2010): 115.

45. Prynne, *White Stones*, 57.

46. Prynne, "The Art of Poetry No. 101 (Interview)," *Paris Review* 218 (2016): 205.

47. Prynne, *White Stones*, 77.

48. In his study of poetic structures as "pictograms" of poetic statements, Justus George Lawler argues that enjambment occurs "when assaying that situation in which, after repeated frustration, the human subject suddenly experiences the overcoming of limitations and an expansion into something beyond those limits"; Lawler, *Celestial Pantomime: Poetic Structures of Transcendence* (New Haven, Conn.: Yale University Press, 1979), 74.

49. Martin Tucker, "Kofi Awoonor's Prison," *Worldview Magazine* 22 (1979): 22.

50. See George Vecsey, "Arrest of a Poet in Ghana Stirs Stony Brook Campus," *New York Times*, http://www.nytimes.com/1976/02/22/archives/arrest-of-a-poet-in-ghana-stirs-stony-brook-campus-ambassador.html.

51. Teju Cole, *Known and Strange Things: Essays* (New York: Random House, 2016), 271.

52. Kofi Awoonor, *The House by the Sea* (New York: Greenfield Review Press, 1978), 25.

53. Qtd. in Tucker, "Kofi Awoonor's Prison," 24.

54. For his translations of Ewe poetry, see Awoonor, *Guardians of the Sacred Word: Ewe Poetry* (New York: NOK, 1974).

55. Fred Moten, "Blackness and Nothingness (Mysticism in the Flesh)," *South Atlantic Quarterly* 112 (2013): 738.

56. Ibid., 738.

57. Awoonor, *House*, 36.

58. Édouard Glissant, *Poetics of Relation*, trans. Betsy Wing (Ann Arbor: University of Michigan Press, 1997), 9.

59. Prashad identifies the elements of what he and others call a "new geography of production": "the breakdown of the factory regimes across the world (post-Fordism), the emergence of the new technological infrastructure (computers, satellites), and the magnetic attraction of all the planet's wealth to the all-powerful financial centers of the North (financialization)"; Prashad, *Poorer Nations*, 88.

60. Natasha Trethewey, *Beyond Katrina: A Meditation on the Mississippi Gulf Coast* (Athens: University of Georgia Press, 2010), 51.

61. Prashad, *Poorer Nations*, 5.

62. Trethewey, *Beyond Katrina*, 2.

63. Ibid., 12.

64. Ibid., 51.

65. Ibid., 50–51.

66. Berlant, *Cruel Optimism*, 100.

67. Trethewey, *Beyond Katrina*, 52.

68. Elliott Colla, "The Poetry of Revolt," *Jadaliyya*, accessed August 26, 2017, http://www.jadaliyya.com/pages/index/506/the-poetry-of-revolt/.

69. Juliana Spahr, *That Winter the Wolf Came* (Oakland, Calif.: Commune, 2015), 11.

70. Spahr, *Winter*, 14.

71. Ibid., 16.

72. Ibid., 16–17.

73. Ibid., 39.

74. Timothy Morton, "Ecology without the Present," *Oxford Literary Review* 34 (2012): 231.

75. Spahr, *Winter*, 42.

76. Ibid., 42.

CODA

1. John Ashbery, *Collected Poems 1956–1987* (New York: Library of America, 2008), 252.

2. See Martin Albrow, *The Global Age: State and Society Beyond Modernity* (Stanford, Calif.: Stanford University Press, 1997).

3. See, in particular, the recent work on the literature of combined and uneven development from the Warwick Research Collective and the responses collected in *Comparative Literature Studies*. The WReC argues, in a deft formulation, that "the effectivity of the world-system will *necessarily* be discernible in any modern literary work, since the world-system exists

unforgoably as the matrix within which all modern literature takes shape and comes into being"; Warwick Research Collective, *Combined and Uneven Development: Towards a New Theory of World-Literature* (Liverpool: Liverpool University Press, 2015), 20.

4. Aamir Mufti writes that "under the conditions of neoliberal capitalism, whenever English rises to dominance in a particular cultural and social sphere for the first time . . . it seems at once to naturalize itself, erasing the scene of politics and power that marks its emergence"; Mufti, *Forget English! Orientalisms and World Literature* (Cambridge, Mass.: Harvard University Press, 2016), 16.

5. *DOD Dictionary of Military and Associated Terms* (Washington, D.C.: Joint Chiefs of Staff, 2007), 318.

6. Zinzi Clemmons, "The Role of the Poet: An Interview with Solmaz Sharif," *Paris Review*, http://www.theparisreview.org/blog/2016/07/27/the -role-of-the-poet-an-interview-with-solmaz-sharif/.

7. Emily Brown Coolidge Toker, "What Makes a Native Speaker? Nativeness, Ownership, and Global Englishes," *minnesota review* 78 (2012): 113.

8. Michael Gordin has written a history of the dominance of English on a global scale in scientific research. Gordin writes that "today, English is not only the dominant form of international scientific publication and oral communication at conferences and in multinational laboratories—it is almost always the *only* language of such communication"; Gordin, *Scientific Babel: How Science Was Done Before and After Global English* (Chicago: University of Chicago Press, 2015), 293–94.

9. David Harvey, *The New Imperialism* (Oxford: Oxford University Press, 2003), 183.

10. Giovanni Arrighi, *The Long Twentieth Century* (London: Verso, 2010), 8.

11. Timothy Mitchell, *Carbon Democracy: Political Power in the Age of Oil* (New York: Verso, 2011), 155.

12. Solmaz Sharif, *Look* (Minneapolis: Graywolf, 2016), 3.

13. Laleh Khalili, *Time in the Shadows: Confinement in Counterinsurgencies* (Stanford, Calif.: Stanford University Press, 2013), 241.

14. Adrienne Rich, *Later Poems: Selected and New, 1971–2012* (New York: W. W. Norton, 2013), 132.

15. Gordin, *Scientific Babel*, 294.

16. *DOD Dictionary*, ii.

17. Khalili, *Time*, 48.

BIBLIOGRAPHY

Aarons, K. "No Selves to Abolish: Afropessimism, Anti-Politics, and the End of the World." *Mute*. Accessed August 26, 2017. http://www.metamute.org/editorial/articles/no-selves-to-abolish-afropessimism-anti-politics-and-end-world.

Abrahamian, Atossa Araxia. *The Cosmopolites: The Coming of the Global Citizen*. New York: Columbia University Press, 2016.

Abrams, M. H. "Structure and Style in the Greater Romantic Lyric." In *From Sensibility to Romanticism: Essays Presented to Frederick A. Pottle*, edited by Frederick W. Hilles and Harold Bloom, 527–60. New York: Oxford University Press, 1965.

Abrams, M. H., and Geoffrey Galt Harpham. *A Glossary of Literary Terms*. Independence, Ky.: Cengage Learning, 2011.

Abu-Lughod, Janet. *Before European Hegemony: The World System A.D. 1250–1350*. Oxford: Oxford University Press, 1989.

Adorno, Theodor. "On Lyric Poetry and Society." In *Notes to Literature*, translated by Shierry Weber Nicholsen, edited by Rolf Tiedemann, 1:37–54. New York: Columbia University Press, 1991.

Agamben, Giorgio. *The End of the Poem*. Translated by Daniel Heller-Roazen. Stanford, Calif.: Stanford University Press, 1999.

Aisbett, Emma. "Why Are the Critics So Convinced That Globalization Is Bad for the Poor?" In *Globalization and Poverty*, edited by Ann Harrison, 33–51. Chicago: University of Chicago Press, 2007.

Albright, Daniel. *Lyricality in English Literature*. Lincoln: University of Nebraska Press, 1985.

Albrow, Martin. *The Global Age: State and Society Beyond Modernity*. Stanford, Calif.: Stanford University Press, 1997.

Ali, Agha Shahid. *Bone-Sculpture*. Calcutta: Writer's Workshop, 1972.
———. *Call Me Ishmael Tonight*. New York: Norton, 2003.
———. *In Memory of Begum Akhtar*. Calcutta: Writer's Workshop, 1979.
———, ed. *Ravishing DisUnities*. Middletown, Conn.: Wesleyan University Press, 2000.

Altieri, Charles. *The Art of Twentieth-Century American Poetry: Modernism and After*. Malden, Mass.: Blackwell, 2006.
———. *Self and Sensibility in Contemporary American Poetry*. Cambridge: Cambridge University Press, 1984.
Anker, Elizabeth. *Fictions of Dignity: Embodying Human Rights in World Literature*. Ithaca, N.Y.: Cornell University Press, 2012.
Appadurai, Arjun. *Banking on Words: The Failure of Language in the Age of Derivative Finance*. Chicago: University of Chicago Press, 2015.
———. "Disjuncture and Difference in the Global Cultural Economy." *Public Culture* 2 (1990): 1–24.
Apter, Emily. *Against World Literature: On the Politics of Untranslatability*. New York: Verso, 2013.
Arac, Jonathan. Conclusion. In *Lyric Poetry: Beyond New Criticism*, edited by Chaviva Hošek and Patricia A. Parker, 344–55. Ithaca, N.Y.: Cornell University Press, 1985.
Arendt, Hannah. *The Origins of Totalitarianism*. New York: Harcourt, Brace, Jovanovich, 1973.
Aristotle. *Rhetoric*. Translated by W. Rhys Roberts. New York: Cosimo, 2010.
Armantrout, Rae. *Money Shot*. Middletown, Conn.: Wesleyan University Press, 2012.
———. "Why Don't Women Do Language-Oriented Writing?" In *In the American Tree: Language, Realism, Poetry*, ed. Ron Silliman, 518–20. Orono, Maine: National Poetry Foundation, 2007.
Arrighi, Giovanni. *The Long Twentieth Century*. London: Verso, 2010.
Ashbery, John. *Collected Poems 1956–1987*. New York: Library of America, 2008.
———. *Planisphere*. New York: Ecco, 2009.
Ashton, Jennifer. "Labor and the Lyric: The Politics of Self-Expression in Contemporary American Poetry." *American Literary History* 25 (2013): 217–30.
Auden, W. H. *Collected Poems*. Edited by Edward Mendelson. New York: Vintage, 1991.
Awoonor, Kofi. *Guardians of the Sacred Word: Ewe Poetry*. New York: NOK, 1974.
———. *The House by the Sea*. New York: Greenfield Review Press, 1978.
Baucom, Ian. "Found Drowned: The Irish Atlantic." *Nineteenth-Century Contexts* 22 (2000): 103–38.
Bayly, C. A. *The Birth of the Modern World: 1780–1914*. Malden, Mass.: Blackwell, 2004.
Bell, Kevin. "Unheard Writing in the Climate of Spectacular Noise: Claudia Rankine on TV." *Global South* 3 (2009): 93–107.
Benjamin, Walter. *Gesammelte Schriften*. Vol. 4. Frankfurt am Main: Suhrkamp Verlag, 1972.

———. *Illuminations*. Translated by Harry Zohn. New York: Schocken, 1968.

Berardi, Franco "Bifo." *The Uprising: On Poetry and Finance*. Los Angeles: Semiotext(e), 2012.

Berlant, Lauren. *Cruel Optimism*. Durham, N.C.: Duke University Press, 2011.

Bernes, Jasper. "John Ashbery's Free Indirect Labor." *Modern Language Quarterly* 74 (2013): 517–40.

———. "Logistics, Counterlogistics, and the Communist Prospect." *Endnotes*. Accessed June 10, 2017. https://endnotes.org.uk/issues/3/en/jasper-bernes-logistics-counterlogistics-and-the-communist-prospect.

———. *The Work of Art in the Age of Deindustrialization*. Stanford, Calif.: Stanford University Press, 2017.

Bernstein, Charles. "Poetics of the Americas." *Modernism/modernity* 3 (1996): 1–23.

———, ed. *The Politics of Poetic Form*. New York: Roof 1990.

Black, Stephanie. *Life and Debt*. Kingston, Jamaica: Tuff Gong Pictures, 2001.

Blasing, Mutlu Konuk. *Lyric Poetry: The Pain and the Pleasure of Words*. Princeton, N.J.: Princeton University Press, 2007.

Bloch, Ariel, and Chana Bloch, trans. *The Song of Songs*. Berkeley: University of California Press, 1995.

Bloomberg-Rissman, John. Review of *The Commons*, by Sean Bonney. *Galatea Resurrects*. Accessed February 24, 2016. http://galatearesurrection17.blogspot.com/2011/12/commons-by-sean-bonney.html.

Boltanski, Luc, and Eve Chiapello. *The New Spirit of Capitalism*. Translated by Gregory Elliott. New York: Verso, 2006.

Bonney, Sean. *Blade Pitch Control Unit*. Cambridge: Salt Press, 2005.

———. *The Commons*. London: Opennned, 2011.

Bourdieu, Pierre. *Acts of Resistance: Against the Tyranny of the Market*. Translated by Richard Nice. Cambridge: Polity, 1998.

Boyer, Anne. *Garments against Women*. Boise, Idaho: Ahsahta, 2015.

Bozovic, Marijeta. *Avant-Garde Post-: Radical Poetics After the Soviet Union*. Forthcoming.

Braudel, Fernand. *The Mediterranean and the Mediterranean World in the Age of Philip II*. Translated by Siân Reynolds. Berkeley: University of California Press, 1995.

———. *The Wheels of Commerce*. Vol. 2, *Civilization and Capitalism: 15th-18th Century*. Translated by Siân Reynolds. Berkeley: University of California Press, 1992.

Brik, Osip M. "Contributions to the Study of Verse Language." Translated by C. H. Severens. In *Readings in Russian Poetics*, edited by Ladislav Matejka and Krystyna Pomorska, 117–25. Chicago: Dalkey Archive Press, 2002.

Brooks, Cleanth. "Criticism and Literary History: Marvell's Horatian Ode." *Sewanee Review* 55 (1947): 199–222.

Brownlow, Timothy. "A Molehill for Parnassus: John Clare and Prospect Poetry." *University of Toronto Quarterly* 48 (1978): 23–40.

Burt, Stephanie. "Agha Shahid Ali: 'Tonight.'" *Poetry Foundation*. Accessed August 27, 2017. https://www.poetryfoundation.org/articles/69597/agha -shahid-ali-tonight.

———. "American Poetry at the End of the Millennium." In *The Cambridge History of American Poetry*, edited by Alfred Bendixen and Stephen Burt, 1144–66. Cambridge: Cambridge University Press, 2015.

———. *From There: Some Thoughts on Poetry and Place*. Vancouver, B.C.: Ronsdale, 2016.

———. "Sestina! Or the Fate of the Idea of Form." *Modern Philology* 105 (2007): 218–41.

Bush, Douglas. "Marvell's 'Horatian Ode.'" *Sewanee Review* 60 (1952): 363–76.

Butler, Judith. *Precarious Life*. New York: Verso, 2004.

———. "Precarious Life, Vulnerability, and the Ethics of Cohabitation." *Journal of Speculative Philosophy* 26 (2012): 134–51.

Caplan, David. *Questions of Possibility: Contemporary Poetry and Poetic Form*. Oxford: Oxford University Press, 2006.

Centano, Miguel A., and Joseph N. Cohen. "The Arc of Neoliberalism." *Annual Review of Sociology* 38 (2012): 317–40.

Chakrabarty, Dipesh. *Provincializing Europe*. Princeton, N.J.: Princeton University Press, 2000.

Chazkel, Amy, and David Serlin. "Editors' Introduction." *Radical History Review* 109 (2010): 1–11.

Chiu, Jeannie. "Identities in Process: The Experimental Poetry of Mei-mei Berssenbrugge and Myung Mi Kim." In *Asian North American Identities: Beyond the Hyphen*, edited by Eleanor Ty and Donald C. Goellnicht, 84–101. Bloomington: Indiana University Press, 2004.

Clancy, Sarah. *The Truth and Other Stories*. Cliffs of Moher, Ireland: Salmon, 2014.

Clayton, Michelle. *Poetry in Pieces: César Vallejo and Lyric Modernity*. Berkeley: University of California Press, 2011.

Clover, Joshua. "*Retcon*: Value and Temporality in Poetics." *Representations* 126 (2014): 9–30.

———. *Riot. Strike. Riot: The New Era of Uprisings*. New York: Verso, 2016.

Cohen, Ralph. "The Augustan Mode in English Poetry." *Eighteenth-Century Studies* 1 (1967): 3–32.

Cole, Rachel. "Rethinking the Value of Lyric Closure: Giorgio Agamben, Wallace Stevens, and the Ethics of Satisfaction." *PMLA* 126 (2011): 383–97.

Cole, Teju. *Known and Strange Things: Essays*. New York: Random House, 2016.

Colla, Elliott. "The Poetry of Revolt." *Jadaliyya*. Accessed August 26, 2017. http://www.jadaliyya.com /pages/index/506/the-poetry-of-revolt/.

Comaroff, John L., and Jean Comaroff. *Ethnicity, Inc.* Chicago: University of Chicago Press, 2009.

Cooke, Jennifer. **not suitable for domestic sublimation*. London: Contraband, 2012.

Costello, Bonnie. "Elizabeth Bishop's Impersonal Personal." *American Literary History* 15 (2003): 334–66.

———. "Lyric Poetry and the First-Person Plural: 'How Unlikely.'" In *Something Understood: Essays and Poetry for Helen Vendler*, edited by Stephanie Burt and Nick Halpern, 193–206. Charlottesville: University of Virginia Press, 2009.

———. "The Plural of Us." *Jacket2*. Accessed August 26, 2017. http://jacket2.org/article/plural-us.

Crutzen, Paul J., and Eugene F. Stoermer. "The 'Anthropocene.'" *IGBP Global Change Newsletter* 41 (2000): 17–18.

Culler, Jonathan. "Apostrophe." *diacritics* 7 (1977): 59–69.

———. "Introduction: Critical Paradigms." *PMLA* 125 (2010): 905–15.

———. "Lyric, History, and Genre." *New Literary History* 40 (2009): 879–99.

———. "The Lyric in Theory: A Conversation with Jonathan Culler." In *Los Angeles Review of Books*. Accessed May 27, 2017. https://lareviewofbooks.org/article/the-lyric-in-theory-a-conversation-with-jonathan-culler/.

———. *Theory of the Lyric*. Cambridge, Mass.: Harvard University Press, 2015.

Cummings, Robert, ed. *Seventeenth-Century Poetry*. New York: Blackwell, 2006.

Damrosch, David. *What Is World Literature?* Princeton, N.J.: Princeton University Press, 2003.

Davidson, Michael. "Introduction: American Poetry, 2000–2009." *Contemporary Literature* 52 (2011): 597–629.

Davis, Heather, and Etienne Turpin. "Art & Death: Lives between the Fifth Assessment and the Sixth Extinction." In *Art in the Anthropocene: Encounters among Aesthetics, Politics, Environments and Epistemologies*, edited by Heather Davis and Étienne Turpin, 3–29. London: Open Humanities, 2015.

Davis, Mike. *Planet of Slums*. New York: Verso, 2006.

De'Ath, Amy. "Unsociable Poetry: Antagonism and Abstraction in Contemporary Feminized Poetics." Ph.D. diss., Simon Fraser University, 2017.

de Man, Paul. "Autobiography as De-facement." *MLN* 94, no. 5 (1979): 919–30.

———. *Blindness and Insight*. Minneapolis: University of Minnesota Press, 1983.

DoD Dictionary of Military and Associated Terms. Washington, D.C.: Joint Chiefs of Staff, 2007.

Desai, Radhika. *Geopolitical Economy: After US Hegemony, Globalization, and Empire*. London: Pluto, 2013.

Diaz, Natalie. "A Poet Subverts the Defense Department's Official Dictionary." *New York Times*. Accessed May 15, 2017. https://www.nytimes.com/2016/08/21/books/review/look-poems-solmaz-sharif.html?_r=0.

Dickinson, Emily. *The Poems of Emily Dickinson*. Edited by R. W. Franklin. Cambridge, Mass.: Harvard University Press, 1999.

Dowdy, Michael. *Broken Souths: Latina/o Poetic Responses to Neoliberalism and Globalization*. Tucson: University of Arizona Press, 2013.

Dowling, Sarah. "Interpolation, Coherence, History: The Works of Myung Mi Kim." In *Nests and Strangers: On Asian American Women Poets*, edited by Timothy Yu, 15–19. Berkeley, Calif.: Kelsey Street Press, 2015.

Edmond, Jacob. *A Common Strangeness: Contemporary Poetry, Cross-Cultural Encounter, Comparative Literature*. New York: Fordham University Press, 2012.

———. "'Their Echoes Split Us': Sean Bonney Rewrites Baudelaire and Rimbaud." *Jacket2*. Accessed February 24, 2016. http://jacket2.org/commentary/%E2%80%9Ctheir-echoes-split-us%E2%80%9D.

Eggan, Taylor A. "Regionalizing the Planet: Horizons of the Introverted Novel at World Literature's End." *PMLA* 131 (2016): 1299–1315.

Eliot, T. S. *The Complete Poetry and Plays, 1909–1950*. New York: Harcourt Brace, 1980.

———. *On Poetry and Poets*. New York: Farrar, Straus and Giroux, 2009.

Federici, Sylvia. *Revolution at Point Zero: Housework, Reproduction, and Feminist Struggle*. Oakland, Calif.: PM Press, 2012.

Feinsod, Harris. *The Poetry of the Americas: From Good Neighbors to Countercultures*. Oxford: Oxford University Press, 2017.

Ferguson, James. *Global Shadows: Africa in the Neoliberal World Order*. Durham, N.C.: Duke University Press, 2006.

Ferguson, Roderick. "On *Citizen*: Ethics and Method." *Los Angeles Review of Books*. Accessed August 26, 2017. https://lareviewofbooks.org/article/reconsidering-claudia-rankines-citizen-an-american-lyric-a-symposium-part-i/.

Fogle, Stephen F., and Paul H. Fry. "Ode." In *Princeton Encyclopedia of Poetry and Poetics*, edited by Roland Greene, 971–73. Princeton, N.J.: Princeton University Press, 2012.

"Forum: Global Poetics." Edited by Walt Hunter. *ASAP/Journal* 1, no. 3 (September 2016): 365–88.

Frye, Northrop. *Anatomy of Criticism: Four Essays*. Toronto: University of Toronto Press, 2006.

Furani, Khaled. *Silencing the Sea: Secular Rhythms in Palestinian Poetry*. Stanford, Calif.: Stanford University Press, 2012.

Galeano, Eduardo. *Soccer in Sun and Shadow*. New York: Nation, 2013.

Galella, Donatella. "(Re)Presenting the South Bronx." *PAJ: A Journal of Performance and Art* 33 (2011): 82–88.

Gallagher, Mary. "Poetics, Ethics, and Globalization." In *World Writing: Poetics, Ethics, Globalization*, edited by Mary Gallagher, 3–61. Toronto: University of Toronto Press, 2008.

Galvin, Rachel. *News of War: Civilian Poetry 1936–1945*. Oxford: Oxford University Press, 2017.

Ganti, Tejaswini. "Neoliberalism." *Annual Review of Anthropology* 43 (2014): 89–104.

Genette, Gérard. *The Architext*. Translated by Jane E. Lewin. Berkeley: University of California Press, 1992.

Ghosh, Amitav. "'The Ghat of the Only World': Agha Shahid Ali in Brooklyn." *Annual of Urdu Studies* 17 (2002): 311–23.

Giddens, Anthony. *The Consequences of Modernity*. Stanford, Calif.: Stanford University Press, 1990.

Gikandi, Simon. "Preface: Modernism in the World." *Modernism/modernity* 13 (2006): 419–24.

Gilroy, Paul. *The Black Atlantic: Modernity and Double Consciousness*. London: Verso, 1993.

Glissant, Édouard. *Caribbean Discourse*. Translated by J. Michael Dash. Charlottesville: University of Virginia Press, 1989.

———. *Poetics of Relation*. Translated by Betsy Wing. Ann Arbor: University of Michigan Press, 1997.

Goodman, Kevis. *Georgic Modernity and British Romanticism: Poetry and the Mediation of History*. Cambridge: Cambridge University Press, 2008.

Gordin, Michael. *Scientific Babel: How Science Was Done Before and After Global English*. Chicago: University of Chicago Press, 2015.

Gray, Thomas. *Selected Poems*. London: Bloomsbury, 1997.

Greene, Roland. "The Lyric." In *The Cambridge History of Literary Criticism*, edited by Glyn P. Norton, 3:216–28. Cambridge: Cambridge University Press, 1999.

———. *Post-Petrarchism: Origins and Innovations of the Western Poetic Sequence*. Princeton, N.J.: Princeton University Press, 1991.

Grossman, Allen. *The Sighted Singer: Two Works on Poetry for Readers and Writers*. Baltimore: Johns Hopkins University Press, 1991.

Hall, Stuart. "Culture, Community, Nation." *Cultural Studies* 7 (1993): 349–63.

Hamilton, Clive, and Jacques Grinevald. "Was the Anthropocene Anticipated?" *Anthropocene Review* 2 (2015): 59–72.

Hardt, Michael, and Antonio Negri. *Multitude: War and Democracy in the Age of Empire.* New York: Penguin, 2004.

Harlow, Barbara, Sarah Brouillette, David Thomas, Maria Elisa Cevasco, Joshua Clover, and David Damrosch. "First Responses." *Comparative Literature Studies* 53 (2016): 503–34.

Hart, Matthew. *Nations of Nothing But Poetry: Modernism, Transnationalism, and Synthetic Vernacular Writing.* New York: Oxford University Press, 2010.

Hartman, Geoffrey, and Daniel T. O'Hara, eds. *The Geoffrey Hartman Reader.* New York: Fordham University Press, 2004.

Hartman, Saidiya. *Scenes of Subjection: Terror, Slavery, and Self-Making in Nineteenth-Century America.* Oxford: Oxford University Press, 1997.

Harvey, David. *A Brief History of Neoliberalism.* Oxford: Oxford University Press, 2007.

———. *The Enigma of Capital and the Crises of Capitalism.* London: Profile, 2010.

———. "The Future of The Commons." *Radical History Review* 109 (2010): 101–7.

———. *The New Imperialism.* Oxford: Oxford University Press, 2003.

Hayot, Eric. *On Literary Worlds.* New York: Oxford University Press, 2012.

Heaney, Seamus. "Banks of a Canal." *Guardian.* Accessed August 15, 2016. https://www.theguardian.com/books/2014/oct/03/seamus-heaney-last -poem-national-gallery-ireland-anthology.

———. "Current Unstated Assumptions about Poetry." *Critical Inquiry* 7 (1981): 645–51.

———. *Opened Ground.* New York: Farrar, Straus and Giroux, 1998.

———. "'Place and Displacement': Recent Poetry from Northern Ireland." *Wordsworth Circle* 16 (1985): 48–56.

———. *The Redress of Poetry.* New York: Farrar, Straus and Giroux, 1995.

Hegel, G. W. F. *Aesthetics: Lectures on Fine Arts.* Vol. 1. Translated by T. M. Knox. Oxford: Oxford University Press, 1975.

Held, David, and Anthony McGrew. "The End of the Old Order? Globalization and the Prospects for World Order." *Review of International Studies* 24 (1998): 219–43.

Hill, Christopher L. *Reformation to Industrial Revolution: A Social and Economic History of Britain, 1530–1780.* New York: Penguin, 1967.

Hölderlin, Friedrich. *Selected Verse.* Translated by Michael Hamburger. London: Anvil Press Poetry, 1986.

Hong, Cathy Park. "Delusions of Whiteness in the Avant-Garde." *Lana Turner.* Accessed February 18, 2016. http://www.lanaturnerjournal.com/ 7/delusions-of-whiteness-in-the-avant-garde.

Hošek, Chaviva, and Patricia A. Parker, eds. *Lyric Poetry: Beyond New Criticism.* Ithaca, N.Y.: Cornell University Press, 1985.

Hume, Angela. "Toward an Anti-Racist Ecopoetics: Waste and Wasting in the Poetry of Claudia Rankine." *Contemporary Literature* 57 (2016): 79–110.

Israel, Nico. "Globalization and Contemporary Literature." *Literature Compass* 104 (2004): 1–5.

Jackson, Virginia. *Dickinson's Misery: A Theory of Lyric Reading*. Princeton, N.J.: Princeton University Press, 2005.

Jackson, Virginia, and Yopie Prins, eds. *The Lyric Theory Reader*. Baltimore: Johns Hopkins University Press, 2013.

Jakobson, Roman. "Closing Statement: Linguistics and Poetics." In *Style in Language*, edited by T. A. Sebeok, 350–77. New York: Wiley and Sons, 1960.

———. *Language in Literature*. Edited by Krystyna Pomorska and Stephen Rudy. Cambridge, Mass.: Harvard University Press, 1987.

Jameson, Fredric. *The Prison House of Language: A Critical Account of Structuralism and Russian Formalism*. Princeton, N.J.: Princeton University Press, 1975.

———. *Valences of the Dialectic*. New York: Verso, 2009.

Jay, Paul. *Global Matters: The Transnational Turn in Literary Studies*. Ithaca, N.Y.: Cornell University Press, 2010.

Jeffreys, Mark. "Ideologies of Lyric: A Problem of Genre in Contemporary Anglophone Poetics." *PMLA* 110 (1995): 196–205.

Jenkins, G. Matthew. *Poetic Obligation: Ethics in Experimental Poetry after 1945*. Iowa City: University of Iowa Press, 2008.

Jeon, Joseph Jonghyun. "Asian American Poetry." In *The Cambridge History of American Poetry*, edited by Alfred Bendixen and Stephanie Burt, 978–1002. Cambridge: Cambridge University Press, 2015.

———. 2012. *Racial Things, Racial Forms: Objecthood in Avant-Garde Asian American Poetry*. Iowa City: University of Iowa Press.

Johnson, Barbara. "Apostrophe, Animation, and Abortion." *diacritics* 16 (1986): 28–47.

Johnson, Samuel. *Lives of the English Poets*. Edited by George Birkbeck Hill. Vol. 3. Oxford: Clarendon, 1945.

Jones, Elizabeth. "Writing for the Market: Keats's Odes as Commodities." *Studies in Romanticism* 34 (1995): 343–64.

Kahn, Hilary E. "Introduction." In *Framing the Global: Entry Points for Research*, edited by Hilary E. Kahn, 1–17. Bloomington: Indiana University Press, 2014.

Kaufman, Robert. "Adorno's Social Lyric, and Literary Criticism Today: Poetics, Aesthetics, Modernity." In *The Cambridge Companion to Adorno*, edited by Tom Huhn, 354–75. Cambridge: Cambridge University Press, 2004.

Keats, John. *The Complete Poems*. New York: Penguin, 1988.

Keith, Jennifer. *Poetry and the Feminine from Behn to Cooper*. Newark: University of Delaware Press, 2005.

Keller, Lynn. "An Interview with Myung Mi Kim." *Contemporary Literature* 49 (2008): 335–56.

Khalili, Laleh. *Time in the Shadows: Confinement in Counterinsurgencies*. Stanford, Calif.: Stanford University Press, 2013.

Kim, Myung Mi. *Commons*. Berkeley: University of California Press, 2002.

Kimberley, Emma. "Politics and Poetics of Fear After 9/11: Claudia Rankine's *Don't Let Me Be Lonely*." *Journal of American Studies* 45 (2011): 777–91.

Kitchin, Rob, Rory Hearne, and Cian O'Callaghan. "Housing in Ireland: From Crisis to Crisis." *NIRSA Working Paper Series* 77 (2015): 2–24.

Krippner, Greta. *Capitalizing on Crisis: The Political Origins of the Rise of Finance*. Cambridge, Mass.: Harvard University Press, 2011.

Komorowski, Michael. "Public Verse and Property: Marvell's 'Horatian Ode' and the Ownership of Politics." *ELH* 79 (2012): 315–40.

Kuhnheim, Jill. *Beyond the Page: Poetry and Performance in Spanish America*. Tucson: University of Arizona Press, 2014.

Lacoue-Labarthe, Philippe. *Musica Ficta (Figures of Wagner)*. Translated by Felicia McCarren. Stanford, Calif.: Stanford University Press, 1991.

———. *Poetry as Experience*. Translated by Andrea Tarnowski. Stanford, Calif.: Stanford University Press, 1999.

Lawler, Justus George. *Celestial Pantomime: Poetic Structures of Transcendence*. New Haven, Conn.: Yale University Press, 1979.

Le Blanc, Guillaume. *Vies ordinaires, vies précaires*. Paris: Éditions du Seuil, 2007.

Levinas, Emmanuel. *Totality and Infinity: An Essay on Exteriority*. Translated by Alphonso Lingis. Pittsburgh, Pa.: Duquesne University Press, 1961.

Levien, Michael. "From Primitive Accumulation to Regimes of Dispossession." *Economic and Political Weekly* 50 (2015): 146–57.

———. "Regimes of Dispossession: From Steel Towns to Special Economic Zones." *Development and Change* 44 (2013): 381–407.

Lewis, Simon L., and Mark A. Maslin. "Defining the Anthropocene." *Nature* 519 (2015): 175–80.

Linebaugh, Peter. *The Magna Carta Manifesto: Liberties and Commons for All*. Berkeley: University of California Press, 2009.

Lisette, Francesca. *Teens*. Cambridge: Mountain Press, 2012.

Lonsdale, Roger, ed. *Eighteenth-Century Verse*. Oxford: Oxford University Press, 1984.

———, ed. *The New Oxford Book of Eighteenth Century Verse*. Oxford: Oxford University Press, 1984.

Lowell, Robert. *Life Studies and For the Union Dead*. New York: Farrar, Straus and Giroux, 1964.

Lorde, Audre. *Sister Outsider*. Trumansburg, N.Y.: Crossing, 1984.

Lorey, Isabell. *State of Insecurity: Government of the Precarious*. Translated by Aileen Derieg. New York: Verso, 2015.

Lotz, Christian. "Poetry as Anti-Discourse: Formalism, Hermeneutics, and the Poetics of Paul Celan." *Continental Philosophy Review* 44 (2011): 491–510.

Lowe, Lisa. *The Intimacies of Four Continents*. Durham, N.C.: Duke University Press, 2015.

Luna, Joe. *Astroturf*. Brighton: Hi Zero, 2012.

Macekura, Stephen. *Of Limits and Growth*. Cambridge: Cambridge University Press, 2015.

MacKenzie, Donald. *An Engine, Not a Camera: How Financial Models Shape Markets*. Cambridge, Mass.: MIT Press, 2006.

Maclean, Norman. "From Action to Image: Theories of the Lyric in the Eighteenth Century." In *Critics and Criticism: Ancient and Modern*, edited by R. S. Crane, 408–50. Chicago: University of Chicago Press, 1952.

Marx, John. *Geopolitics and the Anglophone Novel, 1890–2011*. Cambridge: Cambridge University Press, 2012.

Marx, Karl. *Capital*. Vol. 1, *A Critique of Political Economy*. Translated by Ben Fowkes. New York: Penguin, 1992.

McClanahan, Annie. *Dead Pledges: Debt, Crisis, and Twenty-First-Century Culture*. Stanford, Calif.: Stanford University Press, 2016.

McLane, Maureen. *Mz N: The Serial*. New York: Farrar, Straus and Giroux, 2016.

Medvedev, Kirill. "Beyond the Poetics of Privatization." *New Left Review* 82 (2013): 65–83.

Meehan, Paula. *Painting Rain*. Winston-Salem, N.C.: Wake Forest University Press, 2009.

Meillassoux, Quentin. *The Number and the Siren: A Decipherement of Mallarmé's "Coup de dés."* Translated by Robin Mackay. New York: Sequence/Urbanomic, 2012.

Melamed, Jodi. *Represent and Destroy: Rationalizing Violence in the New Racial Capitalism*. Minneapolis: University of Minnesota Press, 2011.

Mill, John Stuart. "Thoughts on Poetry and its Varieties." *Crayon* 7 (1860): 93–97.

Mitchell, Timothy. *Carbon Democracy: Political Power in the Age of Oil*. New York: Verso, 2011.

Moore, Jason W. *Capitalism in the Web of Life*. New York: Verso, 2015.

Morris, Marianne, Josh Stanley, Luke Roberts, and Sophie Robinson. *Untitled Colossal Parlour Odes*. Cambridge: Bad Press, 2010.

Morton, Timothy. *The Ecological Thought*. Cambridge, Mass.: Harvard University Press, 2010.

———. "Ecology without the Present." *Oxford Literary Review* 34 (2012): 229–38.

Moten, Fred. "Blackness and Nothingness (Mysticism in the Flesh)." *South Atlantic Quarterly* 112 (2013): 737–80.

———. *In the Break: The Aesthetics of the Black Radical Tradition*. Minneapolis: University of Minnesota Press, 2003.

Moten, Fred, and Stefano Harney. "The University and the Undercommons: Seven Theses." *Social Text* 22 (2004): 101–15.

Mufti, Aamir. *Forget English! Orientalisms and World Literature*. Cambridge, Mass.: Harvard University Press, 2016.

Nagy, Gregory. *Pindar's Homer: The Lyric Possession of an Epic Past*. Baltimore: Johns Hopkins University Press, 1990.

Naimou, Angela. *Salvage Work: U.S. and Caribbean Literatures amid the Debris of Legal Personhood*. New York: Fordham University Press, 2015.

Nancy, Jean-Luc. *Being Singular Plural*. Stanford, Calif.: Stanford University Press, 2000.

———. *Multiple Arts: The Muses II*. Edited by Simon Sparks. Stanford, Calif.: Stanford University Press, 2006.

Nealon, Christopher. *The Matter of Capital: Poetry and Crisis in the American Century*. Cambridge, Mass.: Harvard University Press, 2011.

———. *The Victorious Ones*. Oakland, Calif.: Commune Editions, 2015.

Neyrat, Frédéric. *Atopies*. Caen: Éditions Nous, 2014.

Nicholls, Peter. "Of Being Ethical: Reflections on George Oppen." *Journal of American Studies* 31 (1997): 153–70.

Nickels, Joel. *The Poetry of the Possible: Spontaneity, Modernism, and the Multitude*. Minneapolis: University of Minnesota Press, 2012.

Nixon, Rob. *Slow Violence and the Environmentalism of the Poor*. Cambridge, Mass.: Harvard University Press, 2011.

O'Brien, Karen. "'Still at Home': Cowper's Domestic Empires." In *Early Romantics: Perspectives in British Poetry from Pope to Wordsworth*, edited by Thomas Woodman, 134–47. London: Macmillan, 1998.

O'Callaghan, Cian, Mark Boyle, and Rob Kitchin. "Post-Politics, Crisis, and Ireland's Ghost Estates." *Political Geography* 42 (2014): 121–33.

O'Malley, Mary. *Asylum Road*. Cliffs of Moher, Ireland: Salmon, 2001.

Ong, Aihwa. *Neoliberalism as Exception: Mutations in Citizenship and Sovereignty*. Durham, N.C.: Duke University Press, 2005.

Ostrom, Elinor. *Governing the Commons: The Evolution of Institutions for Collective Action*. Cambridge: Cambridge University Press, 1990.

Ostry, Jonathan, Prakash Loungani, and Davide Furceri. "Neoliberalism: Oversold?" *Finance and Development* 53 (2016): 38–41.

Palumbo-Liu, David. *The Deliverance of Others: Reading Literature in a Global Age*. Durham, N.C.: Duke University Press, 2012.

Panitch, Leo, and Sam Gindin. *The Making of Global Capitalism: The Political Economy of American Empire*. New York: Verso, 2012.

Parikh, Crystal. *An Ethics of Betrayal: The Politics of Otherness in Emergent U.S. Literatures and Cultures*. New York: Fordham University Press, 2009.

Perloff, Marjorie. *The Poetics of Indeterminacy: Rimbaud to Cage*. Princeton, N.J.: Princeton University Press, 1981.

Plato. *The Republic*. Translated by Paul Shorey. Cambridge, Mass.: Harvard University Press, 1999.

Potkay, Adam. "Wordsworth and the Ethics of Things." *PMLA* 123 (2008): 390–404.

Powell, D. A. "Long Night Full Moon." *poets.org*. Accessed August 26, 2017. https://www.poets.org/poetsorg/poem/long-night-full-moon.

Prashad, Vijay. *The Poorer Nations: A Possible History of the Global South*. New York: Verso, 2012.

Purdy, Jedediah. *After Nature: A Politics for the Anthropocene*. Cambridge, Mass.: Harvard University Press, 2015.

Prynne, J. H. "The Art of Poetry No. 101 (Interview)." *Paris Review* 218 (2016): 175–207.

———. *The White Stones*. New York: New York Review of Books, 2016.

The Noble Qur'an. Accessed August 27, 2017. https://quran.com/.

Radhakrishnan, R. "Theory, Democracy, and the Public Intellectual." *PMLA* 125 (2010): 785–94.

Ramazani, Jahan. *The Hybrid Muse: Postcolonial Poetry in English*. Chicago: University of Chicago Press, 2001.

———. *Poetry and Its Others: News, Prayer, Song, and the Dialogue of Genres*. Chicago: University of Chicago Press, 2014.

———. *A Transnational Poetics*. Chicago: University of Chicago Press, 2009.

Rancière, Jacques. "The Politics of the Spider." Translated by Emily Rohrbach and Emily Sun. *Studies in Romanticism* 50 (2011): 239–50.

Rankine, Claudia. *Citizen: An American Lyric*. Minneapolis: Graywolf, 2014.

———. "Claudia Rankine in Conversation." *poets.org*. Accessed May 24, 2013. https://www.poets.org/poetsorg/text/claudia-rankine-conversation.

———. *Don't Let Me Be Lonely*. Minneapolis: Graywolf, 2004.

———. "The Provenance of Beauty: A South Bronx Travelogue (Excerpt)." *Nation*. Accessed January 20, 2013. https://www.thenation.com/article/provenance-beauty-south-bronx-travelogue-excerpt/.

Rankine, Claudia, and Lauren Berlant. "Claudia Rankine." *BOMB Magazine*. Accessed July 21, 2015. https://bombmagazine.org/articles/claudia-rankine/.

Rankine, Claudia, and Elizabeth Hoover. "Poet Claudia Rankine on Wounds We Should Not Forget." *Sampsonia Way*. Accessed August 24, 2017. http://

www.sampsoniaway.org/literary-voices/2010/11/12/poet-claudia-rankine
-on-wounds-we-shouldnt-forget/.

Rankine, Claudia and Sandra Lim. "Interview with Claudia Rankine." *National Book Foundation*. Accessed December 1, 2017. http://www.nationalbook.org/ nba2014_p_rankine_interv.html#.V4FxoY7bDhM.

Rankine, Claudia, and Alexandra Schwartz. "On Being Seen: An Interview with Claudia Rankine from Ferguson." *New Yorker*. Accessed July 21, 2015. https://www.newyorker.com/books/page-turner/seen-interview -claudia-rankine-ferguson.

Reed, Anthony. *Freedom Time: The Poetics and Politics of Black Experimental Writing*. Baltimore: Johns Hopkins University Press, 2016.

Reines, Ariana. *Mercury*. Albany, N.Y.: Fence, 2011.

Rich, Adrienne. *Later Poems: Selected and New, 1971–2012*. New York: W. W. Norton, 2013.

Riffaterre, Michael. "Prosopopoeia." *Yale French Studies* 69 (1985): 107–23.

Rilke, Rainer Maria. *Collected Poems*. Translated by Stephen Mitchell. New York: Vintage, 1989.

Robbins, Bruce. "Blaming the System." In *Immanuel Wallerstein and the Problem of the World: System, Scale, Culture*, edited by David Palumbo-Liu, Bruce Robbins, and Nirvana Tanoukhi, 41–66. Durham, N.C.: Duke University Press, 2011.

Robertson, Lisa. *The Men*. Toronto: Book Thug, 2006.

Robertson, Roland. *Globalization: Social Theory and Global Culture*. London: Sage, 1992.

Rockefeller, Stuart Alexander. "Flow." *Current Anthropology* 52 (2011): 557–78.

Ronda, Margaret. "Anthropogenic Poetics." *minnesota review* 83 (2014): 102–11.

———. *Remainders: American Poetry at Nature's End*. Stanford, Calif.: Stanford University Press, 2017.

Rosenberg, Justin. *The Follies of Globalization Theory: Polemical Essays*. New York: Verso, 2002.

Ross, Andrew. *Nice Work If You Can Get It: Life and Labor in Precarious Times*. New York: New York University Press, 2009.

Ross, Kristin. *Communal Luxury: The Political Imaginary of the Paris Commune*. New York: Verso, 2015.

Rubin, Joan Shelley. *Songs of Ourselves: The Uses of Poetry in America*. Cambridge, Mass.: Harvard University Press, 2007.

Said, Edward. *Freud and the Non-European*. New York: Verso, 2004.

Sassen, Saskia. *Expulsions: Brutality and Complexity in the Global Economy*. Cambridge, Mass.: Harvard University Press, 2014.

———. "Global Finance and Its Institutional Spaces." In *Oxford Handbook of the Sociology of Finance*, edited by Karin Knorr Cetina and Alex Preda, 13–32. Oxford: Oxford University Press, 2012.

———. "Global Cities and Survival Circuits." In *Global Woman: Nannies, Maids, and Sex Workers in the New Economy*, edited by Barbara Ehrenreich and Arlie Russell Hochschild, 254–74. New York: Henry Holt, 2002.

Scranton, Roy. *Learning to Die in the Anthropocene: Reflections on the End of a Civilization*. San Francisco: City Light, 2015.

Sedgwick, Eve Kosofsky. *Touching Feeling: Affect, Pedagogy, Performativity*. Durham, N.C.: Duke University Press, 2003.

Sexton, Jared. "The Social Life of Social Death: On Afro-Pessimism and Black Optimism." In *Tensions Journal* 5 (2011): 1–47.

Sharif, Solmaz. *Look*. Minneapolis: Graywolf, 2016.

Shelley, Percy Bysshe. *Shelley's Poetry and Prose*. Edited by Donald H. Reiman and Neil Fraistat. New York: Norton, 2002.

Shockley, Evie. "Race, Reception, and Claudia Rankine's 'American Lyric.'" *Los Angeles Review of Books*. Accessed August 25, 2017. https://lareviewof books.org/article/reconsidering-claudia-rankines-citizen-an-american -lyric-a-symposium-part-i/#!.

Silliman, Ron, Barrett Watten, Steve Benson, Lyn Hejinian, Charles Bernstein, and Bob Perelman. "For *Change*." In *In the American Tree*, edited by Ron Silliman, 468–472. Orono, Maine: National Poetry Foundation, 2007.

Sklair, Leslie. "Competing Conceptions of Globalization." *Journal of World-Systems Research* 5 (1999): 143–63.

Smith, Charlotte. *The Poems of Charlotte Smith*. Oxford: Oxford University Press, 1993.

Smith, Danez. *[INSERT]* BOY. Portland, Ore.: YesYes, 2014.

Sommer, Doris. *Bilingual Aesthetics: A New Sentimental Education*. Durham, N.C.: Duke University Press, 2004.

Spahr, Juliana. "Multilingualism in Contemporary American Poetry." In *The Cambridge History of American Poetry*, edited by Alfred Bendixen and Stephen Burt, 1123–43. Cambridge: Cambridge University Press, 2015.

———. *That Winter the Wolf Came*. Oakland, Calif.: Commune, 2015.

Spiro, Peter. *Beyond Citizenship: American Identity after Globalization*. New York: Oxford University Press, 2008.

Spivak, Gayatri Chakravorty. *An Aesthetic Education in the Age of Globalization*. Cambridge, Mass.: Harvard University Press, 2012.

Standing, Guy. *The Precariat: The New Dangerous Class*. London: Bloomsbury, 2011.

Stewart, Susan. "Lyric Possession." *Critical Inquiry* 22 (1995): 34–63.

———. "What Praise Poems Are For." *PMLA* 20 (2005): 234–45.

Stierle, Karlheinz. "Die Identität des Gedichts—Hölderlin als Paradigma."
   In *Identität (Poetik und Hermeneutik 8)*, edited by Odo Marquard and Karl-
   heinz Stierle, 505–52. Munich: Wilhelm Fink, 1979.
Stilling, Robert. "Multicentric Modernism and Postcolonial Poetry." In *The
   Cambridge Companion to Postcolonial Poetry*, edited by Jahan Ramazani, 127–
   38. Cambridge: Cambridge University Press, 2016.
Strange, Susan. *The Retreat of the State: The Diffusion of Power in the World
   Economy*. Cambridge: Cambridge University Press, 1996.
Suhr-Sytsma, Nathan. "Publishing Postcolonial Poetry." In *The Cambridge
   Companion to Postcolonial Poetry*, 237–48. Cambridge: Cambridge Univer-
   sity Press, 2016.
Sutherland, Keston. "Blocks: Form Since the Crash." Accessed May 20, 2017.
   https://archive.org/details/BlocksSeminarAtNYU13November2015.
———. "Hilarious Absolute Daybreak." *Glossator* 2 (2010): 115–48.
———. *Hot White Andy*. London: Barque, 2009.
———. "Interview with Keston Sutherland." *The White Review*. Accessed
   June 20, 2014. http://www.thewhitereview.org/interviews/interview-with
   -keston-sutherland/.
———. *The Odes to TL61P*. London: Enitharmon, 2013.
———. "Statement for Revolution and/or Poetry." *Revolution and/or Poetry*.
   Accessed June 8, 2014. https://revolutionandorpoetry.wordpress.com/
   2013/10/15/keston-sutherlands-statement-for-revolution-andor-poetry/.
Tageldin, Shaden. "Reversing the Sentence of Impossible Nostalgia: The
   Poetics of Postcolonial Migration in Sakinna Boukhedenna and Agha Sha-
   hid Ali." *Comparative Literature Studies* 40 (2003): 232–64.
Tengour, Habib. *Exile Is My Trade: A Habib Tengour Reader*. Translated by
   Pierre Joris. Boston: Black Widow, 2012.
Terada, Rei. "After the Critique of Lyric." *PMLA* 123 (2008): 195–200.
Toker, Emily Brown Coolidge. "What Makes a Native Speaker? Nativeness,
   Ownership, and Global Englishes." *minnesota review* 78 (2012): 113–29.
Tong, Joanne. "'Pity for the Poor Africans': William Cowper and the Limits of
   Abolitionist Affect." In *Affect and Abolition in the Anglo-Atlantic, 1770–1830*,
   edited by Stephen Ahern, 129–49. Burlington, Vt.: Ashgate, 2013.
Trethewey, Natasha. *Beyond Katrina: A Meditation on the Mississippi Gulf Coast*.
   Athens: University of Georgia Press, 2010.
Trexler, Adam. *Anthropocene Fictions: The Novel in a Time of Climate Change*.
   Charlottesville: University of Virginia Press, 2015.
Tucker, Bram, Amber Huff, Tsiazonera, Jaovola Tombo, Patricia Hajasoa,
   and Charlotte Nagnisaha. "When the Wealthy Are Poor: Poverty Expla-
   nations and Local Perspectives in Southwestern Madagascar." *American
   Anthropologist* 113 (2011): 291–305.

Tucker, Martin. "Kofi Awoonor: Restraint and Release." *English in Africa* 6 (1979): 46–51.

———. "Kofi Awoonor's Prison." *Worldview Magazine* 22 (1979): 22–24.

Turco, Lewis. *The Book of Forms*. Lebanon, N.H.: University Press of New England, 2000.

Turner, Lindsay. "Poetry's Work: Labor and Poiesis, 1950 to the Present." Ph.D. diss., University of Virginia, 2017.

Tynianov, Yuri. "The Ode as an Oratorical Genre." *New Literary History* 34 (2003): 565–96.

United Nations Conference on Trade and Development Report, 2011. New York and Geneva: United Nations, 2011.

Vecsey, George. "Arrest of a Poet in Ghana Stirs Stony Brook Campus." *New York Times*. Accessed December 1, 2017. http://www.nytimes.com/1976/02/22/archives/arrest-of-a-poet-in-ghana-stirs-stony-brook-campus-ambassador.html.

Vendler, Helen. *Invisible Listeners: Lyric Intimacy in Herbert, Whitman, and Ashbery*. Princeton, N.J.: Princeton University Press, 2005.

———. *The Odes of John Keats*. Cambridge, Mass.: Harvard University Press, 1985.

Virno, Paulo. *A Grammar of the Multitude*. Translated by Isabella Bertoletti, James Cascaito, and Andrea Casson. Los Angeles: Semiotext(e), 2004.

von Hallberg, Robert. *American Poetry and Culture 1945–1980*. Cambridge, Mass.: Harvard University Press, 1985.

Wade, Robert H. "Is Globalization Reducing Poverty and Inequality?" *World Development* 32 (2004): 567–89.

———. "The West Remains on Top, Economically and Politically." In *The Global Political Economy of Raúl Prebisch*, edited by Matias E. Margulis, 135–54. New York: Routledge, 2017.

Wallerstein, Immanuel. *The Modern World-System*. Vol. 4, *Centrist Liberalism Triumphant*. Berkeley: University of California Press, 2011.

Wang, Dorothy. *Thinking Its Presence: Form, Race, and Subjectivity in Contemporary Asian American Poetry*. Stanford, Calif.: Stanford University Press, 2013.

Warwick Research Collective. *Combined and Uneven Development: Towards a New Theory of World-Literature*. Liverpool: Liverpool University Press, 2015.

Waters, William. *Poetry's Touch: On Lyric Address*. Ithaca, N.Y.: Cornell University Press, 2003.

Wellek, René. "Genre Theory, the Lyric, and 'Erlebnis.'" In *Festschrift für Richard Alewyn*. Cologne: Böhlau-Verlag, 1967.

White, Gillian. *Lyric Shame: The "Lyric" Subject of Contemporary American Poetry*. Cambridge, Mass.: Harvard University Press, 2014.

Whitman, Walt. *Complete Poetry and Collected Prose*. New York: Library of
America, 1982.

Woloch, Alex. *The One vs. The Many: Minor Characters and the Space of the
Protagonist in the Novel*. Princeton, N.J.: Princeton University Press, 2003.

Wood, Marcus. *Slavery, Empathy, and Pornography*. Oxford: Oxford University Press, 2002.

Woodland, Malcolm. "Memory's Homeland: Agha Shahid Ali and the
Hybrid Ghazal." *English Studies in Canada* 31 (2005): 249–72.

Woods, Tim. *The Poetics of the Limit: Ethics and Politics in Modern and Contemporary American Poetry*. New York: Palgrave, 2002.

Wright, C. D. "The New American Ode." *Antioch Review* 47 (1989): 287–96.

Wrighton, John. *Ethics and Politics in Modern American Poetry*. New York:
Routledge, 2010.

Yu, Timothy. *Race and the Avant-Garde: Experimental and Asian American
Poetry Since 1965*. Stanford, Calif.: Stanford University Press, 2009.

Zhou, Xiaojing. *The Ethics and Poetics of Alterity in Asian American Poetry*. Iowa
City: University of Iowa Press, 2006.

Zirin, Dave. *Brazil's Dance with the Devil: The World Cup, the Olympics, and the
Right for Democracy*. Chicago: Haymarket, 2014.

Žižek, Slavoj. *The Sublime Object of Ideology*. London: Verso, 1989.

Zuromskis, Catherine. "Complicating Images." *Los Angeles Review of Books*.
Accessed August 26, 2017. https://lareviewofbooks.org/article/recon
sidering-claudia-rankines-citizen-an-american-lyric-a-symposium-part-i/.

INDEX

Aarons, K., 139n42
Abrahamian, Atossa Araxia, 49
Abrams, M. H., 32–33, 52, 97–98, 147–48n37
Adams, Jean, 98
Adorno, Theodor, 68–70
afropessimism, 12, 139n42
"Again Ode," 142n44
Agamben, Giorgio, 34
Aisbett, Emma, 152n38
Albright, Daniel, 147n33
Albrow, Martin, 120
Ali, Agha Shahid, 65, 83–88, 125–26, 156–57nn108–9, 157n123
Ali, Hussayn Ibn, 87
Al-Kassim, Dina, 86
Al-Sheikh, Manal, 39–43
Altieri, Charles, 4, 135n7
anaphora, 111, 123–24
"And Yet We Must Live in These Times," 26
Anglophone poetry, and globalization, 3, 120–21
Anglophone poets, and globalization, 2–3
"The Animal Model of Inescapable Shock," 39–41
Anthropocene, the, 158nn4,12; the human damage of, 117; a love song for, 115; overview, 91–92; poetry of, 92
Anthropocene Fictions: The Novel in a Time of Climate Change (Trexler), 158n12
Antígona Gonzalez (Uribe), 125
Antigone (Sophocles), 125
anti-racism, and a global capitalist agenda, 48
apostrophe, 58–59
Appadurai, Arjun, 9, 30
Apter, Emily, 32
Arac, Jonathan, 54
Arendt, Hannah, 43, 95, 159n19

Aristotle, 67
Armantrout, Rae, 154–55n83
Arrighi, Giovanni, 9, 24, 29
The Art of Twentieth-Century American Poetry (Altieri), 135n7
Ashbery, John, 35, 68, 119–20
Ashton, Jennifer, 45
Astrophel (Sidney), 40
Astroturf (Luna), 142n44
Asylum Road (O'Malley), 24–25
"At Night the States," 142n44
Auden, W.H., 33, 37–38
Austin, J. L., 113
"Autumn," 33
Avant-Garde Post-: Radical Poetics After the Soviet Union (Bozovic), 138n16
avant-gardes, and race, 134–35n5
Awoonor, Kofi, 101, 105–9, 112

"Banana Republics of Poetry," 13–14
Banking Act of 1933, Regulation Q, 7
"Banks of a Canal," 26–28
"Banks of a Canal near Naples," 27–28
Baucom, Ian, 24
Baudelaire, Charles, 65, 69, 70, 101
Beachy Head (Smith), 98–99
Beardsley, Monroe, 34
beauty, 62–64
Bell, Kevin, 52
Benjamin, Walter, 65, 68–69, 70, 101
Berardi, Franco, 30, 71, 144n62
Berlant, Lauren, 71, 112
Bernes, Jasper, 5, 30, 133–34n3, 137–38n16, 159n16
Bernstein, Charles, 155n93
Beyond Katrina: A Meditation on the Mississippi Gulf Coast (Tretheway), 109–13
"Beyond the Poetics of Privatization," 144–45n64
Black, Stephanie, 21

The Black Atlantic: Modernity and Double Consciousness (Gilroy), 149n68
Blade Pitch Control Unit (Bonney), 142n44
Blake, William, 81
Bloomberg-Rissman, John, 153n52
Bonney, Sean, 66, 72–78, 142n44, 154n75
The Bounty (Kim), 79
Bourdieu, Pierre, 71
Boyer, Anne, 39–41, 42–43
Bozovic, Marijeta, 138n16
Braudel, Fernand, 9, 28
Broken Harbour (French), 22
Broken Souths (Dowdy), 137–38n16
Brouillette, Sarah, 139–40n47
Brown, Michael, 8
Burt, Steph, 90, 133n2
Butler, Judith, 70, 71, 96, 145n75, 160n36

Caillebotte, Gustave, 27–28
Call Me Ishmael Tonight (Ali), 85
"Calling You Here," 115–17
The Cambridge History of American Poetry (Bendixen and Burt), 133n2
Capital (Marx), 36
capitalism: damage wrought by, 91; in earlier historical periods, 133–34n3
Capitalism in the Web of Life (Moore), 91
Capitalizing on Crisis, 9
Caplan, David, 156–57n108
Celestial Pantomime (Lawler), 161n48
"Ceres in Caherlistrane," 24–25
Chakrabarty, Dipesh, 136n10
Chiu, Jeannie, 155n88
Chukhrov, Keti, 145n64
Citizen: An American Lyric (Rankine), 44–46, 50–52, 55–57, 58
citizen lyric, 46, 49–50. *See also* citizenship; lyric poetry
citizenship: active vs. passive, 47; by birth or by bloodline, 50; as a commodity, 49; Comoro Islands, 49; as a concept, 47; expansion of, 48–49, 57; global, 49; and lyric poetry, 44–47, 53; and market forces, 146n18; and race, 50
Civilization and Capitalism (Braudel), 23–24
Clancy, Sarah, 21, 26
cli-fi. *See* climate fiction
climate fiction, 92–93
Clover, Joshua, 144n59
Cohen, Ralph, 160n22
Cole, Teju, 106
Colla, Elliott, 113

combined and uneven development, literature of, 162–63n3
commodities, 36
Common Place (Halpern), 125
commoning, 66
commons, 72
The Commons (Bonney), 66, 73–78, 153n52
Commons (Kim), 66, 78–83
Comoro Islands, citizenship, 49
conceptual poetry, 4, 11
"Concerning Quality, Again," 103
confessional lyric poetry, 4
The Consequences of Modernity (Giddens), 7–8
Cooke, Jennifer, 36, 142n44
Cooper's Hill (Denham), 97–98, 160n24
cosmopolites, 49
Costello, Bonnie, 150n6
Cowper, William, 31, 142n43
critical theory, and narrative, 3–4
crowd, the, 65
Crutzen, Paul J., 91
"The Cuckoo Bird," 74, 75
Culler, Jonathan, 4, 12, 46, 52–53, 67, 147–48n37
"Culture, Community, Nation," 47–48

Davidson, Michael, relationship between critical theory and narrative, 3–4
Davis, Heather, 92
Davis, Mike, 21
Dawes, Kwame, 107
De Man, Paul, 59
De'Ath, Amy, 137–38n16
"Death of a Field," 22–23
Delaney, Beauford, 12
"Delusions of Whiteness in the Avant-Garde," 134–35n5
Denham, John, 97–98
Denkbilder (Benjamin), 101
Desai, Radhika, 6
"Destitution," 39, 41–42
Dickinson, Emily, 86
Dickinson's Misery (Jackson), 53–54, 149n61
Dictionary of Military and Associated Terms, 121, 126
displacement without moving, 23, 27
dispossession, 19–21; accumulation by, 23; and the consequences of financialization, 37; Indian regimes of, 20; and Irish poetry, 21–23; and subprime housing markets, 29

Don't Let Me Be Lonely: An American Lyric (Rankine), 51–52
Doolittle, Hilda (H. D.), 99
Dowdy, Michael, 5, 137–38n16
Dowling, Sarah, 156n96
"Downhill," 101
"A Dream, or the Type of the Rising Sun," 98

earth system science, 92
ecological thought, 8
Edmond, Jacob, 154n75
"Eighth Elegy," 100–1
Eliot, T. S., 106, 147n33
Endnotes (Bernes), 133–34n3
English, dominance of, 163n8
The Enigma of Capital and the Crises of Capitalism (Harvey), 23
epideixis, 67
Erschütterung, 101
ethics and poetry, 148n54
exhortation, rhetoric of, 66–68
expulsion from place, 21. *See also* dispossession

"The Famine Year," 22
Fanon, Frantz, 74
Ferguson, Roderick, 64
Festschrift für Richard Alewyn (Wellek), 52
"Filter OD," 142n44
financialization, 8–9, 37; and neoliberalism, 10–11
Finch, Anne, 98
"For the Union Dead," 142n44
For the Union Dead (Lowell), 49
Forget English! Orientalisms and World Literature (Mufti), 163n4
Four Quartets (Eliot), 106
Framing the Global (Kahn), 8
Freedom Time (Reed), 6
French, Tana, 22
"From Action to Image: Theories of the Lyric in the Eighteenth Century," 143n46
Frye, Northrop, 55
Furani, Khaled, 5, 137–38n16

Gallagher, Mary, 133n1
Genette, Gérard, 147n33
ghazals, 84, 85, 86–87, 156n106, 157n109
ghost estates, 22, 140n10
Giddens, Anthony, 7–8

Gilroy, Paul, 61, 149n68
Gindin, Sam, 7, 63
Ginsberg, Allen, 123, 124
Giscombe, C.S., 90
"The Glacial Question, Unsolved," 102
gleaning, 66, 73
Glissant, Édouard, 109
global English, 122, 125
globalization: and Anglophone poetry, 3, 120–21; and English-writing poets, 2–3; Ireland and, 23–24; as a world-system, 133–34n3
globalization theory, 7–8
globe, 150n10
glocalization, 8
Gordin, Michael, 163n8
Governing the Commons: The Evolution of Institutions for Collective Action (Ostrom), 152–53n45
Graham, Jorie, 67
Gray, Thomas, 98
"The Great Hunger," 22
Great Hunger, the, 24
Grineveld, Jacques, 92, 158n4
Grossman, Allen, 88
Guardians of the Sacred World (Awoonor), 106

Hall, Stuart, 47–48, 100
Halpern, Rob, 125
Hamilton, Clive, 92, 158n4
Hammons, David, 59
Hancock, Butch, 115, 116
Hardin, Garrett, 152–53n45
Harney, Stefano, 137n11
Harpham, Geoffrey Galt, 97–98
Hartman, Geoffrey, 12
Hartman, Saidiya, 11, 46, 136n10
Harvey, David, 6, 10–11, 73, 122, 140–41n11
"Having Coke with You," 36, 142n44
H. D. (Hilda Doolittle), 99
Heaney, Seamus, 21, 26–28
Hegel, G. W. F., 54–55, 64
Hejinian, Lyn, 155n93
"Heroin," 74
hill, the, 97, 99–100, 116
Hölderlin, Friedrich, 33
"Homecoming," 108–9
Hong, Cathy Park, 134–35n5
Hope, Laurence, 86
Horatian odes, 142–43n45

"An Horation Ode Upon Cromwell's Return from Ireland," 31
"Horation Ode," 144n57
hortatory rhetoric, 66–67, 72. *See also* exhortation, rhetoric of
Hošek, Chaviva, 53
The House by the Sea (Awoonor), 105–9
Howe, Fanny, 33
"Howl," 123
Hugo, Richard, 49
Hume, Angela, 58, 62
Hunger, the. *See* Great Hunger, the
Hurricane Camille, 109
Hurricane Katrina, 56, 58

"I" pronoun, 68, 84, 155n88
"I stood tiptoe upon a little hill," 99
"Identities in Process," 155n88
"If You Were a Bluebird," 115
imperialism, U.S., 122. *See also* militarism, U.S.
"In Praise of Limestone," 33
[INSERT] BOY (Smith), 12–13
In the Break (Moten), 12
"In the Hood," 59
International Monetary Fund, 72
The Intimacies of Four Continents (Lowe), 5
Introductory Lectures on Aesthetics (Hegel), 54–55
Ion (Plato), 20
Irish poetry, and dispossession, 21–23
Israel, Nico, 150n10

Jackson, Virginia, 4, 53, 59, 149n61
Jacobsson, Per, 10
Jameson, Fredric, 38–39, 145n74
Jay, Paul, 7
Jeffreys, Mark, 55
Jeon, Joseph Jonghyun, 79
Johnson, Barbara, 59
Johnson, Samuel, 52
Jones, Claudia, 57

Kahn, Hilary E., 8
"Kashmiri Song," 86
Kaufman, Robert, 69
Kavanagh, Patrick, 22
Keats, John, 27–28, 33, 36, 95, 99; the odes of, 143n47
Keith, Jennifer, 98
kettling, 31
Khalili, Laleh, 124, 126

Kim, Myung Mi, 66, 72–73, 78–83, 155n89, 156n96
Kimberley, Emma, 51–52
Komorowski, Michael, 144n57
Krippner, Greta, 6, 7, 9, 11, 25
Kunitz, Stanley, 105

L=A=N=G=U=A=G=E poetry, 4, 11, 68, 79
The Lady in Kicking Horse Reservoir (Hugo), 49
"Lamenta," 82, 156n96
landscape poetry, 19, 29. *See also* dispossession
language-oriented writing, 154–55n83
lateral agency, 112, 145n75
Lawler, Justus George, 161n48
Le Blanc, Guillaume, 71
Le Testament (Villon), 125
Learning to Die in the Anthropocene (Scranton), 159n17
Leaves of Grass (Whitman), 67
Levien, Michael, 20
Levinas, Emmanuel, 38, 151n27
Lewis, Simon L., 91, 94–95, 158n4
liberalism, critique of, 5
Life and Debt (Black), 21
Life Studies (Lowell), 49
Linebaugh, Peter, 83, 156n98
Lisette, Francesca, 36, 142n44
Lives of the Poets (Johnson), 52
loco-descriptive poetry, 22, 97, 103, 107
"Long Night Full Moon," 8
The Long Twentieth Century (Arrighi), 9, 24
Look (Sharif), 121–26
Lorde, Audre, 48
Lorey, Isabell, 71
"L'Orgie Parisienne," 74
Lotz, Christian, 76
Lowe, Lisa, 5
Lowell, Robert, 49, 55–56, 142n44
"Lullaby," 37–38
Luna, Joe, 36, 142n44
"Lunar Fork Ode," 142n44
lyric poetry: and citizenship, 44–47, 53; as a genre, 147–48n37; Greek, 67; and the language of capital, 69–70; malleability of lyric as a genre, 51–52; as a meditative space, 54, 55, 60; and New Criticism, 52, 53; New Lyric Studies, 64; subjective voice, 147n33; vocal effects, 52–53. *See also* citizen lyric

Lyric Poetry: Beyond New Criticism (Hošek and Parker), 53, 54
lyric reading, 53
lyric situations, 54–55, 60
Lyric Theory Reader, 4
lyricization, 11–12, 53–54

MacKenzie, Donald, 9
Maclean, Norman, 143n46
The Magna Carta Manifesto: Liberties and Commons for All (Linebaugh), 156n98
The Making of Global Capitalism (Panitch and Gindin), 7
"Man and Wife," 55–56
Martin, Dawn Lundy, 35
Marvell, Andrew, 30, 31, 144n57
Marx, Karl, 36
Maslin, Mark A., 91, 94–95, 158n4
Materazzi, Marco, 60
Mayer, Bernadette, 33, 106
McLane, Maureen, 93–94
Medvedev, Kirill, 144–45n64
Meehan, Paula, 21, 22–23
Melamed, Jodi, 10–11, 48, 140n48
militarism, U.S., 122–23, 125–26
Mill, John Stuart, 55
Mitchell, Timothy, 6, 91
Miz N (McLane), 93–94
monetization of water, 22
Moore, Jason, 91, 103
Morris, Marianne, 142n44
Morton, Timothy, 8, 116
Moten, Fred, 11, 12, 35, 108, 137n11
Mufti, Aamir, 14, 84, 157–58nn123–24, 163n4
Music for Porn (Halpern), 125
Mutu, Wangechi, 59–60

Nagy, Gregory, 142–43n45
Naimou, Angela, 46
NAMA. *See* National Asset Management Association
narrative, and critical theory, 3–4
narrative genres, 92–93
National Asset Management Association, 25, 141n23
Native Guard (Trethewey), 109
Natural Disaster (Trethewey), 109
Nealon, Christopher, 4, 5, 9–10, 13, 135n6
neoliberalism, 10–11; and multiculturalism, 48

Neoliberalism as Exception: Mutations in Citizenship and Sovereignty (Ong), 146n18
"Neoliberalism: Oversold?," 72
New Criticism, and lyric poetry, 52, 53
Nixon, Rob, 23, 27, 92–93
"A Nocturnal Reverie," 98
nonexchangeability, poetry as, 144n62
"North American Time," 125
Notley, Alice, 106, 142n44
*not suitable for domestic sublimation (Cooke), 142n44

occupation of the commons, 37
"October 10, 2006/World Cup," 60
"The Ode as an Oratorical Genre," 143n51
"Ode Farage," 142n44
"Ode: Intimations of Immortality from Recollections of Early Childhood," 31
"Ode on a Distant Prospect of Eton College," 98
"Ode on a Grecian Urn," 27
"Ode on Indolence," 33
"Ode to Psyche," 36
odes: as an act of oratory, 143n51; history of, 143n46; Horatian, 142–43n45; modern English odes, 31; new American odes, 33; Pindaric, 142–43n45; subject matter, 31–32; Keston Sutherland and, 30–31, 42; victory, 142–43n45. *See also qasida*
Odes (Olds), 142n44
The Odes of John Keats (Vendler), 143n47
The Odes to TL61P, 33–39
O'Hara, Frank, 33, 36, 142n44
Olds, Sharon, 142n44
Olson, Charles, 35
O'Malley, Mary, 21, 24–25
"On First Looking into Chapman's Homer," 95
"On Lyric Poetry and Society," 69
"On Some Motifs in Baudelaire," 69
Ong, Aihwa, 146n18
"Oread," 99
The Origins of Totalitarianism (Arendt), 159n19
Ostrom, Elinor, 152–53n45

Painting Rain (Meehan), 22–23
"Palinode," 93–94
Panitch, Leo, 7, 63
Paris Commune, 61
Parker, Patricia A., 53
Patterson, Orlando, 12

Pavlov, Aleksei, 91
Penury (Kim), 79
Perloff, Marjorie, 4, 135n7
Philip, M. NourbeSe, 13–14
Pindaric odes, 142–43n45
Pindarique Odes (Cowley), 31
Pindar's Homer: The Lyric Possession of an Epic Past (Nagy), 142–43n45
"Place and Displacement: Recent Poetry from Northern Ireland," 26–27
planetary dysphoria, 32
Planisphere (Ashbery), 68
Plato, 20, 161n41
Poe, Edgar Allan, 106
poetic surplus, 12. *See also* surplus
Poetics of Indeterminacy (Perloff), 135n7
poetry, problem of defining, 2
Poetry and Its Others (Ramazani), 155n86
poetry of revolt, 113
Poetry's Work: Labor and Poiesis (Turner), 138n16
"Pollen Fossil Record," 79–80, 81
The Poorer Nations (Prashad), 21, 159n19, 162n59
postcolonial theory, and the critique of liberalism, 136n10
Powell, D. A., 8
Prashad, Vijay, 6–7, 21, 133–34n3, 159n19, 162n59
"Precarious Life, Vulnerability, and the Ethics of Cohabitation," 145n75, 160n36
precarity, 70–74, 160n36
Prins, Yopie, 4
The Prison House of Language (Jameson), 145n74
Prometheus Unbound (Shelley), 74
prose anecdotes, 50–52
prose poems, 41, 60
prosopopoeia, 58–59
prospect poems, 94–101, 116–17
prospect view, 160n22
Proust, Marcel, 101
"The Provenance of Beauty: A South Bronx Travelogue," 63–64, 67
Provincializing Europe (Chakrabarty), 136n10
Prynne, J.H., 35, 101–5, 109, 112
Purdy, Jedediah, 91

qasida, 41
Qur'an, 85

race: absence of from accounts of twentieth-century poetry, 134–35n5; and citizenship, 50
racial violence, 44
racism: anti-racism and a global capitalist agenda, 48; and citizenship, 45–46
Ramazani, Jahan, 85, 155n86, 157n109
Rankine, Claudia, 35, 43, 59–64, 67, 134–35n5; citizenship and lyric poetry, 44–46, 49–50; lyric as a meditative space, 54, 55; the lyric pronominal "I," 56–57; prose anecdotes, 50–52
Real Estate Investment Trusts, 25
Reddy, Srikanth, 125
Reed, Anthony, 6, 46
Remainders: American Poetry at Nature's End (Ronda), 138n16
Represent and Destroy: Rationalizing Violence in the New Racial Capitalism (Melamed), 48, 140n48
Republic (Plato), 20, 161n41
Rhetoric (Aristotle), 67
Rich, Adrienne, 26, 125
Rilke, Rainer Maria, 100–1
Riot. Strike. Riot: The New Era of Uprisings (Clover), 144n59
riots, 33–34
Roberts, Luke, 142n44
Robertson, Lisa, 35
Robinson, Sophie, 142n44
Ronda, Margaret, 90, 95, 138n16
Ross, Andrew, 71
Ross, Kristin, 6, 61
Rubin, Joan Shelley, 133n2
Rule of Experts (Mitchell), 91

Said, Edward, 86
Sassen, Saskia, 6, 9, 21, 71
Scenes of Subjection (Hartman), 11, 136n10
Scientific Babel (Gordin), 163n8
Scranton, Roy, 95, 159n17
securitization, 25
semio-capitalism, 30
Sexton, Jared, 12
SEZ (Special Economic Zone), 21
Sharif, Solmaz, 121–26
Shockley, Evie, 46, 57
Sidney, Philip, 40
Silencing the Sea (Furani), 137–38n16
Simpson, Louis, 105
The Slave Ship (Turner), 59
Sleeping Heads (Mutu), 60

Smith, Bessie, 112
Smith, Charlotte, 98–99
Smith, Danez, 12–13
Sommer, Doris, 99
The Song of Songs, 67
"Song of the Wreckage," 12–13
Songs of Ourselves: The Uses of Poetry in America (Rubin), 133n2
Sophocles, 125
Spahr, Juliana, 101–2, 109, 113–17, 155n89
Speranza, 22
Spillers, Hortense, 12
Spiro, Peter, 50
Stanley, Josh, 142n44
Station Island (Heaney), 27
Stedman Jones, Daniel, 11
Stevens, Wallace, 124
Stewart, Susan, 20, 35, 144n62
Stierle, Karlheinz, 76
Stilling, Robert, 157n123
Stoermer, Eugene F., 91
"The Stolen Child," 22
"Structure and Style in the Greater Romantic Lyric," 32–33
subject, 11
Suhr-Sytsma, Nathan, 139–40n47
Surah Al-Fatihah, 85
surplus, 11; anti-racist global critique and poetic criticism and, 12
sustainability, 115
Sutherland, Keston, 30–31, 33–39, 42, 102–3

Tageldin, Shaden, 156–57n108
Teens (Lisette), 142n44
Tengour, Habib, 20
Terada, Rei, 53, 54
That Winter the Wolf Came (Spahr), 109, 113–17
"Theories of Time and Space," 109–10
Theory of the Lyric (Culler), 12, 52–53
"They Knew What They Wanted," 68
"Thirteen Ways of Looking at a Blackbird," 124
Thomas, David, 139–40n47
"Thoughts on the Esterházy Court Uniform," 103–5
Three Poems (Ashbery), 119–20
"The Three Ravens," 75
"The Three Voices of Poetry," 147n33
togetherness, 57
Toker, Emily Brown Coolidge, 122

"Tonight," 84, 85, 87–88
"The Tragedy of the Commons," 152–53n45
transgression, 76
"Transitory, Momentary," 113–15
A Transnational Poetics (Ramazani), 157n109
transversal translations, 82
Trethewey, Natasha, 101–2, 109–13, 134–35n5
Trexler, Adam, 158n12
Tucker, Bram, 152n39
Tucker, Martin, 107
Turco, Lewis, 147n33
Turner, J. M. W., 59
Turner, Lindsay, 138n16
Turpin, Étienne, 92
Two Citizens (Wright), 49
Tynianov, Yuri, 143n51

unchosen cohabitation, 70
Under Flag (Kim), 79
United Nations Conference on Trade and Development, 151n31
universalistic language, 48
"The University and the Undercommons," 137n11
"Unsociable Poetry: Antagonism and Abstraction in Contemporary Feminized Poetics," 137–38n16
Untitled Colossal Parlour Odes, 142n44
The Uprising (Berardi), 144n62
Uribe, Sara, 125
"us" pronoun, 84

Valéry, Paul, 34
The Velvet Underground, 74
Vendler, Helen, 4, 31, 143n47
venture capital, 22
The Victorious Ones (Nealon), 9–10
victory odes, 142–43n45
Villon, François, 125
Virno, Paulo, 71
voice in poetry, 12
Von Hallberg, Robert, 49–50
Voyager (Reddy), 125

Wade, Robert H., 72
Wagner, Catherine, 35
Waldheim, Kurt, 125
Wallerstein, Immanuel, 47, 57, 147–48n37, 148n52

Wang, Dorothy, 134–35n5
Warwick Research Collective, 162–63n3
The Waste Land, 76
Waters, William, 59
"The Wayfarer Comes Home," 106
"we" pronoun, 68–69, 84, 86, 88, 150n6
Wellek, René, 52
"What Kind of Times Are These," 26
"What Praise Poems Are For," 144n62
The White Stones (Prynne), 102–3, 109
Whitman, Walt, 35, 67–68, 123, 124
Wieners, John, 33
Wimsatt, W.K., 34
Woodland, Malcolm, 156n106
Wordsworth, William, 31

*The Work of Art in the Age of Deindustrial-
   ization* (Bernes), 138n16
World Writing: Poetics, Ethics, Globalization
   (Gallagher), 133n1
The Wretched of the Earth (Fanon), 74
Wright, C. D., 33, 90
Wright, James, 49

Yeats, W. B., 22
Yu, Timothy, 134–35n5

Zidane, Zinedine, 60, 62
Zirin, Dave, 60
Žižek, Slavoj, 99
Zuromskis, Catherine, 59